CW00552939

The Robin Hood 500 Route

Neil Hallam

THE
ROBIN HOOD 500
ROUTE

Neil Hallam

Contents

About the Author..Page i
Route Maps..Page iii

Author's Foreword..Page 1
Introduction..Page 3
Route Overview..Page 7

PART 1: South Nottinghamshire – Leicestershire
        and Lincoln..Page 22
PART 2: Nottinghamshire..................................Page 49
PART 3: North Yorkshire Coast & Moors................Page 111
PART 4: South Yorkshire..................................Page 179
PART 5: Derbyshire & Nottingham........................Page 235

Just the Directions..Page 373

Author's Afterword..Page 459
Useful Websites...Page 461

About the Author

Neil Hallam MSc, MEPS, MCIOJ

Neil Hallam is a freelance writer and photojournalist based in Nottingham, England. His media career began in the 1980s as a photographer for Mansfield Brewery's trade magazine. He shot his first wedding in 1987, leading to many years of experience with weddings, events, portraiture and commercial photography.

Neil is a contributor to magazines as diverse as *Police World* and *Cycling Active*. A keen motorcyclist throughout his adult life, Neil contributes to motorcycle magazines in Australia, the USA and Britain. His published work includes touring articles, road tests and technical features.

Neil's knowledge of the outdoors is built on a lifetime of outdoor pursuits and expeditions to remote areas including the Himalayas and Mongolia. An experienced Scout Instructor, he advises the county leadership on climbing, walking and mountain biking. He holds National Governing Body awards in all three disciplines.

His published outdoor features include: cycling, mountaineering, trekking, and shooting in locations throughout the world.

Neil's professional career began in the law, as a Chartered Legal Executive, moving to the Police, for a 22 year career chasing real-life outlaws. His journalism experience includes five years seconded to the Home Office as Communications Officer at the Police National CBRN Centre.

Since retirement, Neil has pursued his interests in travelling, writing and the media. Neil's Police experience has found ongoing work as the Police Technical advisor to the scriptwriters of ITV's *Coronation Street* and BBC's *Waterloo Road.*

He has an MSc in Disaster Management and is a full member of the Emergency Planning Society. Neil is a member of the Chartered Institute of Journalists (MCIJ), the world's oldest organisation for journalists.

For more information about Neil and his work, please visit his website at: **www.neilhallam.com**

The Robin Hood 500 (**500RH**) Route

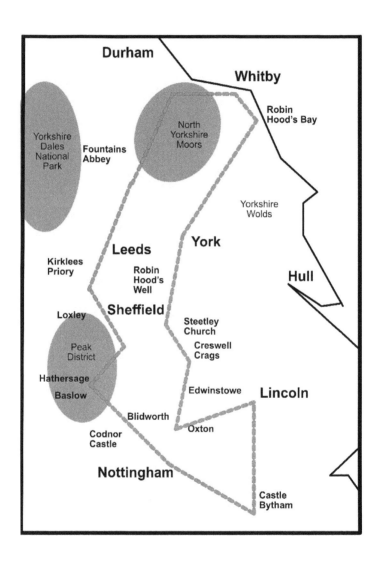

Durham

Whitby

Robin
Hood's Bay

Yorkshire
Dales
National
Park

Fountains
Abbey

North
Yorkshire
Moors

Yorkshire
Wolds

Leeds

York

Kirklees
Priory

Robin
Hood's
Well

Hull

Loxley

Sheffield

Steetley
Church

Peak
District

Creswell
Crags

Hathersage

Baslow

Edwinstowe

Lincoln

Blidworth

Codnor
Castle

Oxton

Nottingham

Castle
Bytham

THE
ROBIN HOOD 500
ROUTE

Neil Hallam

Author's Foreword

500RH

I GREW up in Nottinghamshire, so from early childhood I was immersed in the legends of Robin Hood. Whenever my parents hosted visitors, Nottingham Castle and The Major Oak were always on the itinerary.

I remember being bought Robin Hood hats, wooden swords and bow & arrow sets as a child. Then, as a teenager, I even tried archery for real with a friend of my mum's.

With only three TV channels to choose from, there was always a film or TV series about Robin Hood playing during my childhood. I seemed to be surrounded by the legends throughout my formative years.

The **500RH** journey started by walking the Robin Hood Way – Long Distance Footpath. This 84 mile walking route was created in 1984 by members of the Nottingham Wayfarers' Rambling Club, linking places in Nottinghamshire with connections to the legend.

I also enjoy cycling, but being a walker's route, much of the Robin Hood Way is off limits to cyclists, so I set about adapting the route to use nearby cycle-friendly roads and tracks. This became my Robin Hood Cycle Way, which is available in a separate book.

The final step towards the **500RH** came with the popularity of Scotland's NC500, SWC300 and Heart 200. It was not too big a leap for my imagination to begin extending my cycling route to something more suited to motorised transport.

Initially, I expected my Robin Hood Route to be around 200 miles, taking in the more obvious locations in Nottinghamshire, Derbyshire and Lincoln. The research proved every bit as interesting as the travelling, since I learned so many more legends and factual connections to Robin Hood and his story.

The research provided destinations much further into Lincolnshire, as well as north through most of the Ridings of Yorkshire.

There are many different ways to enjoy The Robin Hood 500. The following Introduction sets out some of them. As the project progresses, I will add more ideas to the **500RH** website. I hope you enjoy your journey, in whatever way you travel.

Introduction

500RH

WELCOME to the **500RH**: The Robin Hood Route.

At first, I planned only to link the locations in Nottinghamshire and Derbyshire. But, as I researched deeper, I found the connection with Castle Bytham in a stunning part of Lincolnshire.

I also took a closer look at Yorkshire, which has long held competitive claims to being Robin Hood's home county.

I knew of Robin Hood's Bay, on the North Yorkshire coast, but did not know of any firm link to the legends. Digging deeper, I learned about the sites at Stoop Brow and Whitby Laithes, which gave extra purpose to a drive through North Yorkshire.

In the end, I came up with the 540 mile route presented to you in this book.

Northern Scotland is graced with sparse population, making navigation around the north coast a straightforward affair. The trade-off for that ease of navigation, is the many hours of travel in reaching even the starting point at Inverness. Navigation around my **500RH** does take a bit more planning, but the route is central to Great Britain, and rather more accessible to those of us in England.

I began with a route linking only places with significance to the Robin Hood legend. But as I travelled around the route, I realised that I would do our beautiful country an injustice by not mentioning the many interesting places I passed through.

It would take a long holiday to visit everywhere I recommend during a single journey, which leaves you with options about how to use the **500RH**:

- The journey could be completed over a few days, in the same way that travellers use the NC500. This would entail picking out the highlights and travelling past everything else.
- The option I chose was to complete the journey in several sections, spending time exploring the places along the way.

Your method of travel is also open to your personal choice. I used a mix of motorcycle and small camper van to travel the route. The entire route can be completed by either form of transport (except the few locations where the final approach must be on foot or by cycle). If you have a caravan, or a large motor home, I have suggested where a diversion around the narrower roads might be appropriate.

As I planned and travelled the route, I became fascinated with the legends, and how they have developed over the centuries.

My previous career was as a Police Officer. We often said that there were three versions to every story. Each person in a dispute had their own version, and the truth would inevitably fall somewhere in between.

This appears to be the case with the legends of Robin Hood. There are some people who write it all off as pure fantasy, while others favour a closer link with real people. As with most things, the truth will occupy the middle ground.

The medieval peasantry justifiably disliked the taxation regime they lived under. They would have provided a combination of produce, money and labour to a hierarchy of overlords. Any story about someone getting the better of this system would have gained traction as a folk-hero. During a time when stories were sung, rather than written down, many versions appear to have merged into a single narrative.

There are a few occasions where I have found links from the legends to real people.

The most notable is through Robert Hode, who lived in the village of Loxley, near Sheffield, during the 14th century. Robert Hode does not appear to have stolen from the rich and given to the poor. In fact, his outlaw status was due to an accidental killing on the family farm.

Over the centuries, the idea of "Robin of Loxley" has entered the popular re-telling.

Long after Robert Hode's death, his family inherited the title "Earl of Huntingdon." This title too has become part of the legend, with male heirs still carrying Robin Hood among their several given names.

There is some speculation that a real person named Robert Hode was buried in the grounds of Kirklees Priory in South Yorkshire. Even Tony Robinson's *Time Team* became involved in this discussion, which has not been properly resolved.

Nottinghamshire historian Brian Benison spent many years researching connections of real Nottinghamshire men to the legends. Benison came up with a candidate named Roger Godberd, who was outlawed during the 13th century. This claim has added credibility when linked to Reynold de Grey, who was one of the feudal barons of Derbyshire's Codnor Castle, and was a very unpopular Sheriff of Nottingham.

I recount all of these stories, and many others with less credibility, during our journey. While some are more fanciful than others, they all made for a very interesting research project.

I make no claims to the accuracy in any of my stories. These are legends, which have been embellished over many hundreds of years. They do, however, add some colour to our journey through five beautiful English counties.

I hope you enjoy reading about, and travelling around, the **500RH** as much as I have.

Route Overview

500RH

I N this overview section, I list only the locations with connections to the legends of Robin Hood. There are a great many places of tourist interest between these locations, which I detail within the book's narrative.

The distances and times quoted are approximate, for the scenic routes I recommend. In most cases, more direct routes can be plotted along major roads.

Part One

South Nottinghamshire – Leicestershire & Lincoln
106 Miles ⁓ 3 Hours travelling
Travelling time does not include time spent exploring the attractions en-route

Nottingham to Castle Bytham 36 miles – 1 hour

Robyn Hoddes Crosse, Castle Bytham: Station Rd, Castle Bytham, Grantham, NG33 4SJ
This was the former location of Robyn Hoddes Crosse. The cross is no longer there, but its inclusion in a 1524 letter places it among the 10 earliest mentions of Robin Hood.

Castle Bytham to Lincoln 40 miles - 1 hour

Lincoln: Castle Hill, Lincoln, LN1 3AA
This city was the source of Lincoln Green cloth, worn by Robin Hood and his men.

Lincoln to Oxton 30 miles - 1 hour

Robin Hood Theatre, Averham: Church Lane, Averham, NG23 5RB
This independent village theatre shares only its name with Robin Hood.

Robin Hood Hill: Oxton: Blind Lane, Oxton, Southwell, NG25 0SS
An historic site on the edge of Sherwood Forest, formerly known as "Robin Hood's Piss Pot".

Part Two

Nottinghamshire
92 Miles - 3 Hours 10 Minutes travelling
Travelling time does not include time spent exploring the attractions en-route

Oxton to Blidworth 4 miles - 10 minutes

Blidworth: Mansfield Rd, Blidworth, NG21 0PN
This village was reputed to be home to Maid Marian, and the place from where Will Scarlet collected her to marry Robin Hood in Edwinstowe.

Church of St Mary of the Purification: Main Street, Blidworth, NG21 0QX
The churchyard has a Memorial to Will Scarlet.

Blidworth to Bestwood Country Park 9 miles - 20 minutes

Bestwood Lodge, Bestwood Lodge Drive, Arnold, Nottingham, NG5 8HT
This former royal hunting lodge, which is now a hotel, has carvings of Robin and his Merrie Men.

Bestwood Country Park to Papplewick 7 miles 20 minutes

Saint James' Church Papplewick: Off Main Street, Papplewick, NG15 8FE
Legend says that Robin Hood's minstrel Alan a Dale was married by Robin in this church.

Robin Hood's Stables: Hall Lane, Papplewick, NG15 8EY
This is a well-hidden cave, set into the sandstone near the Lodge of Papplewick Hall. It is reputed to be where Robin hid his horses when visiting Nottingham. Sadly, it is now sits on private land.

Papplewick to Thieves Wood & Fountaindale 4 miles - 7 minutes

Fountain Dale: Nottingham Rd, Harlow Wood, Mansfield, NG18 4TJ

This area, associated with Friar Tuck, is a 10 minute walk along the Robin Hood Way from the A60, Nottingham Road. It is one of two locations where folk tales place the fight between Robin and Friar Tuck.

Thieves Wood & Fountaindale to Old Clipstone 8 miles - 16 minutes

Kings Mill, Mansfield: Kings Mill Reservoir, Sutton-in-Ashfield, NG17 4PA
This area was the site of the King's Mill, associated with Much the miller's son, in the ballad of the King and the Miller of Mansfield.

King John's Palace: Main Road, Kings Clipstone, NG21 9BT
King John held hostages in this former royal hunting lodge. Then, hearing that Robin Hood was at Creswell Crags, the King led his men to the Crags to capture Robin.

King's Clipstone to Edwinstowe 3 miles 5 minutes

Sherwood Forest and Visitor Centre, Edwinstowe: Sherwood Forest, Edwinstowe, NG21 9RN
A purpose built visitors centre, accessing Sherwood Forest and the Major Oak.

Major Oak, Edwinstowe: Sherwood Forest, Edwinstowe, NG21 9RN

The hollow trunk of this ancient oak was said to have been used as a hiding place by Robin and his Merrie Men.

Saint Mary's Church, Edwinstowe: Church St, Edwinstowe, NG21 9QA
Edwinstowe's medieval church stands against Barnsdale's claim to have hosted Robin and Marian's wedding. The High Street has a statue in their honour.

Edwinstowe to Walesby - 5 miles 10 minutes

Robin Hood's Cave: Brake Rd, Walesby, Newark NG22 9NG
Robin Hood's Cave forms a low cliff over the bank of the river Maun. It is said to have sheltered Robin Hood. The cave is 500 metres along a Bridleway, which is part of the Robin Hood Way.

Walesby to Creswell 12 miles 20 minutes

Church Warsop: Church Rd, Church Warsop, NG20 0SF
Legend says that the people of Church Warsop never locked the doors of their homes, because Robin Hood was always welcome.

Creswell Crags: Crags Rd, Creswell, Worksop, S80 3LH
Creswell Crags was reputedly frequented by Robin Hood, and one of the caves bears his name. It is also a site of prehistoric importance.

Creswell to Steetley Church 3 miles 9 minutes

All Saints' Chapel (AKA Steetley Church): 3 Field
View, Steetley, Worksop S80 3DZ
Legend says the Church Clerk was Friar Tuck, who
entertained the Black Prince (King Richard I) there.

Steetley Church to Skellbrook / Barnsdale 37 miles 1
hour

Saint Mary Magdalane Church: High St, Campsall,
Doncaster, DN6 9LH
Locals claim that Robin Hood married Maid Marian at
this church.

Robin Hood's Well: Skelbrooke, Doncaster DN6 8LS
This ornate well head dates from the early 1600s. Robin Hood is said to have drunk from the spring which
feeds the well, while robbing along the Great North
Road.

Part Three

North Yorkshire Coast & Moors
75 Miles - 2 Hours 30 Minutes travelling
Travelling time does not include time spent exploring
the attractions en-route

Barnsdale to Ravenscar 84 miles 1 hour 48 minutes

Robin Hood's Butts: Scarborough Road, Ravenscar, YO13 0ER
These are historic burial mounds, on Brow Moor. Local legends say Robin Hood and his men used the low tumuli as targets for archery practice.

Robin Hood's Bay: Robin Hood's Bay Road, Robin Hood's Bay, Whitby, YO22 4QN
As with all the legends, there are conflicting versions of how this part of the North Yorkshire coast became associated with Robin Hood. One version simply makes an association between sea-going pirates and our hero, while another has Robin fleeing Nottinghamshire to escape the King's men.

Robin Hood's Bay to Whitby Laithes 4 miles 10 minutes

Robin Hood Closes, and Little John Closes: Whitby Laithes, Hawsker Lane, Whitby YO22 4JZ
A story goes, that Robin and Little John shot two arrows from the top of Whitby Abbey. Two stones mark where their arrows fell. The fields became known as Robin Hood Closes, and Little John Closes.

Whitby Laithes to Fountains Abbey 70 miles 1 hour 30 minutes

Whitby Abbey: Abbey Lane, Whitby, YO22 4JT
A tale goes, that Robin and Little John were dining with the Abbot of Whitby, who asked how far each of them could shoot an arrow. The two outlaws loosed

their arrows from the top of the Abbey. Their arrows travelled 1.3 miles, to the area we visited above.

Guisborough: TS14 6BA
Guisborough is a pretty market town, which enters the Robin Hood legend as a possible home for Guy of Gisborne.

Robin Hood Wood and Robinhood Field, Ripon: Hell Wath Grove, Ripon, HG4 2JT.
This wood and field form part of Hell Wath Nature Reserve, with walks around the River Skell. The Skell is one of two claimants for Robin Hood and Friar Tuck's first meeting, and battle in the river.

Fountains Abbey (including Robin Hood's Well & Robin Hood's Wood): Ripon, HG4 3DY
This National Trust site claims Robin Hood and Friar Tuck's battle in the River Skell, which flows past the ruined abbey.
Robin Hood's Well is also alongside the ruined abbey. It is an ornamental Victorian folly, built to entertain tourists.

Part Four

South Yorkshire
47 Miles - 2 Hours travelling
Travelling time does not include time spent exploring the attractions en-route

Fountains Abbey to Robin Hood Village (Wakefield)
35 miles 1 hour 20 minutes

The village of Robin Hood: Leeds Rd, Robin Hood,
Wakefield, WF3 3AB
Halfway between Leeds and Wakefield, this village developed during the Industrial Revolution, adopting the
name of a nearby spring.

Robin Hood Athletic Football Club: The Coach
Ground, behind the Coach and Horses pub, 71 Wakefield Rd, Rothwell, Leeds LS26 0SF

Robin Hood Village (Wakefield) To Kirklees Priory 16
miles – 40 minutes

Kirklees Priory & Robin Hood's Grave: Leeds Road,
Mirfield, WF14 0BY
Robin Hood's Grave a monument in Kirklees Park Estate, near the now-ruined Kirklees Priory. The estate is
not open to the public, but several pleasant walks surround the area.

Robin Hood's Cottage: Leeds Road, Mirfield, WF14
0BY
Robin Hood's Cottage is in Bottom Wood within the
Kirklees estate. It was known as Robin Hood Malt Kiln
until 1949. Like the grave, it cannot be seen from outside the estate's boundary. You can however catch a
bus from a bus-stop on the A644 Wakefield Road,
named Robin Hood's Cottage.

Kirklees Priory to Loxley 30 miles 1 hour

Loxley: Rodney Hill, Loxley, Sheffield, S6 6SG
Loxley village was the birthplace of Robert Hode, who received a King's pardon in 1382. Aside from being an outlaw, Hode has two tentative claims for his entry into the Robin Hood Legend.
His cousin became the Prioress of Kirklees in 1402, possibly linking her with Robin's murder.
His mother was a descendant of King David, the Earl of Huntingdon. This title has become linked with more recent versions of the Robin Hood story, with current Earls of Huntingdon still having Robin Hood among their several given names.

Robin Wood: Garland Drive, Loxley, Sheffield, S6 6SS
Robin Wood is an area of ancient woodland, which is owned by Loxley Primary School. This is where a local teacher found a marker stone, which he believes marks to location of Robin Hood's birth. A pleasant walk can be had within the wood.

Part Five

Derbyshire & Nottingham
80 Miles - 3 Hours travelling
Travelling time does not include time spent exploring the attractions en-route

Loxley to Hathersage 16 miles 30 minutes

Robin Hood's Cross, Abney Moor: Abney, Derbyshire, S32 1AH
The Ordinance Survey maps from 1883 to 1923 show
Robin Hood's Cross, but it has disappeared from modern editions. I have not personally been able to find it
on my walks in the area.

Little John's Grave: Church of St Michael the Archangel, Church Bank, Hathersage, S32 1AJ
A grave-stone in the churchyard marks the grave of
Little John, where a thigh bone measuring 28 inches
was said to have been unearthed. This would have
made Little John eight feet tall.

Robin Hood's Cave, Stanage Edge: Hope Valley, S32
1BR
Robin Hood's Cave is set within Stanage Edge, the cliff
face that towers over Hathersage.

Hathersage to Baslow 7 miles 15 minutes

Robin Hood's Stoop: Highlow, Hathersage, S32 1AX
Robin Hood's Stoop is a marker stone on the north facing hillside of Offerton Edge. It had an alternative
name, linked to Robin's second in command, of Little
John's Flight. This is thought to be a version of Robin
Hood's last arrow shot at Kirklees Priory, crediting Little John with a similar shot to his grave at Hathersage.

The Hamlet of Robin Hood (Baslow): Chesterfield
Road, Baslow, DE45 1PQ

This hamlet contains: The Robin Hood Inn, Robin Hood Farm B&B, Robin Hood Bar (a strip of land south of the A619) and Robin Hood Plantations.

Baslow to Annesley 26 miles 40 minutes

Hamlet of Robin Hood (Whatstandwell): Robin Hood Road, Robin Hood, Whatstandwell, Matlock, DE4 5HF
The hamlet has a historic sawmill, part of which has been converted into a B&B, called Robin Hood Tower.

Annesley Hall: Mansfield Road, Annesley, NG15 0EA
Annesley Hall is a Grade II listed building, which dates from the 13th century. Robin Hood's boots were reputed to have once been kept at the Hall.

Robin Hood's Hills, Chair & Cave (Kirkby in Ashfield): Derby Road, Kirkby in Ashfield, Nottingham, NG17 9AT
There are pleasant walks onto and around this hill, to the south of Kirkby in Ashfield. The cave was known as Friar Tuck's Cell when it was visited by author, Washington Irving.

Annesley to Beauvale Priory 7 miles 15 minutes

Robin Hood's Well, Beauvale Priory: Beauvale Abbey Farm, New Road, Moorgreen, Nottingham, NG16 2AA
Robin Hood's Well sits in the private High Park Wood, overlooking Beauvale Priory from the north.

D.H. Lawrence used the well as a location for two of his novels. There is a pleasant tea-room within the grounds.

Beauvale Priory to Codnor Castle 7 miles 25 minutes

Codnor Castle: Castle Lane, Codnor Park, Ironville, Derbyshire, NG16 5PQ
Reynold de Grey, a Baron of Codnor Castle, was a prime candidate for the legendary evil Sheriff of Nottingham.

Codnor Castle to Nottingham: 16 miles - 1 hour

Nottingham Castle & Robin Hood's Statue: Castle Road, Nottingham, NG1 6AA
Nottingham Castle needs no introduction. The statue, outside the old castle walls, is a popular photo-opportunity.

Old Market Square: Nottingham, NG1 2BS
Nottingham's Old Market Square is the location of Robin Hood's best known appearance. Folklore says that it was in the Market Square where Robin Hood took advantage of an amnesty and won the silver arrow, in a contest devised by the Sheriff of Nottingham.

The Robin Hood 500: 500RH

Part One

South Nottinghamshire – Leicestershire & Lincoln

106 Miles - 3 Hours travelling

Travelling time does not include time spent exploring the
attractions en-route

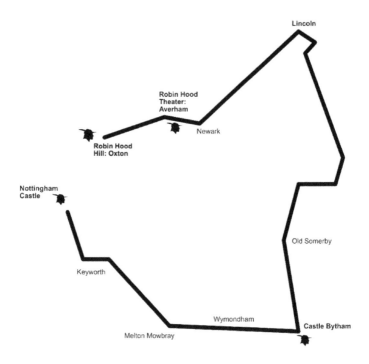

Nottingham Castle to Robin Hood Hill: Oxton

Nottingham to Castle Bytham: 36 miles – 1 hour

"Where do I begin," I asked myself. "At the beginning," some of you might answer. However, this is a circular route, or perhaps polygonal is more correct, since it makes a very irregular circle. Nottingham was my first thought, because the city has worked so hard at owning the Robin Hood legend. There was also something symbolic for me in riding out of Nottingham, because I had recently left Nottingham after retiring from the Police. Nottingham Castle seemed more of a finishing point than a start, since the Sheriff of Nottingham expended so much energy trying to get Robin Hood there. In the end, I settled for starting my journey in Nottingham, and since I would have to return there, ending the tour with the city's Robin Hood highlights.

The Robin Hood statue at Nottingham Castle

I planned the **500RH** to be suitable for campervans, cars, or motorcycles. For this first stage, a motorcycling friend was available, and the choice of vehicle was made.

- Leaving Nottingham to the south is much like leaving any city. Once out of the historic centre, all there is to see is modern-day industrial and retail sprawl. Luckily, it is a fairly short ride along the A52 Trunk Road, before you turn south on the A606 into more rural Nottinghamshire.

The first place of interest along the A606, is Keyworth.

Keyworth
One or more of the many candidates for Robin's mantel might well have visited Keyworth, since it is old enough for a mention in the *Domesday Book*. However, its modern claim to fame is the British Geological Survey (BGS), which is headquartered there. During office hours, you can visit their Geological Walk and by appointment, you can sometimes visit their excellent indoor exhibition. I visited the BGS for a seminar of Emergency Planners whilst I was a Police Officer. It is a fascinating place. Their Geological Walk squeezes three billion years of Earth's history into a 130 metre long stone concourse, with each step bringing you about 25 million years closer to the present day. **www.bgs.ac.uk**

The British Geological Survey's Geological Walk

Back on the A606 we are into agricultural country, riding through some of the best scenery South Nottinghamshire and North Leicestershire has to offer.

Ab Kettleby
The views are striking, but the unusual place names along the road are also attention grabbing. Just three miles across the Leicestershire border is the village of Ab Kettleby, whose Danish name translates to Ketil's homestead.

Burton Lazars
Just off our route, as it is two miles south of Melton Mowbray, but worthy of a mention for its unusual name, is Burton Lazars. The Anglo-Saxon village was listed simply as Burtone in the *Domesday Book*. Its name was changed to Burton Saint Lazarus, when the Order of Saint Lazarus founded a Leper Hospital on a hill overlooking the village, during the 12th century Crusades. The village has a natural sulphurous spring,

which probably accounts for its choice as a hospital location. The hospital became the Order's English headquarters, raising large amounts of money to fund their military and hospitaller activities in the Holy Land. The village's name became abbreviated to Burton Lazars.

Given the prominence that Richard the Lionheart and the Crusades play in the Robin Hood legends, it is entirely possible that Robin visited Burton Saint Lazarus.

Melton Mowbray

Back on our ride towards Melton Mowbray, it becomes apparent this is something of a foodie destination. The Melton Mowbray Pork Pie is a celebrity among pies, being protected under the Government's Geographic Indication List for food and drink. The brown tourist sign for Brockleby's Food and Pie experience prompted further investigation by this particular pie lover. Brockleby's are a pie-making firm, who sell at Farmers Markets all around the area, as well as delivering from their on-line shop. The "Experience" is an opportunity to learn how to make your own Melton Mowbray Pork Pie, which you get to take home. They also use a wide range of other fillings, including a Penguin Pie, which I had to assure someone very close to me, was not made from penguins. The Melton Mowbray version of the Pork Pie is thought to have been made for 18th century fox-hunters, but the basic cured meat pie dates from medieval times, when Robin and his Merrie Men might well have feasted on them.

Cheese has also contributed to Melton Mowbray's popularity as a food destination. Just off the A606 is the village of Long Clawson, famous for its Stilton Cheese, the second of Melton Mowbray's geographically protected food names. The Long Clawson Creamery (**www.clawson.co.uk**)

has been making Stilton since 1911, and I can say they have become particularly good at it. A detour to their factory shop is a must-do for any cheese lover. The cheese is said to have originated in Wymondham, a little further along our route, so more about it when we get there.

The Long Clawson Creamery has been making Stilton since 1911

Melton Mowbray is the biggest town we have visited since leaving Nottingham. Aside from its food connections, the town's markets are worthy of a mention. A Cattle &

Sheep Market is held every Tuesday, which is said to be one of the largest remaining in England. The Fur & Feather auc-tion, held alongside the Cattle Market, on the first and third Saturdays of the month, sells parrots, peacocks, chickens, rab-bits and a multitude of other pets. There is a Farmers' Market each Tuesday and Friday, and a traditional street market on Tuesday and Saturday. For those with more eclectic tastes in market shopping, Tuesday's Cattle Market also hosts an An-tique & Collectors Fair. On Wednesdays you can rummage for bargains at the Antique & Bric-a-Brac Market in the Market Place, and on the first Wednesday of each month the Cattle Market hosts an evening equestrian equipment sale. Then to really overdose on bargain hunting, you could join the 3,000 people at each Sunday's Car Boot Sale. **www.visitleicester.info**

- We leave Melton Mowbray, initially on the busy A607 towards Grantham, branching off very soon onto the much quieter B676 Saxby Road.

This section, through to Castle Bytham, is possibly the high-light of today's ride, being a series of chocolate box villages linked by winding rural roads.

- Just before the village of Saxby, take a right turn onto the unclassified Melton Road, towards Wymondham.

The scenery just gets better along this stretch, as I repeatedly activated my GoPro camera.

Wymondham

I promised I would tell you more about the Leicestershire village of Wymondham, and we have now reached that part of our route. The entire parish has just over 600 residents, although its busy village centre is significantly boosted by tourists. Aside from its picturesque appearance, there are two big draws to Wymondham. First, as alluded to earlier, is its part in the story of Stilton Cheese.

Stilton, if anyone does not know, is produced in two varieties: Blue, which has Penicillium Roqueforti (a fungus of the penicillin family) added to create its unique smell and taste, and White, which does not have the fungus. The ripening process for Blue Stilton takes between nine and 12 weeks. To make the Government's Geographic Indication List and use the name Stilton, the cheese must be made in either Derbyshire, Leicestershire or Nottinghamshire, from pasteurised local milk. Just six dairies are licenced to make Stilton: three in Leicestershire, two in Nottinghamshire, and one in Derbyshire. Two of Leicestershire's dairies are near Melton Mowbray, at Saxelby near Brockleby's Pie Shop and at Long Clawson, which we visited earlier.

Wymondham's place in the story comes from village cheesemaker Frances Pawlett, who is credited with creating the cheese in the 1720s. According to the Stilton Cheesemaker's Association, the wider popularity of Stilton is thanks to Cooper Thornhill, landlord of the Bell Inn at Stilton in Huntingdonshire. Association tradition says that in 1730, Cooper discovered the distinctive blue cheese while visiting Wymondham. He loved the cheese and contracted for the Bell Inn to have exclusive marketing rights. Cooper Thornhill's pub sat on the Great North Road, the main stagecoach route to London, enabling Cooper to quickly promote Stilton Cheese along the length of England.

Wymondham's second visitor draw is its windmill, which dates from 1814. The former flour mill and its grounds now contain a tearoom, craft centre, boutique shops and a caravan site. The tearoom does get incredibly busy. **www.wymondhamwindmill.co.uk**

Although I was not lucky enough to meet them, llamas Mr Peru and Lopez, occasionally escape from a village farm for a trot around the village.

Wymondham Windmill

- Another staggered crossroads takes you past the village of South Witham, before passing under the A1 and reaching our Robin Hood destination of Castle Bytham.

Castle Bytham

Castle Bytham is another small village, of about 300 houses. It is a pretty village, with two pubs in the old village centre and little else.

There is an obvious risk in recommending an attraction, in that it may close after publication. However, the efforts of the locals in bringing a shop and café to their village are worth recording. My recommendation for a drink and snack is the Bytham Community Shop, to the south of the village centre on Station Road (postcode NG33 4SJ). Opened in 2020, the Community Shop is exactly what it sounds like: a shop and café developed by the local people, when the commercial operators moved out. It has all the wares of any small supermarket, along with a little café. We very much enjoyed our bacon cobs.

Bytham comes from the Old English word bythme, meaning valley bottom. It is listed in the *Domesday Book* as West Bytham (and the nearby Little Bytham – as East Bytham) since its castle had yet to be built. The mound of its 11th century Norman castle overlooks the village. A simpler Saxon castle was home to a Chief called Morcar, who was related by marriage to King Harold. William the Conqueror's barons improved the castle, which was destroyed by fire during the War of the Roses.

Castle Bytham's Robin Hood connection is sadly no longer there to be seen; it is also subject to a little academic speculation. The Editor of Henry VIII's State Papers described a letter written by Thomas Wolsey in 1524 to Thomas Howard, the 3rd Duke of Norfolk, discussing "Robyn Hoddes Crosse". There is speculation that Wolsey described a cross in either Northumberland or Barnsdale, but academics examining the duke's travels put him in Lincolnshire at the time. The actual location of an ancient boundary stone known as Robin Hood's Cross is a little tenuous. It is not shown on any OS map and nothing can be seen on the ground. However, its inclusion in the 1524 letter, places it among the 10 earliest mentions of Robin Hood. **www.castlebytham.com**

Castle Bytham Community Shop

Castle Bytham to Lincoln: 40 miles - 1 hour

The next leg of our journey turns north towards Lincoln. Setting a satnav to Lincoln will plot a less interesting route, avoiding several pretty villages. If, like me, you are not technical enough to program a bespoke route, I recommend setting it first to Old Somerby.

- There is a choice of equally scenic routes from Castle Bytham.
- Turning right, the satnav will route you through Little Bytham.
- Turning left will take you back to the village centre, then north on A151 Water Lane.
- Then the B1176 takes us through Bitchfield, which is actually little more than two hamlets.
- The next village is Boothby Pagnal.

Here you can see the Grade I Listed fragment of a Norman style manor house, dating from about 1200. Boothby Pagnal's other claim to fame, is that Isaac Newton lived at the rectory for a time.

- We are now at Old Somerby, about three miles south of Grantham, where I stopped to reset my satnav for RAF Waddington (giving an indication of the area we are about to enter).

Old Somerby has its origins with the Danes, who founded a colony after making peace with King Alfred in 878. It remains a tiny settlement of around 300 people.

- From Old Somerby, we take the dead straight B6403 High Dyke, through Ancaster.

Ancaster
The straightness of the road attests to its Roman origins, with Ancaster sitting at the junction of Ermine Street and King Street. Tony Robinson's *Time Team* TV program visited Ancaster in 2002, uncovering Iron Age artifacts, as well as

the expected Roman remains. We will encounter the *Time Team* again, when the **500RH** reaches Codnor Castle and again in Nottingham.

Just before reaching Ancaster, we pass the first of today's air bases. Looking around, you see how flat this part of Lincolnshire really is, making it an ideal location for the long runways needed by Bomber Command. There are a great many excellent books about Lincolnshire's part in the war, written by far more knowledgeable people than I. So, I will endeavour only to give a flavour of the bases we pass along the way.

It is not just the flat plain of Lincolnshire that attracted aviators. A high limestone escarpment, called The Lincoln Edge, was also a useful feature. The escarpment runs along the edge of the Trent Valley, rising from 22 feet to 200 feet. It is a significant feature when seen against the pancake-flat fens of Lincolnshire, Cambridgeshire and East Anglia, and early pilots used it to help provide extra lift for their aircraft.

Many consider Lincolnshire as the spiritual home of military aviation. During WWI, pilots of the Army's Royal Flying Corps and Royal Naval Air Service flew from here to defend against the Zeppelin threat. During WWII, Lincolnshire became known as Bomber County, then during the Cold War, it became home to Britain's nuclear-armed Thor missiles and Vulcan bombers. By the end of WWI there were 37 military aerodromes in Lincolnshire, with Lincoln itself becoming a major centre for aircraft production.

RAF Barkston Heath

The first of today's airbases is RAF Barkston Heath. Today, it is a flying school for all three of our Armed Forces. Built in 1938, it was first used by the bombers of RAF Number 7

Group, before being loaned to the USAF from 1943 until the end of WWII.

- The old Roman road joins the A17 at the hamlet of Byard's Leap.

Byard's Leap

The hamlet was once the location of a Knights Templar Preceptory, and jousting tournaments could once be watched here.

A more colourful story concerns a witch called Old Meg, who plagued the local villagers from her cave near Ermine Street, often causing crops to whither. A retired soldier came forward offering to kill her. His rather bizarre choice of horse for the venture was known as Blind Byard, because he was blind. The champion went to the witch's cave, but she crept up behind him, sinking her long nails into the horse, who leapt over 60 feet. The champion regained control of his horse near a pond, where he thrust his sword into the witch, who fell into the pond and drowned. The spot where Blind Byard landed, is marked by a memorial.

Today, rather than knights or witches, you will receive a much warmer welcome at Byard's Leap.

- Facing you, on the other side of the A17, is the second of our RAF bases. This time it is the Air Force's Staff College at Cranwell.

The spot where Blind Byard landed is marked by four horseshoes

Cranwell is where the RAF trains its officers, making it the RAF equivalent of the Army's Sandhurst Military Academy. **www.raf.mod.uk**

- At this point, there is an option for anyone not wishing to visit Lincoln. By remaining on the A17, you miss out Lincoln and join the A47 on its way to Newark.
- For those heading for Lincoln, we turn left for a brief spell along the A17, before turning

right and driving north along the A607 towards RAF Waddington.

RAF Waddington (Waddington, Lincoln, LN5 9NB)
Like all of Lincolnshire's bases, Waddington served through-out WWII, continuing to the present day as a base for surveil-lance aircraft. Rather than repeat the base's military history, I will say a few words about its part in the Falklands War. Three aircraft took part in a long-range bombing raid on Port Stanley airfield. The three Vulcan B2s were already 22 years old and were selected for their powerful Olympus 301 engines. A complicated air-to-air refuelling plan, involving 14 tankers, was developed for them to reach the remote islands. **www.raf.mod.uk**

- Another four miles brings us into the centre of Lin-coln and another stop on our Robin Hood journey.

Lincoln's major part in our hero's legend comes from its cloth-making industry.

Lincoln
Many of Robin's tales have our hero and his Merrie Men wearing "Lincoln Green". I never gave the title much thought, assuming it to generally refer to the forest colour of the area. However, there is a much stronger tie between Robin's signa-ture colour and Lincoln's medieval wool trade.

Lincoln in the Middle Ages was a prosperous city, be-cause of its farming and its variety of merchants. Possibly the most famous of Lincoln's wares were its beautifully coloured textiles. Two shades of cloth were most coveted: Lincoln Green and Lincoln Scarlet. Lincoln became renowned throughout England for the high quality of the dyes used and for the consistency of their colour. By comparison, Kendal Green was also popular, but was notoriously inconsistent in its colour.

Green, (or grene / greene as it was known in the Middle Ages), was the less expensive of Lincoln's two coloured fabrics. The green colour was created by first dying the wool with woad, giving the fabric a deep blue colour, and then giving it a second dye with a yellow plant, known as Dyers Broom or Waxen Wood. The two pigments combined to give a consistent and attractive light olive green colour.

The city's other fabric was much more of a luxury item, due to the higher raw material cost. The green fabric cost 3 Shillings for an Ell (or 15 pence for 1.14 square metres in today's equivalent). Lincoln Scarlet cost more than double at 6 Shillings & 8 Pence per Ell (or 37 pence for 1.14 square metres). The reason for this cost difference was due to the difficulty in sourcing the necessary dyes. Lincoln Scarlet was created with a dye from Turkey called Kermes (from which the English word crimson developed). This dye was made by crushing the dried bodies of female Kermes Vermilio insects, which gave a richer colour than could be created with the pigments native to Britain.

Lincoln Scarlet was aimed at the more affluent members of society, but Robin Hood did sometimes dress in scarlet, according to at least one 18th century ballad. The ballad reported that while in the forest, Robin wore the same Lincoln Green outfit as his men. But, when at court or similar social events, he wore Lincoln Scarlet, symbolically showcasing his higher rank.

Lincoln Castle (Castle Hill, Lincoln, LN1 3AA) is worthy of a visit while exploring the city. Built in the 11th century by William the Conqueror, on the site of an earlier Roman fortress, the castle is unusual in that it has two mottes. Lincoln's is one of only two such castles in the country; the other is at Lewes in Sussex. The castle has been used as a prison and court, right up to modern times. The castle grounds still house Lincoln's Crown Court, in their own Grade II Listed building. The castle is open to the public most days and visitors can walk around the walls, enjoying views of the castle complex, cathedral and surrounding countryside. **www.lincolncastle.com**

Lincoln's Anglican Cathedral (Minster Yard, Lincoln, LN2 1PX) is the city's other famous building. Building began in 1072, but like all projects of the time, it went on for decades. It is said to have been the tallest building in the world for 238 years. The central spire collapsed in 1548, ending its claim to the title. Had the central spire remained intact, or been rebuilt, Lincoln Cathedral would have retained its world's tallest status until the Eiffel Tower was completed in 1889. The Cathedral did once hold one of four remaining copies of the original *Magna Carta*, which has since been moved to Lincoln Castle.

A stone carving of the Lincoln Imp, a much loved icon of the county, can also be found within the Cathedral. According to 14th century legend, two mischievous imps were sent to Earth by Satan. The two imps headed to Lincoln Cathedral, where they smashed tables and chairs and tripped up the Bishop. An angel appeared and ordered them to stop, but one of the imps sat atop a stone pillar, throwing stones at the angel. The angel turned that imp to stone, who can still be seen atop his column in the Angel Choir. **www.lincolncathedral.com**

Lincoln to Oxton: 30 miles - 1 hour

There is much to be seen in the surrounds of Lincoln, but lit-tle of it is connected with our hero.

- I took the busy A46 Trunk Road away from Lincoln, towards Newark and back into Nottinghamshire.

Newark Air Museum (Drove Lane, Winthorpe, Codding-ton, Newark, NG24 2NY)
One highlight I do recommend is Newark Air Museum at Winthorpe, in the triangle where A46 and A17 meet. This museum, set on a wartime training base, is volunteer run and is a great antidote to today's over-commercialised tourist at-tractions.

Based in the RAF's WWII heartland, there is a focus on wartime exhibits, with volunteers often dressing up to add a sense of realism.

The author at Newark Air Museum

Pride of place near the museum entrance, is a Cold War Vulcan bomber, which you can sometimes see inside. At six feet tall, I was surprised by how cramped the cockpit of the huge aircraft was, probably to leave room for a large nuclear payload. **www.newarkairmuseum.org**

Inside the cramped Vulcan Bomber cockpit

Newark

Newark itself has little in the way of official Robin Hood heritage, although the town is certainly in the geographic area of the legends. It does have a Grade II Listed hotel bearing our hero's name. There is a very pretty Market Place, with regular market days. The market also hosts an annual literary fair, where you might see me on a stall.

The ruined castle, alongside the River Trent, is also worthy of a visit – as is the unusual Castle Barge public house, converted from a Dutch Barge, which has been moored opposite the castle since 1980.

Newark's Castle Barge public house

Newark's Civil War Museum (14 Appleton Gate, Newark, NG24 1JY) also gets a thumbs up from my grandchildren. Newark was a Royalist stronghold during the Civil War, the museum holds lots of interest for all ages, although the girls especially enjoyed the opportunity to dress up. **www.nationalcivilwarcentre.com**

- We leave Newark on the A617 Kelham Road, sign-posted for Mansfield, although we turn off before reaching there.

Kelham

Kelham itself is a tiny, but picturesque village, whose most imposing feature is Kelham Hall (Main Street, Kelham, Newark, NG23 5QP). The estate itself dates to the Civil War years, when King Charles I was imprisoned there in 1647, after surrendering at nearby Southwell. The current Hall is Grade I Listed, and was for many years the HQ of Newark & Sherwood District Council. The local authority has now moved out and the estate is a popular wedding venue, as well as hosting craft and Xmas fayres.

- Soon after passing through Kelham, you will see a brown tourist sign, pointing to the Robin Hood Theatre at Averham.

The Robin Hood Theatre: Averham (Church Lane, Averham, Newark, NG23 5RB)

Although sharing nothing but its name with our hero, the theatre is worth a short detour for its curiosity. The theatre was built by a local carpenter in 1913, within the grounds of the very grand Averham Rectory. A section from an article written for the theatre's 21st anniversary describes it very well: "The exterior was simple and functional, but the interior surprised and delighted all who entered it. The ample three foot high stage with a depth of 24 feet and a width of 16 feet, was framed by an ornate arch painted in gold leaf, flanked by more beautiful plaster work. The handsome front drop tabs were of dark green velvet, and the orchestra pit was surrounded by a heavy brass rail hung with curtains of the same material." The simplified version of that prose is that the theatre looks far better from inside than out. **www.rhtc.co.uk**

The Robin Hood Theatre: Averham

- Back on the A617, we very soon turn left onto A612, towards Southwell.

Upton

Our first stop on the way to Southwell is at Upton, where the delightful Upton Hall (Main Street, Upton, Newark, NG23 5TE) has a very unusual function. The Victorian hall is home to the British Horological Institute and their Museum of Timekeeping. Among the museum's many exhibits is the watch worn by Captain Scott, on his ill-fated polar expedition of 1912. Upton Hall as you see it today was built by Thomas Wright in 1828. He was part of a Nottingham banking family and was High Sheriff of Nottingham in 1811, somewhat later than the evil sheriff connected to our hero. **www.bhi.co.uk**

British Horological Institute: Upton Hall

- After leaving Upton, we pass through Eastthorpe and Westthorpe, before reaching the market town of Southwell.

Southwell

As the site of an Anglican cathedral, Southwell is sometimes taken as a city; however, its city status is not recognised by the government. Southwell Minster (Church Street, South-well, NG25 0HD) is a magnificent building and a draw for many, but the town has lots more to offer.

We mentioned earlier the surrender of King Charles I. You can visit the inn where the King spent his last night of freedom. The Saracen's Head (Market Place, Southwell, NG25 0HE) was then called the King's Head, and was the place at which the King surrendered to the Scottish Army, stationed at Kelham.

There is also a Workhouse Museum, run by the National Trust (Upton Road, Southwell, NG25 0PT), where visitors can experience how the poor once lived. **www.nationaltrust.org.uk**

Southwell has a popular racecourse (postcode NG25 0TS), hosting jump and flat racing events. **www.southwell-racecourse.co.uk**

Being something of a food-lover, my favourite bit of Southwell history is the Bramley cooking apple. It was first seeded in 1809, by Mary Ann Brailsford. Henry Merryweather, a Southwell nurseryman, saw potential and cultivated it from cuttings. The apple is now widely used and renowned for its acidic taste and for cooking into a smooth purée. The original tree now looks in poor condition, but does still bear fruit.

- We leave Southwell on the B6386 Oxton Road.

This road holds unusual memories for me, as I most often travelled it during a cycle race. The annual Southwell Triathlon uses the out and back stretch to Oxton for its cycling section. The Race Director always described it as "undulating," which – to you and me – means "hilly."

Along the way, we pass Brackenhurst Agricultural College (Brackenhurst Lane, Southwell, NG25 0QF), which is now part of Nottingham Trent University. Starting life as a Victorian private residence in 1828, the hall eventually became a WWI military hospital (commemorated with a Blue Plaque), a working farm and in 1948, an agricultural college.

- Finally, just before reaching the roundabout with the busy A6097, we turn right into Oxton Village (postcode NG25 0SS).

Robin Hood Hill - Oxton

The 20-foot-high, 80-foot-diameter hill is actually a 3,000-year-old burial mound, and part of a larger complex of ancient structures. The Iron Age settlement would have been close to the boundary of Sherwood Forest, which followed the Dover Beck. The views from the summit are excellent and would have assisted Robin in his travels through the forest. The hill was marked on early maps as "Robin Hood's Piss-Pot," named for a basin-shaped stone that once sat on the summit. Victorian mapmakers apparently disliked the hill's vulgar colloquial name. They removed any reference to piss-pots from their cartography, re-naming the Oxton site "Robin Hood's Hill."

The burial mound is visible from the A6097 Ollerton Road and Oxton Bypass, but the more adventurous can walk up to enjoy the view enjoyed by our hero. A public footpath ascends the hill from Oxton's Old Green Dragon Pub (Blind Lane, Oxton, NG25 0SS). Unusual for many ancient sites, this one has no entry fee, no car park and no information signs. It sits within a working farm.

From the pub, follow a lane called Windmill Hill until it becomes a farm track.

After about a mile, the track ends at a gate. A Bronze Age settlement called Oldox Camp is visible on your right, and Robin Hood's Hill is straight ahead. The public footpath continues over the hill to a bench and viewpoint, although from here, the path is not always obvious.

Robin Hood Hill: Oxton

The Robin Hood 500: 500RH

Part Two

Nottinghamshire

92 Miles - 3 Hours 10 Minutes travelling

Travelling time does not include time spent exploring the attractions en-route

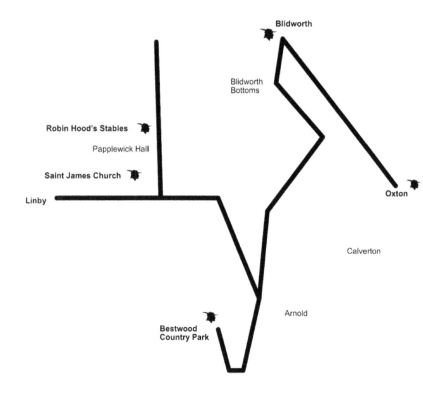

Blidworth

Blidworth
Bottoms

Robin Hood's Stables

Papplewick Hall

Saint James Church

Linby

Oxton

Calverton

Arnold

Bestwood
Country Park

Oxton to Papplewick

Oxton to Blidworth: 4 miles - 10 minutes

- Follow Forest Road north out of Oxton. Looking up to our right, we get a view onto the tree-lined top of Robin Hood Hill.
- We meet and cross the busy Oxton By-Pass into Oaks Lane, passing Oakmere Golf Course (postcode NG25 0RH).
- Then we cross the busy A614 into Haywood Oaks, driving through the woods from which the lane takes its name.

The hamlet of Haywood Oaks (meaning enclosed wood) was once considered an Extra-Parochial Area, meaning its residents paid no tithes to any clergy. Today it is included in the nearby Parish of Blidworth.

- After about a mile of forest and farmland, we reach houses at the edge of Blidworth.
- Turn left onto Dale Lane, then left again at the petrol station, uphill on Main Street.
- Saint Mary of the Purification & Saint Lawrence Church (Main Street, Blidworth, NG21 0QX) is on your left, opposite the junction with Ricket Lane.

Blidworth

Blidworth has a double claim for inclusion in the Robin Hood legends. Both Maid Marian and Will Scarlet are said to have lived here. It was from this village that Will took Marian away to marry Robin at Edwinstowe.

Then later in their story, Will Scarlet was thought to be buried somewhere in the churchyard of Blidworth's

Church of Saint Mary of the Purification (Main Street, Blidworth, NG21 0QX). The exact location of his grave is lost to time, but a piece of the earlier church building stands as a memorial to him.

Memorial to Will Scarlet: Blidworth

The original church was built in the 15th century, but only the west tower survives from the medieval church. The church was rebuilt in 1739, with additions in 1839 and is Grade I Listed.

Saint Mary of the Purification is the only church which continues the 13th century custom of The Rocking Ceremony. The ceremony re-enacts a story from Luke's Gospel, when Joseph and Mary went to the Temple in Jerusalem for Mary's ritual purification and to perform the redemption of the first born, by sacrificing two doves.

The Sunday nearest Candlemas (2nd February) is known as the Feast of the Purification of Mary. On this day, whichever baby boy from Blidworth was born closest to Christmas Day, is chosen to be rocked in the church's cradle. The practice dates from a time when few people could read, so Bible stories were acted out in church. You will be pleased to hear that doves are no longer sacrificed, but each boy's name is recorded on a board inside the church.

Saint Mary of the Purification & Saint Lawrence Church: Blidworth

Blidworth to Bestwood Country Park: 9 miles - 20 minutes

- Backtrack slightly along Main Street until you reach the Black Bull pub (Main St, Blidworth, NG21 0QH), and turn right, downhill, onto Field Lane and back into open countryside.

The Black Bull is another of this area's historic pubs. The owners have deeds dating back to 1730, which show that The Black Bull was already an ale house, and paying a preband to the Parish of Oxton and Netherhall. A conveyance dated 1878 marks the date when the pub was bought by Nottingham's Shipstones Brewery. Several transfers of ownership between successively bigger breweries followed, until 2012 when the pub returned to private ownership.

- At the T junction at the bottom of the hill, turn left onto Blidworth Lane, entering the hamlet of Blidworth Bottoms, and passing the Fox & Hounds pub on your left (Calverton Rd, Blidworth Bottoms, NG21 0NW).

Blidworth Bottoms

The Fox & Hounds became a public house in the early 1800's, having previously been a farmhouse. The Fox and Hounds Beer House was originally in a nearby nail maker's shop before moving to the current premises. Pubs are prone to change hands, but at time of writing, this has been a consistently good place to eat. The inside is a quaint country inn, and the outside has a large and scenic beer garden.

- We are now on Calverton Road, passing through Blidworth Woods, another surviving section of Sherwood Forest, with walks, cycle rides and horse trails (car-park postcode NG21 0NZ).

Calverton

The nearby town of Calverton is worthy of a mention for its place in the history of Frame Knitting. Today, it is a sizeable former mining town, but at the time of the Domesday survey, it was a small forest village, in the part of Sherwood known as Thorney Wood Chase. Although the town's name means "the farm of the calves," the area's rural economy was limited by a lack of grazing land. So, handicrafts like woodworking and the knitting of stockings took on a greater importance.

William Lee is credited with inventing the Stocking Frame, and Calverton has one of several claims to be Lee's hometown and birthplace of his invention. There is an element of mystery around Lee and his invention, with Queen Elizabeth I's refusal to grant a patent to his wife being the invention's catalyst. In the archives of the Historical Manuscript Commission is a 1600 partnership agreement between William Lee and George Brooke, which describes the invention. In 1831, Gravener Henson, a workers' leader of the time, wrote a book called *A History of the Framework Knitters*. In his book, Henson quoted several "ancient stocking makers" as crediting Lee with inventing the Stocking Frame. Failing to find much enthusiasm in England for his invention, Lee went to Rouen in France and set up Stocking Frames there. By the end of the 17th century, his Stocking Frames, the most complex machinery of the pre-industrial age, were in widespread use in England.

If you visit the gallery in Nottingham Castle, you will see an 1847 painting by Alfred Elmore, entitled *The Origin of the Stocking Loom*.

- Calverton Road becomes Blidworth Lane, running parallel to Haywood Oaks, along which we earlier entered Blidworth.
- Meeting the busy A614 Old Rufford Road, we turn right, crossing a roundabout after which the A614 becomes Ollerton Road.

The A614 itself has some historic significance. In Robin's time, this was known as The King's Highway, and was the main route north to York. Just off the A614, towards Calverton, lay a lost hamlet of Salterford, which still existed at the time of the Domesday Survey. There are two suggestions for the area's name. The most likely being that the ford was used by Salt Carriers. However, given its position in a royal hunting ground, it might refer to a saltery, or deer-leap, from the Latin saltatorium.

- At the next roundabout, we turn left on A60 Mansfield Road, towards Nottingham. These are the suburbs of Nottingham, and our route becomes more urban.

Arnold

The area around this roundabout is known as Leapool and Redhill, which now form part of Arnold. The local history group provides some information which ties in with the Framework Knitters we encountered earlier. Cottages on either side of the A60 Mansfield Road once housed Framework

Knitters. There is debate over when the cottages were built, but the history group favours a date around 1750.

Laburnum Cottages (postcode NG5 8LW) is a terrace of four Framework Knitters' cottages on the west side of Mansfield Road. In the 18th century, Nottingham's thriving hosiery industry saw developers build rows of such cottages, incorporating workshops with long windows. In this case the long windows are on the ground floor, which meant the upper floors did not have to be strengthened to support the frames. The cottages are currently numbered 271 – 277.

Mansfield Road: Framework Knitters' Cottages

For the motorcyclists among our **500RH** travellers, 1939 records show a resident of interest. Behind our Framework Knitters' cottages sat a larger house called The Mount. This was home to George Brough, the founder of Brough Superior Motorcycles, which had its works on Haydn Road in Nottingham. Brough lived at The Mount until his death in 1970. A road built adjacent to The Mount was named

Pendine Close (postcode NG5 8NS), after the Brough Superi-
or motorcycle model "Pendine", which broke lap records at
Brooklands in 1939.

We now move on to Bestwood Lodge and Bestwood
Country Park (Bestwood Lodge Drive, Arnold, Nottingham,
NG5 8HT). The former royal hunting estate would no doubt
have been a favoured poaching area for Robin Hood. The
hunting lodge, which is now a hotel, commemorates Robin
and his Merrie Men with carvings above its main entrance.

- At a very busy traffic light controlled junction, turn
  right onto B6004 Oxclose Lane.
- Then, take the first turn right onto Queens Bower
  Road. You may think you are going wrong as you
  drive into a Council Estate, but Bestwood Country
  Park is signposted from here.
- Take your first turning right onto Bestwood Lodge
  Drive. After a short distance, houses continue on
  your left, but farmland opens up on your right.
- After driving through an avenue of trees, the houses
  continue on Woodchurch Road to your left, and
  Bestwood Lodge Drive turns off to the right, becom-
  ing more rural. Bestwood Lodge Hotel is signposted
  at this junction.

High vehicles should park on the unmade layby at this
junction, as the official car park has a height restriction.

- Approximately 100 metres from the junction, a car
  park and toilets are on your right (car-park postcode
  NG5 8NQ).

A forest footpath opposite the toilet block leads first into the gardens of Bestwood Lodge, then into the Country Park. Cyclists should continue up the tarmac drive.

Path to Bestwood Lodge

Bestwood Country Park

Bestwood Lodge & Park was originally 4,000 acres of Sherwood Forest, which served as a royal hunting forest from medieval times until the 17th century. It would certainly have featured in our hero's poaching activities, and the Bestwood Lodge Hotel is decorated with carvings of Sherwood's outlaws.

Both the Robin Hood Way long distance footpath, and National Cycle Route 6 pass through Bestwood Park. The park is a splendid place to walk and cycle. There are well landscaped trails. But there are also areas with "bomb holes", which make for interesting mountain bike challenges.

At the top of the main drive is the Bestwood Lodge Hotel, which was built on the site of the old Bestwood Hall. The hall was built around 1363, as a royal hunting lodge, which saw lots of royal entertaining. The hall was demolished, and Bestwood Lodge was built on its site in 1865.

The present building is an example of Gothic Revival designed by Samuel Sanders Tuelon, complete with towers and turrets. In the 1800s, Prince Albert Edward, the Prince of Wales, made several visits to Bestwood, and was so impressed with Teulon's work that he employed him to work at Sandringham.

The inside and outside of the lodge are decorated with relief sculptures. Above the main entrance are seven sculptures depicting the heads of Robin Hood and his Merry Men. Elsewhere around the building are carvings of foresters and a depiction of a bull crashing into a well, after which the nearby town of Bulwell was named.

Bestwood Lodge was once a royal residence, used for hunting purposes. Henry I granted Lenton Priory "the right of having two carts to fetch dead-wood daily out of the Royal Forest of Bestwood". This grant might appear to be a petty privilege, but his Forest Laws were stricter than any laws since. Within the forests, the animals subject to royal hunting, such as red deer, fallow deer and wild boar, were protected against poaching by harsh penalties. To poach a deer from the Royal Forest of Bestwood put your life at peril. It was not only the game that was protected, but also the timber, which could not be cut without permission, and neither could the land itself be ploughed.

The first lodge was built around 1363, on the instruction of King Edward III.

Edward IV stayed at Nottingham Castle during 1469, and is recorded as having "availed himself of the joys of hunting in Bestwood, while in residence at the Castle."

Richard III also hunted there while staying at Nottingham Castle. His last visit was on 16th August 1485 when he rode out with friends to visit the Lodge.

In 1683 King Charles II granted Bestwood Lodge to his illegitimate son Henry Beauclerk, the 1st Duke of St Albans. Henry's mother was the King's mistress, the infamous Nell Gwynn.

During the last century, Sir Frank Bowden, head of Raleigh Cycles, lived at Bestwood Lodge. Then, when it ceased to be a private home, it became an Army HQ during WWII. It remained Ministry of Defence property until the mid-1970s, when it was converted into The Bestwood Lodge Hotel.

Carvings at Bestwood Lodge

During the Victorian era, Bestwood Colliery was established. The mine became the first in the world to produce one million tonnes of coal in a single year, but closed in 1967. The winding house still stands and can be visited on the Bestwood Village side of the park.

Bestwood Country Park to Papplewick: 7 miles - 20 minutes

- Retrace your route back through the suburbs of Nottingham to the A60 / A614 roundabout.
- This time, take the A60 Mansfield Road northwards, towards Mansfield and returning into rural scenery.

Sherwood Lodge (postcode NG5 8PP)
To your right is Sherwood Lodge, which is now the headquarters of Nottinghamshire Police and Nottinghamshire Fire & Rescue Service.

The original Sherwood Lodge was built on land allotted in Arnold's 1791 Enclosure Award to William Coape Sherbrooke. The Lodge and grounds passed through the hands of several families before being sold to the National Coal Board in 1947.

In 1973 Nottinghamshire County Council bought the 96 acre estate from the Coal Board for £100,000 and demolished the house and church. The Police were initially accommodated in a series of temporary huts, which survived until redevelopment in 2019. A single stained glass window from the old house survived as a feature in the new Police Headquarters building, which I was sad to see removed during the

2019 development while I was stationed there. The window did go to descendants of the last family to live in the house.

- Soon after passing Police Headquarters, turn left on B6011 Forest Lane, signposted for Papplewick Village.

We are back into farmland, and on our way to another hot-spot of Robin Hood locations.

Linby (postcode NG15 8AE)
A short detour beyond Papplewick, along the B6011 Linby Lane brings us to the pretty village of Linby, which won Nottinghamshire's Best Kept Village Award in 2013.

Linby was established around mills on the River Leen, from which village's name is derived. Smaller streams known as Linby Docks run on either side of the main street and give an unusual appearance to the village.

Top Cross: Linby

Many villages can boast of having a village cross, but Linby has two. The Top Cross dates from the 14th century and is Grade II Listed. It suffered vandalism during the Commonwealth period and was restored in 1869. The base is original and is possibly the only surviving example of an even-sided base in the country.

The Bottom Cross has some dispute over its date, with the defaced date inscription being interpreted as 1469 or 1663. Local historians favour the later date, thinking the cross may have been one of many erected in testimony to the Restoration in 1660. The Cross is set on a square base through which one of the village streams flows, symbolising the Living Water through the Cross of Christ.

Like many of Nottinghamshire's old churches, the parish church of Saint Michael is a Grade II Listed building. The oldest parts date from the 13th century, although it has been extended several times.

Walkers and cyclists can use Linby as another point to join both the Robin Hood Way and the National Cycle Network. The Linby Trail is a 2 km section of the National Cycle Route, which starts opposite the church and ends at nearby Newstead Village, with access into Newstead Abbey Park. Several of the local walking and cycling trails were once mineral railways, built during the Victorian heyday of coal mining. These railways were: the Great Northern Leen Valley Line, the Great Central Main Line and the Midland Railway.

Papplewick Village (postcode NG15 8FD)
The village of Papplewick is now a conservation area, and in medieval times was the southern gateway to Sherwood Forest. Parking can be difficult around the narrow lanes.

There is a layby opposite the Griffin's Head on Moor Road (postcode NG15 8EN), and another larger layby 200 metres further along the B6011 Linby Lane (postcode NG15 8FB). I recommend the larger lay-by, as it gives access to the Papplewick Trail and Saint James' Church.

Papplewick and its neighbour, Linby, are doing a reasonable job of avoiding becoming suburbs of Hucknall. There is still a fair amount of green belt around them, although this is being eroded by new housing developments. If we cast our imagination back 200 to 300 years, things were rather different, and these were very much "quintessential English villages in the heart of the countryside." We can still see some of the area's history, by exploring the green belt along the path of the River Leen.

The Leen rises from a series of springs within the Robin Hood Hills, near Annesley, which we will visit later on our journey. It flows through the grounds of Newstead Abbey before reaching where we are now, and continues through Nottingham and its suburbs to join the River Trent, covering a distance of around 15 miles.

The River Leen was a big draw for the builders of mills, utilising the river's energy to drive their water wheels. It is this mill heritage that forms the basis of the Papplewick Trail. The first recorded reference of a water-powered mill in the area dates to 1232, when Linby was known as Lindeby. Then, between 1615 and 1773, iron refining was happening at Forge Mill in nearby Bulwell. During the latter part of the 18th century the River Leen was said to have more mills than any similar stretch of water in England. Around 70 acres of water control was constructed along the Lean to drive the mill wheels. One of the country's largest water wheels meas uring 44 feet in diameter (almost 13.5 metres) was constructed at Papplewick.

The collection of reservoirs and water courses we see today, as we wander around the Papplewick Trail, were built by George Robinson and his associate David Melvin, who began bleaching and cleaning cotton at Bulwell in 1742. The Robinson empire grew, and they began converting corn mills and building new mills along the Leen from 1776. At one point the Robinson family employed 800 people along the Leen Valley.

The Robinsons were hampered by the 5th Lord Byron (great uncle of the poet, who succeeded him), who demanded payments for using the River Leen, which passed through his grounds at Newstead Abbey. In order to enforce his payment demands, Byron dammed the lower lake at Newstead, refusing to allow them to regulate the flow of water; he even threatened to open the sluice gates in a "sudden violent eruption of water", which would have caused serious damage to their workings. Their case was heard in court, but the Robinsons were unable to recover damages because Byron pleaded poverty. Due to the disagreements with Byron, Robinson bought a steam engine in 1785, installing it at his mill on Grange Farm. This was the first rotative steam engine to be used in a cotton mill anywhere in the world. In 1828 Robinson's cotton spinning business ended, and most of the disused mills were demolished.

The remains of the mills and water infrastructure have been preserved as the Moor Woods Project. At the far north of the area, alongside the layby on the B6011 Linby Lane, is a pond known as Papplewick Dam. On the south of the pond a weir allows water from the dam to fall into the river, which flows through the wooded valley below. During the years of the Robinson mills, this whole valley was flooded as a water supply for the mills.

Footpaths from the layby also take you on a pleasant walk to Saint James' Church, where legend says that Robin Hood's minstrel Alan a Dale was married.

Directly opposite the layby, the building that was once Robinson's Castle Mill (AKA Top Mill) has been converted into a residential house. The reservoir once came right up to this building, where its waters were held by a dam. The original road ran along the top of this dam, with the River Leen passing under the mill to power its water wheel.

To the left of the Castle Mill building, a kissing-gate allows access into the rest of the Moor Pond Woods project. Within this woodland are many traces of the water control workings, including several more ponds. The area has a series of information boards, maintained by the Parish Council.

A dam on the Papplewick Trail

- Opposite the 300 year old Griffin's Head Pub (post-code NG15 8EN), turn onto Main Street.
- After 200 metres, Main Street takes a sharp right, and then left turn, becoming B683 Blidworth Waye.
- Taking a left turn at this point, is a lane leading to Saint James' Church (postcode NG15 8FE). The lane is a private road but is designated as a Public Footpath and reaches the church in about 200 metres.

Saint James' Church Papplewick (postcode NG15 8FE)
Legend says that Robin Hood's minstrel Alan a Dale was married by Robin in this church.

The wandering minstrel Alan a Dale was a relatively late addition to the legend, first appearing in a 17th century ballad. In this tale, Robin rescues Alan's sweetheart from an unwanted marriage to an old knight. They stop the bishop from completing the ceremony, then Robin Hood, dressed in the bishop's robes, marries Alan to his bride.

Saint James' Church Papplewick

The churchyard also contains medieval grave-stones for forest wardens, which are carved with bow & arrow, sling, knife and hunting horns.

Papplewick Hall (postcode NG15 8FE) is a little further along Blidworth Waye, on your left. The hall is too recent for a Robin Hood connection, having been built in 1787, but it is a lovely building. It was built for the Whig MP Frederick Montague, and is still privately owned.

Papplewick Hall

Robin Hood's Stables

Robin Hood's Stables is a well-hidden cave, set into the sandstone near Papplewick Hall. It is one of many caves said to have been used by Robin Hood. This one is reputed to be where Robin hid his horses when visiting Nottingham. Sadly, it is another landmark that sits on private land. The cave is within a small wooded hillside, called The Firs. The edge of the wood can be followed by walking along Hall Lane, from Top Farm (which forms part of the Robin Hood Way). The landowner has tantalisingly placed an ornate bench just inside the fence, but it remains stubbornly out of legitimate reach.

The Firs – Papplewick

Newstead Abbey (postcode NG15 8NA)
Behind Papplewick Hall is an ornate iron gate, leading into
Newstead Abbey Park. This is a Public Footpath (the gate's
design prevents cycles from passing through – or over). It
forms part of the Robin Hood Way, long distance footpath.

Newstead Abbey is somewhat incorrectly named, since
it was a priory, not an abbey, founded in 1170 by the Augustinian Order. After Henry VIII's dissolution of the monasteries, it became a private dwelling, most famous as the poet
Lord Byron's (mad, bad and dangerous to know) ancestral
home.

The former priory is now a partially ruined shell, but
the grand house is still intact, and I enjoyed my daughter's
medieval themed wedding there some years ago. The park and
gardens are kept well maintained by their current owners,

Nottingham City Council, and are a popular picnic spot for families. **www.newsteadabbey.org.uk**

The author on his motorcycle at Newstead Abbey

King's
Clipstone

Edwinstowe

King John's
Palace

Mansfield

Fountaindale

Papplewick
Hall

Papplewick Hall to Edwinstowe

Papplewick to Thieves Wood & Fountaindale: 4 miles - 7 minutes

- Continue uphill from Papplewick Hall on Blidworth Waye, until you reach the T junction with A60 (at a point where it changes from Mansfield Road to Nottingham Road).
- Turn left towards Mansfield, passing the main vehicle entrance to Newstead Abbey on your left.

The A60 Nottingham Road drops downhill through farmland, before climbing again between Thieves Wood on your left and Harlow Wood (postcode NG18 4TJ) on your right.

Thieves Wood and Harlow Wood (postcode NG18 4TJ)
We are following the ancient road between Nottingham and Mansfield, which ran past Bestwood Park through Papplewick and Newstead Abbey, before continuing through Thieves' Wood into Mansfield.

There is roadside parking alongside the A60 and a larger car park in Thieves' Wood, from which the Friar Tuck locations can be reached.

Both woods have a fine selection of walking and cycling trails, but despite the name Thieves' Wood suggesting an outlaw connection, it is Harlow Wood into which we venture.

Bessie Sheppard's Stone is a good setting off point into Harlow Wood, sitting almost at the bottom of the hill, where the Robin Hood Way crosses the A60.

This memorial stone was erected in 1819 to remember the murder of a 17 year old Elizabeth "Bessie" Sheppard from

Papplewick. She failed to return home after looking for work in Mansfield, having been beaten to death with a hedge stake by Charles Rotherham, a Napoleonic War veteran, who had been drinking in the nearby Hutt public house.

Rotherham stole Bessie's shoes and umbrella, and disposed of her body in a ditch. He returned to the Hutt (opposite Newstead Abbey gates), where he failed to sell the stolen goods. He finally sold the umbrella and shoes at a pub in Redhill, close to where we passed the Framework Knitters cottages.

After a manhunt on an unprecedented scale, Rotherham was apprehended and sent back to Nottingham, where his trial and public hanging drew a large crowd.

Bessie Sheppard's Stone

Visitors to Bessie's memorial should know that her ghost is said to appear every time the stone is disturbed. The A60 was widened in the 1930s and the stone moved back several feet. An eerie figure was seen around the spot for several days afterwards. Similar sightings were reported 20 years later after the stone was hit by a car. A final spooky event happened in 1988, when vandals attacked Bessie's grave in Papplewick, moving her gravestone. A Police Officer was photographed by the Bessie Sheppard Stone for a newspaper article about the vandalism. The Officer touched the stone and was drawn back to Papplewick, where he found the missing gravestone in vegetation 200 feet from the grave.

Fountain Dale

This area associated with Friar Tuck, is a 10 minute walk along the Robin Hood Way from Bessie Sheppard's Stone.

The friar is said to have lived as a hermit in a nearby cave. A well, with supposedly healing waters, bears Tuck's name. Most importantly, it is said to be the place where folk tales place the fight between Robin and Tuck (alternative versions locate their fight at Fountains Abbey, which we visit later in our journey).

A sign on your approach to Fountaindale, along the Robin Hood Way

The ballad of Robin Hood and the Curtal Friar describes Robin seeking out the infamous friar, to test his mettle. The story goes that, after the holy man refused to carry Robin across the water, the two fought, before becoming firm friends.

Fountain Dale itself is the remains of a 12th century dwelling. The 40 feet wide ancient moat encloses what was once a large artificial island. The moat dates to at least 1251, when the island was the site of a hunting lodge. The moat and its structures are listed as a Scheduled Monument of National Importance by Historic England.

About 100 metres from the moat, we find the ruins of Friar Tuck's Well. The well was once surrounded by iron railings, which are now missing. All that remains are over-grown parts of a brick cascade that once channelled the spring water. There is some historic evidence that the spring was formerly named after Saint Lawrence, before becoming linked to Friar Tuck.

There are many other legends about Fountain Dale. One story says that when Tuck left his hermitage, he cursed the spring, making it flow only once every seven years. The groundwater in this valley is somewhat erratic, although this probably has more to do with the water needs of nearby Mansfield. Other tales claim that Vikings cursed the spring when they found no treasure in the island's shine.

The Lake at Fountaindale

Washington Irving, American author, famous for *The Legend of Sleepy Hollow* and *Rip Van Winkle*, visited Nottinghamshire in 1824. He stayed at Fountaindale House (postcode NG21 oND), close to Friar Tuck's legendary hermitage. Sir Walter Scott also spent time at Fountaindale House, working on his 1819 *Ivanhoe* novel. The Robin Hood legends had great influence on Scott's *Ivanhoe* story, with Robin appearing for the first time under the name Loxley. The grand eight bedroom house still stands, and was last on the market at £1.75 million.

Irving later wrote about his experiences of following the haunts of Robin Hood in his book, *Abbotsford and Newstead Abbey*. He said, "there is scarce a hill or dale, a cliff or cavern, a well or fountain, in this part of the country, that is not connected with his memory". Whilst in Scotland, Irving bought a collection of Robin Hood ballads, illustrated with woodcuts, from an old Scotch peddler. He is said to have "devoured its pages," which filled his mind with "picturings of merry Sherwood, and the revelling of Robin Hood, Little John and Friar Tuck".

Thieves Wood & Fountaindale to Old Clipstone: 8 miles - 16 minutes

- After walking back to the road, and our vehicles, we continue on the A60 Nottingham Road, towards Mansfield.

Mansfield

We turn east before reaching Mansfield, but in 1824 Washington Irving rode close to the town on his return to Fountaindale House. He heard "the chime of evening bells on the breeze across the heath from a distant village," which his companion identified as the evening bells of Mansfield. Irving remembered the town's association with Much the miller's son, in the *Ballad of the King and the Miller of Mansfield.* The long demolished mill is immortalised in the names of both Kingsmill Reservoir (postcode NG18 5HY) and its adjacent Kingsmill Hospital.

Mill Stone at Kings Mill: Mansfield

- At the outskirts of Mansfield, turn right at a busy traffic light junction, onto A617. This is a newly built by-pass road.
- At the first roundabout on the A617 by-pass road, turn left on A6117 Adamsway, towards Forest Town.
- The A6117 crosses the A617 at a busy traffic light junction, then continues downhill as Oak Tree Lane.

- At the traffic light controlled crossroads in Forest Town, turn right on B6030 Clipstone Road West, towards Clipstone.

A lane to your right in Clipstone takes you to Vicar Water.

Vicar Water (postcode NG21 9AS)
Vicar Water is a tributary of the River Maun, which runs through the ancient royal hunting ground of Clipstone Park. The stream was known as Warmebroke, until 1870 when it was dammed to become a trout fishery for Welbeck Abbey, which we will visit later in our journey.

The pool became a popular location for swimming and boating during the First World War, when it was used by the 20,000 soldiers stationed nearby.

After Clipstone Colliery opened in 1922, bathers were swelled by the 2,000 people who moved into the specially built pit village of New Clipstone. Fishing became more popular when the Duke of Portland awarded fishing rights to Clipstone Colliery Angling Club.

Spoil tips from Clipstone Colliery gradually surrounded the lake, until tipping ceased in 1976. The local authorities began to transform the area into a country park and designated as a Local Nature Reserve. **www.newarksherwooddc.gov.uk/vicarwater**

- We return up the Vicar Water access lane to re-join the B6030, now named Mansfield Road, turning right towards Kings Clipstone (postcode NG21 9BT).

The place names of Clipstone are worthy of mention here, if only to avoid confusion. The name itself combines a

Viking personal name, Klyppr, with an Old English word, tun, meaning farmstead. So Clipstone translates to, Klyppr's Farm.

The pit village we are just leaving is now known simply as Clipstone. At the time of its creation in the 1920s, as you read above, it was named New Clipstone.

- As we drive down a spiralling set of bends known as The Rat Hole, we reach a much smaller village sharing the name Clipstone.

This older village was once simply Clipstone, but the creation of New Clipstone caused this to become known as Old Clipstone. Then, as New slipped from use in the pit village's name, Old Clipstone became known as King's Clipstone, in reference to the nearby King John's Palace.

Driving out of the Rat Hole bends, spare a thought for drivers in the 1960s. The bends of today are challenging enough, but they have been significantly smoothed out in this century. Many drivers met their end in the Rat Hole, including one of my family members, who was hit by a lorry descending the hill too quickly.

- Soon after the Rat Hole bends, we see the Dog & Duck pub on our right.

King John's Palace (postcode NG21 9BT).
King John's Palace is on private land, but can be seen from the Bridleway between Vicar Water and the pub.

If using the pub, the ruins are a short walk. Otherwise, you should park for a slightly longer walk from Vicar Water.

King John's Palace is the ruin of a medieval royal house and hunting lodge. Before the 18ᵗʰ century, the site was known as the King's Houses. King John spent a grand total of nine days here, so the adoption of his name probably has more to do with the King's association with Robin Hood.

The earliest reference to the King's Houses dates from 1164 during the reign of Henry II, when King Henry ordered £500 to be spent on the creation of a deer park.

The ruins that are visible today are the remains of a Romanesque chamber dating from around 1180. Geophysical survey and archaeological excavation show that this chamber was a small part of a large complex of buildings. These included a gatehouse, tower, individual hall and chambers for the King and Queen, kitchens, several chapels, stabling for 200 horses, and lodgings for their many royal retainers. Today's remains are Grade II Listed and a scheduled ancient monument. The ruin is one of several sites in the region to have featured in Tony Robinson's *Time Team* TV show.

King John's Palace

King John's Palace is linked to the Robin Hood legend through a story about King John holding hostages in the Palace, then hearing that Robin Hood was at Creswell Crags, led his men to the Crags to capture Robin. An embellishment of the legend tells of Robin Hood and his men disguising themselves as minstrels, to rescue the hostages from King John's Palace.

King's Clipstone to Edwinstowe: 3 miles - 5 minutes

- Continue on B6030 through a rural area, then after a short distance turn left onto Mill Lane, signposted Edwinstowe.
- You will see Sherwood Pines Forest Park (postcode NG21 9JL) on your right, which is worthy of a visit.

Sherwood Pines has many walking and cycling trails, a café and visitors centre, and accommodation in the form of forest lodges. **www.forestryengland.uk/sherwood-pines**

- Mill Lane ends at a T junction in Edwinstowe, which is another hot spot of Robin Hood locations.
- Turn left and negotiate the one way system, to reach the Sherwood Forest Visitors' Centre car park (postcode NG21 9JZ).

Sherwood Forest and Visitor Centre (postcode NG21 9JZ) Originally covering about 100,000 acres, Sherwood Forest is now a 450 acre woodland to the north and west of Edwinstowe. Large areas were cleared in the mid-17th century, after it ceased to be used as a royal hunting forest.

The Visitor Centre hosts exhibitions about the Forest and Robin Hood. Film shows and talks are held on summer weekends, and the Forest Rangers lead guided walks. There is also a café and toilets. **www.visitsherwood.co.uk**

Several ancient oak trees in the forest either bear the name of Robin Hood, or are associated with his legend.

Major Oak: This is reputed to be the largest oak tree in England. The hollow tree has a circumference of 10 metres (32 feet) and its branches spread to cover a ring of 85 meters (278 feet). The hollow in its trunk was said to have been used as a hiding place by Robin and his Merrie Men.

The tree is now protected by fencing, but as a small boy, I enjoyed climbing inside the hollow tree.

The Major Oak

Robin Hood's Larder (also known as the Butcher's Oak and the Slaughter Tree): This ancient tree once measured seven meters (24 feet) in circumference. The tree was hollow and is said to have been used by Robin Hood as a larder for poached meat. It was damaged by fire in the late 19th and early 20th centuries and fell in a gale during 1961. Sadly, no trace of it remains.

Sherwood Forest Art & Craft Centre (postcode NG21 9RN): The Craft Centre is directly opposite the Visitors Centre, in Edwinstowe. The historic stable block has a range of shops selling locally produced crafts, gifts, and pamper products. The covered atrium has a cafe where you can enjoy a meal or drink protected from the weather. **www.newark-sherwooddc.gov.uk/sfacc**

Edwinstowe Craft Centre

Saint Mary's Church (Church Street, Edwinstowe, NG21 9QA): Edwinstowe's medieval church stands against Barns-dale's claim to have hosted Robin and Marian's wedding. The High Street has a statue in their honour.

Some form of church has stood here since 633, when Edwin, the Saxon king of Northumbria, was killed in the Battle of Hatfield Chase. He was buried here so that his enemies could not find his body, and a small wooden chapel was built. The current Church of Saint Mary's was rebuilt in stone in 1175. The main church building is Grade I Listed, and the boundary wall, gate, steps and overthrow are Grade II Listed.

Saint Mary's Church: Edwinstowe

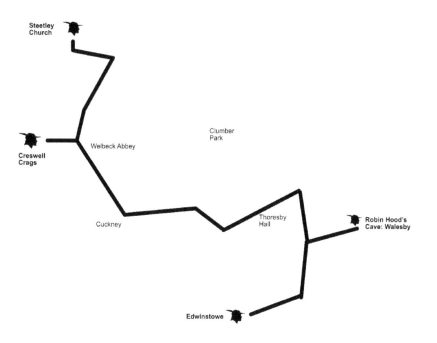

Steetley
Church

Creswell
Crags

Welbeck Abbey

Clumber
Park

Cuckney

Thoresby
Hall

Robin Hood's
Cave: Walesby

Edwinstowe

Edwinstowe to Steetley Church

Edwinstowe to Walesby: 5 miles - 10 minutes

- Leave Edwinstowe on B6075 Ollerton Road. At the busy five-way roundabout, take A614 Blyth Rd (second exit).
- After about two miles, opposite one of the gates to Clumber Park, turn right onto Whitewater Lane, towards Walesby.
- Just after the hump-back bridge, there are several rough parking areas outside Walesby Forest Scout Camp (postcode NG22 9NG).

Founded in 1938, the Scout Camp is set in 250 acres of forest. Of course, archery is one of the many activities on offer to the Scouts.

- At a point where Whitewater Lane turns a sharp right, park on the rough layby.

Robin Hood's Cave (off Whitewater Lane, Walesby, NG22 9NG)
A Public Bridleway, which is part of the Robin Hood Way, heads north from the layby. About 500 metres along this Bridleway, the rock forms a low cliff over the bank of the river Maun. This is Robin Hood's Cave, which is said to have sheltered Robin Hood.

This area has an extensive network of footpaths and bridleways within the Robin Hood Way. Keen walkers and cyclists could easily spend a good day in this area.

Robin Hood's Cave

Walesby to Creswell: 12 miles ⁓ 20 minutes

- Retrace your route along Whitewater Lane and turn right onto A614.

We are now in the part of north Nottinghamshire known as the Dukeries. The area got its name from the five ducal es-tates which were established close together. Worksop Manor was home to the Dukes of Norfolk. Welbeck Abbey was owned by the Dukes of Portland. Thoresby Hall was established by the Dukes of Kingston, and later taken over by the Earls Manvers. The now-demolished Clumber House was the seat of the Dukes of Newcastle, who were responsible for remodelling Nottingham Castle. Rufford Abbey belonged to the Savile baronets.

Clumber Park (postcode S80 3AZ)

The 3,800 acre Clumber Park, which is facing us as we return to the A614, was the seat of the Dukes of Newcastle, until it was bought by the National Trust in 1946. It is listed as Grade I on the Register of Historic Parks and Gardens. A visit to Clumber Park is well worth adding to your itinerary. There are many options for walking, cycling or picnicking among the park's fields and forest. In the 19th century, the 5th Duke of Newcastle created the longest double avenue of lime trees in Europe, which extends for more than two miles. Clumber Lake is a serpentine lake covering 87 acres.

Limetree Avenue – Clumber Park

The Duke's Study is all that survives of the main house, and now houses the Clumber Café. The building is listed Grade II on the National Heritage List for England. **www.nationaltrust.org.uk/clumber-park**

- After passing Clumber Park, we turn left onto Netherfield Lane, passing Thoresby Hall (postcode NG22 9WH) on our left.

Thoresby Hall & Courtyard (The Courtyard, Thoresby park, NG22 9EP)
Thoresby Hall, another of the Dukeries ducal seats, is a Grade I Listed 19th century country house. The 1st Earl of Kingston-upon-Hull acquired the Thoresby lands in 1633, but he was killed in the Civil War, so his son Henry, the 2nd Earl, built the first grand house. It went through several phases of alteration, before being demolished and rebuilt in 1871.

Thoresby Hall

The house is now a luxury hotel and spa, but the rear courtyard is open to the public, with a café and shops. The courtyard also houses the museum of The Queen's Royal Lancers and Nottinghamshire Yeomanry, which is well worth a visit. **www.whatsonatthoresby.co.uk**

- At the end of Netherfield Lane, we reach a pair of roundabouts, turning left at the first, then right at the second.
- Follow A616 Budby Road into the pretty village of Cuckney (postcode NG20 9NQ) which has lots of history.

Cuckney

The grounds of Cuckney Parish Church (postcode NG20 9JP), itself a Grade I Listed building, contains the remains of Cuckney Castle.

In the 17th century, George Sitwell mined iron locally and built a blast furnace here. During the 19th century, there were two large watermills on the River Poulter in Cuckney, one for cotton and another for corn. The upstream mill is now a primary school.

- The village of Church Warsop (postcode NG20 0SF) is a short detour to your left.

Legend says that the people of Church Warsop never locked the doors of their homes, because Robin Hood was always welcome.

- For those of us not visiting Church Warsop, turn right onto A60, towards Worksop.

- Before long, we reach the Dukeries Garden Centre (postcode S80 3LT), set around the former Welbeck Abbey.

Welbeck Estate (postcode S80 3LL)

Welbeck Abbey was once a Premonstratensian monastery, then after the Dissolution of the Monasteries, it became a country residence of the Dukes of Portland. The house is a Grade I Listed building. After WWII, Welbeck was leased to the Ministry of Defence and was run as an Army sixth form college until 2005.

One of Welbeck's stranger claims to fame, is that Archduke Franz Ferdinand stayed here in 1913. The Archduke narrowly avoided death during his stay, when a loader stumbled, causing a shotgun to go off. Had the Archduke died accidentally in England, his assassination in Sarajevo could not have triggered WWI.

American author Bill Bryson describes a visit to the Abbey in his book *Notes from a Small Island*.

Welbeck's most substantial building works were commissioned by the 5th Duke of Portland. He built a huge riding house, which was the second largest in the world, beaten only by the Manege at Moscow's Kremlin. The 422 yards long Tan Gallops was lit by 4,000 gas jets, and was heated to allow riding at night and in winter. The Tan Gallops was named after the oak chips that covered its floor, which were a by-product of leather tanning and provided a good surface for the horses to run on.

A 1,000 yard long tunnel ran from the house to the riding school, which was wide enough for several people to walk side by side.

A longer and more elaborate tunnel ran for one and a half miles towards Worksop. This was intended as a carriage drive, broad enough for two carriages to pass, and was abandoned in the late 19th century when a section forming part of the lake dam failed. Sections of tunnel survive on either side of the lake, and you can still see the tunnel's skylights when walking the Robin Hood Way.

The 5th Duke's excavations became more elaborate than simple tunnels, becoming a whole suite of underground apartments. The largest is a Great Hall, 160 feet (49 m) long and 63 feet (19 m) wide, which was used as a picture gallery and occasionally as a ballroom. A suite of five adjacent underground rooms housed the duke's library.

When I wrote my Loxley series of crime thrillers, bringing Robin Hood into the modern age, these tunnels inspired part of my fictional Loxley Hall. My modern characters use the tunnels in a Batcave-like fashion, to operate in secret against organised crime. **www.welbeck.co.uk**

The Harley Gallery at Welbeck

- Soon after passing Welbeck Garden Centre, turn left on B6042 Hennymoor Lane.
- At a T junction turn right on Craggs Rd, to see the Creswell Crags Visitors Centre car park on your left (postcode S80 3LH).

Creswell Crags (Crags Rd, Creswell, S80 3LH)

Creswell Crags was reputedly frequented by Robin Hood, and one of the caves bears his name. However, human habitation at the Crags pre-dates our hero by a very long time.

This is a limestone gorge, whose cliffs contain several caves occupied during the last ice age (between 43,000 and 10,000 years ago). The caves contain the most northerly cave art in Europe. Evidence of occupation found in the sediment that accumulated over thousands of years is considered internationally unique, in the way it demonstrates how prehistoric people survived at the extreme limits of their territory.

Creswell Crags is designated as a Site of Special Scientific Interest (SSSI). It has also been put forward as a potential World Heritage Site. **www.creswell-crags.org.uk**

Creswell Crags

Creswell to Steetley Church: 3 miles ‑ 9 minutes

- Leave Creswell Crags, turning right from the car park, and retrace your route back to the A60.
- Turn left onto A60 towards Worksop.
- At an oddly shaped roundabout, turn left onto A619.
- After approximately one mile, Steetley Lane is on your right, signposted Shireoaks and Thorpe.

Beware, parking and turning for larger vehicles will be difficult after taking this turn. We are now less than 500 me‑ tres from the church, so parking a motor‑home and walking in is not an onerous task.

- After about 500m, turn left into Scratta Lane, then almost immediately left into the church's unmade car park (postcode S80 3DZ).

All Saints' Chapel Steetley (3 Field View, Steetley, Work‑ sop, S80 3DZ)
All Saints' Chapel's official address is Field View, Steetley. The church certainly does have a field view. It struck me that the road lay‑out must have changed orientation since the church was first built. The elevation facing Scratta Lane is a fine example of Norman stonework, but the much more im‑ pressive carved doorway faces onto open fields. One can imag‑ ine the Norman Barons approaching from this direction, get‑ ting the full benefit of a splendid building.

Steetley Church is considered among the finest exam‑ ples of Norman village church architecture. I certainly agree with this opinion; the Grade I Listed church is a small, but very pretty package all round. It was built around 1150, and was referred to in Sir Waiter Scott's *Ivanhoe* as Copman-hurst. Legend says the Church Clerk was Friar Tuck, who entertained the Black Prince (King Richard I) there, when the church was just 50 years old.

All Saints' Chapel: Steetley

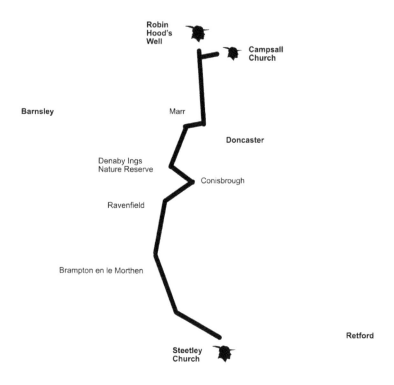

Robin
Hood's
Well

Campsall
Church

Barnsley

Marr

Doncaster

Denaby Ings
Nature Reserve

Conisbrough

Ravenfield

Brampton en le Morthen

Retford

Steetley
Church

Steetley Church to Robin Hood's Well: Skellbrook

Steetley Church to Skellbrook / Barnsdale: 37 miles - 1 hour

This is a long section, which could be driven along major roads to reach Robin Hood's Well quite quickly. The most straightforward route covers the distance in 35 minutes. However, you would miss out on many nice roads and villages along my recommended route. By necessity, we skirt the edges of some industrial towns along the way, but we are through them quickly and back into rural scenery and along lightly used roads. So, for those coming with me on the scenic route, get out your map, or program your sat-nav.

- Retrace your route from Steetley to the A619, turning left towards Worksop. Then, join the A60 Mansfield Road towards Worksop.
- At a large roundabout, take the second exit, onto A57.
- Stay on the A57, going straight through the next three roundabouts.
- The A57 begins as a dual carriageway, but quickly becomes a more rural single carriageway.
- At the fourth roundabout, with the Red Lion pub (postcode S26 1DJ) on your left, turn right, taking the fourth exit for B6463 Todwick Road.
- After 500 metres on Todwick Road, turn left onto the delightfully named Pocket Handkerchief Lane (postcode S26 1HD).

Local sources claim Pocket Handkerchief Lane to be the only road bearing this unusual name, but they provide no ideas of its origin. The road is just as delightful as its name suggests.

- Reaching a T junction with Common Road, turn left.
- The road name soon changes to Long Road then once again becomes Common Lane as we enter the village of Brampton-en-le-Morthen (postcode S66 9AT).

Brampton-en-le-Morthen (postcode S66 9AT)
This tiny village of stone built houses declares a population of just 80 people. As you might expect so close to the steel working cities of Sheffield and Rotherham, Brampton-en-le-Morthen has a connection to this industry. The village is part of Victorian Ironworker George Sitwell's estate.

- Our short journey through Brampton-en-le-Morthen takes an inverted S shape, and we leave the village on Brampton Road.
- Reaching a roundabout, with a hotel (postcode S66 9JA) on your left, take the first exit onto B6060 Morthen Road and cross over M18.
- Continue on B6060 Morthen Road as it bends to the right and passes through a modern, but pleasant, residential area into Wickersley (postcode S66 1JL).

Wickersley (postcode S66 1JL)
In contrast to Brampton's 80 residents, Wickersley has grown considerably, now housing around 8,000 people. First settled in Roman times, the village was once held by the founder of Roche Abbey, Richard FitzTurgis, who adopted the surname 'de Wickersley.

Saint Alban's, the oldest of Wickersley's three church-es, has a history dating back to 1150, although the current nave dates from 1833. Richard 'de Wickersley stayed in the village, having been laid to rest in Saint Alban's nave.

Of significance to our fellow travellers is a mention in a 1419 document of a Lamp of Saint Nicholas, mounted in the tower of Wickersley Church. This served as a guide to travel-lers along the route from Bawtry, which was a significant port at the time, to Sheffield, Rotherham and North Derbyshire.

- At the roundabout in Wickersley, take the fourth ex-it, onto A631 Bawtry Road.
- This is an area where historic villages have grown to join with each other as suburbs of nearby conurba-tions, and Wickersley blends seamlessly into Bramley.
- We turn left onto Church Lane, immediately before Bramley Park (postcode S66 2RU) and head towards open countryside.
- At the first roundabout, we take the first exit, onto B6093 Main Street, entering Ravenfield (postcode S65 4LZ), another of Rotherham's villages turned suburb.

Ravenfield (postcode S65 4LZ)
Ravenfield began as an agricultural community, and green fingers seem to have been passed along, as the village regularly does well in the Britain in Bloom competition.

- At the next roundabout, take the second exit, turning right, remaining on the B6093 Moor Lane.
- As the name suggests, we are about to get a view of moorland.

- Houses remain to our left, but the view to our right opens up nicely.
- This is quite a long section, but is easy to navigate since Moor Lane ends at a T junction with A630.
- At the T junction, turn right onto A630 Doncaster Road.
- Immediately before the Hilltop pub (postcode DN12 2AY), turn left onto Old Road.
- Then after about 500m, at a school's green railings (postcode DN12 3LR), turn left onto Hill Top Road.
- We are still navigating Rotherham's suburbs as we reach a roundabout in the former village of Conisbrough. On the roundabout is an Asda supermarket (postcode DN12 4TJ).
- At the roundabout, take the first exit, turning left onto A6023 Doncaster Road.
- The River Don has split into two channels here and we cross over both of them.
- At traffic lights, soon after the second river crossing, turn right onto Pastures Road and back into the countryside.
- Just like the Don, the River Dearne has also split into two channels, which we cross, passing through the Denaby Ings Nature Reserve (postcode S64 0JJ).
- After the second crossing of the River Dearne, turn left onto Melton Mill Lane (postcode DN5 7TF).
- At the end of Melton Mill Lane, we navigate two junctions close together, both of which are formed around triangles of grass.
- At the first of these junctions, turn left onto Doncaster Road.

- Then, after 100m, turn right at a similar junction, onto Hangman Stone Road (postcode DN5 7EE).
- This is a long rural section, and the road name changes to Blacksmith's Lane as we drive through a wind farm.
- Navigating off Blacksmith's Lane is easy, as it ends in a T junction with A635 Barnsley Road (postcode DN5 7AX).

The village of Marr is another small one, with around 150 residents. It is old enough to have featured in the *Domesday Book*.

- Turn right onto A635 Barnsley Road, then after 100m turn left onto Church Lane.
- At a rather complicated five-way junction, take the one-o-clock option, onto Red House Lane, which runs parallel with A1M.
- We are now almost opposite Robin Hood's Well, but on the wrong side of the A1, so our next section loops us onto the southbound A1.
- Turn left onto A638 Doncaster Road, then at roundabout, turn right onto A6201 Wrangbrook Lane. This brings us to Barnsdale Bar roundabout (postcode WF8 3JF).

We are now in an area of South Yorkshire known as Barnsdale. The region has for a long time contested Sherwood Forest with an alternative claim to Robin Hood. The most modern manifestation of this claim was in naming Doncaster's airport as Robin Hood Airport. (First Ave, Doncaster DN9 3RH). Sadly, at time of writing (late 2022) Robin Hood Airport was in financial difficulties, and its future looked uncertain.

Doncaster Sheffield (Robin Hood) Airport

Robin Hood's Statue inside the airport

Historically, Yorkshire's claim originates from 15th century ballads which connect several places in Barnsdale with Robin Hood. The ballads credit him with building a chapel in Skellbrooke, and suggests nearby Campsall Church as an alternative claim to Robin & Marion's wedding venue.

- From Barnsdale Bar roundabout, we can take a 10 minute detour to a church with an alternative claim to Robin & Marion's wedding venue.
- Cross straight on from the roundabout, into Woodfield Road.
- At the T junction in Campsall village, turn left, then right onto High Street, which takes us straight to Saint Mary Magdalene Church (postcode DN6 9LH).

Saint Mary Magdalene Church, at Campsall (High St, Campsall, Doncaster, DN6 9LH)

The present church was built towards the end of the 11th century and contains features of almost every style of architecture since that time.

Locals claim that Robin Hood married Maid Marian at this church. They base their claim on the description of a church in one of the ballads, believing that Saint Mary Magdalene is the only church in the area to fit the description. However, since much of Robin's story is shrouded in legend, no firm evidence exists to support their assertion.

In 2013, when the National Churches Trust compiled a list of Britain's favourite places of worship, local MP Ed Miliband nominated Saint Mary Magdalene because of its connection with Robin Hood.

Saint Mary Magdalane Church, at Campsall

- After visiting the church at Campsall, we retrace our route back to Barnsdale Bar roundabout (postcode WF8 3JF), where we take the A1 south.
- Our destination is a minor road on our left, called Robin Hood's Well. (Skelbrooke, DN6 8LS). NB: the road has a street-sign calling it Robin Hood's Well, but Google Maps shows it as Great North Road.

This village of Skelbrook was bisected by the A1, leaving Robin Hood's Well as little more than a lay-by. There is a light industrial works and a couple of houses. The remainder of the road stub is hidden behind a screen of trees, making a useful camper-van stop.

Robin Hood's Well (postcode DN6 8LS)
Robin Hood's Well was first recorded in 1622, but there had been a water source here for a very long time. Aerial photography shows evidence of Iron Age and Roman settlements here, which would have taken their water from the spring. There is also evidence of two, or possibly three, Roman forts on the site. They were built on what was once Ermine Street, which linked York to Lincoln, before the road was extended to become the Great North Road. A journal entry from 1638 reads "Thirst knowes neither meane nor measure, Robin Hood's Well was my treasure." The journal also records the Well Keeper charging the traveller two farthings for the quenching of his thirst.

By the early 18th century, the small hamlet of Robin Hood's Well had begun to develop. This growth was due do the popularity of coach travel, as up to 30 coaches per day passed through the hamlet. Two coaching inns developed to serve this trade, the Robin Hood Inn on the west side and the New Inn on the east.

The Robin Hood Inn was demolished to make way for widening of the A1 in the 20th century. Horses were changed at the inns, for the next 12 mile stretch, where they were changed again. After being rested, the horses were attached to a carriage returning in the direction they had come from.

Although neither are now present, the hamlet once had a tree and a boundary stone named after Robin Hood, adding weight to Barnsdale's claim.

The Stone of Robert Hode between Burghwallis and Skellbrook is next to the Robin Hood's Well original location on the 1893 Ordnance Survey map. But the stone can no longer be physically found.

A tree that once stood in nearby Skelbrooke Park also links this village with our hero. Known as both Robin Hood's Oak and The Bishop's Tree, it is credited as being where Robin Hood robbed the Bishop of Hereford on his journey up The Great North Road (A1).

Although our hero may have drunk from Robin Hood's Well, the ornate well house post-dates him by a very long time. The Grade II Listed structure was built in 1710 by the 3rd Earl of Carlisle. He commissioned famous architect John Vanbrugh (Castle Howard and Blenheim Palace are among Vanbrugh's other works) to design the structure, celebrating Robin Hood's local connections.

Robin Hood's Well

The original well actually stood about 150m north-west of its current position. Widening of the A1 in the 1960s necessitated capping the well and moving Vanbrugh's well head building.

During my visit to Robin Hood's Well, I spoke to an elderly resident of the hamlet, who had lived there for most of his life. Many of the photographs displayed on the information board are his, with a few actually featuring him. He had clearly taken an interest in the hamlet's history, adding to the information I had read on the sign.

The Robin Hood 500: 500RH

Part Three

North Yorkshire Coast & Moors

75 Miles - 2 Hours 30 Minutes travelling

Travelling time does not include time spent exploring the attractions en-route

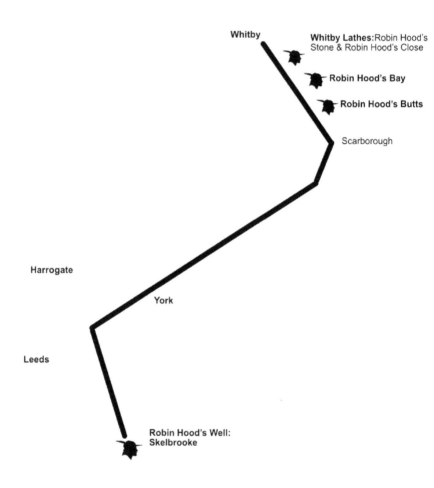

Whitby

Whitby Lathes: Robin Hood's
Stone & Robin Hood's Close

🌑 **Robin Hood's Bay**

🌑 **Robin Hood's Butts**

Scarborough

Harrogate

York

Leeds

**Robin Hood's Well:
Skelbrooke**

Skelbrooke to Whitby

Barnsdale to Ravenscar: 84 miles - 1 hour 48 minutes

- The most straightforward route allows a stop in York.
- Take the A1 north, then the A64 to York.

York

York is a cathedral city and the county town of historic York-shire, which lies at the confluence of the rivers Ouse and Foss. The city has many historic buildings worthy of a visit, includ-ing its minster, castle and ancient city walls.

York was founded by the Romans as Eboracum in 71 AD, although archaeological evidence suggests that Mesolith-ic people settled in the area between 8,000 and 7,000 BC. The Romans used York as the capital of the Roman province of Britannia Inferior.

After the Roman's left Britain, it became capital of the kingdoms of Deira, Northumbria and Jórvík.

During the Middle Ages, York grew as a major wool-trading centre and became the northern administration centre for the Church of England.

The Vikings, led by Ivar the Boneless, captured York in 866. They renamed their captured city from the Saxon Eoforwic to Jorvik, making it the capital of Viking territory in Britain. At its peak, Jorvik had more than 10,000 inhabitants, a population second only to London at the time. Archaeolo-gists have found evidence of craft workshops around the cen-tral Coppergate area. These workshops were used for textile production, metalwork, carving, glasswork and jewellery-making. Materials from as far away as the Persian Gulf have been discovered, suggesting that Jorvik was part of an interna-tional trading network.

The last ruler of an independent Jórvík, Eric Bloodaxe, was driven from the city in 954 by King Eadred, completing his unification of England.

After an unsuccessful rebellion by the city's inhabitants in 1068, William the Conqueror put his stamp on York by building a wooden fortress on a motte. This, and another timber fort, were destroyed in subsequent rebellions. William responded by building a stone castle, as part of the ravaging of Northumbria that became known as the "Harrying of the North".

Along with William's early forts, the first stone minster church was damaged by fire in the uprisings. So, the Normans built a minster on a new site. In 1080, Archbishop Thomas started building the cathedral, which became the current York Minster.

Arrival of the railway in 1839 brought new prosperity to York. Railway promoter George Hudson favoured York over Leeds as the base for his York and North Midland Railway Company. This helped establish York as a major railway centre by the late 19th century.

By the turn of the 20th century, the North Eastern Railway had its headquarters in York, employing more than 5,500 people.

If you love chocolate as much as I do, you will be interested in hearing that railways were instrumental in the growth of The Rowntree's Cocoa Company. The company was founded in 1862 by Henry & Joseph Rowntree. Terry's of York soon joined the Rowntrees as York confectioners. By 1900, railways and confectionery had become York's two biggest industries.

With the emergence of tourism, York's historic core became the city's best asset, and in 1968 it was designated a conservation area. The historic attractions were supplemented by the addition of the National Railway Museum **www.railwaymuseum.org** in 1975, the Jorvik Viking Centre **www.jorvikvikingcentre.co.uk** in 1984, and York Dungeon **www.thedungeons.com/york** in 1986. York's Chocolate Story **www.yorkschocolatestory.com** followed in 2012.

York has earned many tourism accolades. In 2007, York was voted European Tourism City of the Year by European Cities Marketing, beating 130 other European cities. It was also voted safest place to visit in the 2010 Condé Nast Traveller Readers' Choice Awards. In 2018, The Sunday Times declared York to be the "Best Place to Live in Britain." A 2018 YouGov survey reported that 92% of respondents liked York better than any of 56 other British cities.

York's historic city walls, and Minster

In a motor touring guide, I should mention the Romans' contribution to England's road network. Like most cities founded by the Romans, York is well served by long-distance trunk roads. It sits at the intersection of the A19 between Doncaster and the River Tyne, the A59 from Liverpool to York, the A64 from Leeds to Scarborough and the A1079 from York to Hull.

Historic York was not built for modern traffic, though. The street plan within the walls dates from medieval times and is not suitable for motor vehicles. Most routes inside the city walls are now designated as car-free during business hours, or restrict motor vehicles entirely. To ease access into York, six bus-based park and ride sites are located at the edge of the urban area, with easy access from the ring road. **www.visityork.org**

- From York take the A64 and A170 towards Scarborough.

I have not described the junctions along this section of the route, as it is straightforward to navigate.

Scarborough
With a population of just over 61,000, Scarborough is the largest holiday resort on the Yorkshire Coast.

Despite the lack of any archaeological evidence, claims were made during the 1960s that the town was founded around 966 AD as Skarðaborg, by a Viking raider named Thorgils Skarthi.

There was certainly a Roman signal station on the headland during the 4th century, and there is evidence of much earlier Stone Age and Bronze Age settlements.

Today, tourism is the town's greatest draw; an industry boosted by the craze for Spa Towns. A stream of acidic water was discovered running from the cliffs in 1626, which led to the building of Scarborough Spa. Dr Robert Wittie's 1660 book about the spa waters attracted a flood of visitors. Scarborough Spa became Britain's first seaside resort, although it took until 1735 for the first bathing machines to appear on the beaches.

Arrival of the Scarborough to York railway in 1845 increased the tide of visitors. This increase in passengers clearly needed a very large seat. Scarborough railway station claims a record for the world's longest platform bench, at 139 metres long.

For about 40 years, up to the start of WWI, Scarborough was a regular destination for Burton on Trent's Bass Brewery. The company used 15 trains to take around 9,000 employees on an annual trip to the seaside.

The town's most striking feature is the high promontory, pointing east into the North Sea, which supports the 11th century ruins of historic Scarborough Castle (Castle Road, Scarborough, YO11 1HY) **www.english-heritage.org.uk/visit/places/scarborough-castle** and divides the seafront into its North and South bays.

Scarborough Castle

The South Bay was the location of the original medieval settlement and harbour, which form the old town. This is
still the main tourist area, with a sandy beach, cafés, amuse-
ments, arcades, theatres and entertainment facilities.

North Bay and South Bay are linked by Marine Drive
(postcode YO11 1PJ), a Victorian promenade, built around
the headland. Both bays have popular sandy beaches and lots
of rock-pools at low tide.

The North Bay is the more peaceful end of the town. It
is home to the Japanese-themed Peasholm Park (North Bay,
Scarborough, YO12 7TR).

A miniature railway runs from Peasholm Park, through
Northstead Manor Gardens, to the Sea Life Centre at Scalby
Mills. The North Bay Railway (Burniston Road, Scarborough, YO12 6PF) boasts the oldest operational diesel-
hydraulic locomotive in the world, which was built in 1931.

Along with the miniature railway, Northstead Manor
Gardens (postcode YO12 6PQ) has three other attractions: a
water chute, a boating lake and the open-air theatre. The water chute is Grade II Listed and is one of the oldest surviving
water chutes in Britain. The ride of today is just the same as
when it first opened in the 1930s.

Perhaps not fitting terribly well with North Bay's
claim to be "peaceful," a mock sea battle, based on the Battle
of the River Plate, is re-enacted on the boating lake throughout the summer holiday season. **www.peasholmpark.com**

Scarborough Council has described its tourism industry
as "punching above its weight." Visit England collected data
between 2013 and 2015, finding that Scarborough came second
only to London as the most-visited destination in England.
The area had 1.4 million trips per year, compared to 3.7 million visits to London, and 594,000 to Skegness.

The town has several museums, operating under the banner of Scarborough Museums Trust. The Woodend Museum is a creative centre, with workspace for artists and digital businesses, plus an exhibition space. The Rotunda is now a national centre for geology. Scarborough Art Gallery is located in a Grade II* Italianate villa, which was built in the 1840s. It has displayed fine art collections since 1947. **www.scarboroughmuseumsandgalleries.org.uk**

Scarborough's Open Air Theatre, in Northstead Manor Gardens, has had an up and down history. The Lord Mayor of London opened the theatre in 1932, when audiences flocked to see the opera, *Merrie England*. Regular performances stopped in 1968 after *West Side Story*. A final concert was staged by James Last and his orchestra, before it closed in 1986. The theatre has now been restored and was officially opened to the public by Queen Elizabeth II in 2010. **www.scarboroughopenairtheatre.com**

Music from very different ends of the spectrum is celebrated in Scarborough. The Grade II Listed Scarborough Spa is home to the Scarborough Spa Orchestra, the last remaining seaside orchestra in the UK.

The internationally successful pop singer Robert Palmer spent his teenage years in the town, attending Scarborough High School for Boys. **www.scarboroughspa.co.uk**

Continuing on a musical theme, many of you will have heard the song *Scarborough Fair*: "Are you going to Scarborough Fair? Parsley, sage, rosemary and thyme..."

This song is based on a real fair, granted a Royal Charter in 1253. Scarborough Fair was a six-week festival attracting merchants from all over Europe. It ran from Assumption Day (15th August) until Michaelmas Day (29th September). The long-running fair lasted for 500 years, between the 13th and 18th centuries.

The TV and film industry could not have overlooked Scarborough. The 1998 film *Little Voice*, starring Jane Horrocks, is the most successful of several films made in Scarborough.

Other films set in and around the area included: *An Inspector Calls*, *Dancing Queen* and *The Damned United*.

Television series filmed in the area include BBC's *Rosie*, and an episode each of *Coronation Street* and *Last of the Summer Wine*.

The town even hosted its own sitcom, when the creator of ITV's *Benidorm* brought his format closer to home in 2019. The BBC show "*Scarborough*" was based on a group of friends attending karaoke nights in the town. The show was given a primetime Friday night slot at 9:30 pm. Locals got a sneak preview, when the first two episodes were premiered two days earlier at the Stephen Joseph Theatre.

Later in our journey, we will visit Oakwell Hall, near Wakefield, which Charlotte Brontë used as the manor house, Fieldhead, in her novel *Shirley*.

Scarborough marks a period at the end of the Brontë story. Charlotte's sister Anne lived for a time in the Grand Hotel (Saint Nicholas Cliff, Scarborough, YO11 2ET). At the time of its opening, this was the largest hotel in Europe. A blue plaque outside the hotel marks where the novelist Anne Brontë died in 1849. She was buried in the graveyard of Saint Mary's Church, near the castle. **www.visitscarborough.com**

- From Scarborough take the A171 north.

This appears to be a coastal road on a map, but high ground prevents a view of the sea. Even without a sea-view, it is still a stunning section of North Yorkshire road.

Scalby village (postcode YO13 0NW) is the first sign of rural Yorkshire after leaving Scarborough. The village is almost joined to Scarborough, but it has a village feel about it. Concentrated housing ends after Scalby, although we still cannot see the sea over the hills to the right

As we enter Burniston village (postcode YO13 0HJ), it has rather more modern housing than Scalby, though you can still see the village's history in its dry stone walls and the remaining sections of village green. As we drive further through the village, the buildings become older with several quaint stone cottages.

The whole coast has a prehistoric legacy. Burniston is part of this legacy, as dinosaur footprints have been found in its rocks.

Dalby Forest (Dalby Forest Drive, Low Dalby, Pickering, YO18 7LT)
Dalby Forest is signposted by a brown tourist sign off the A171. The forest park is about 20 miles inland. It is a Forestry Commission park, with a number of hiking trails and a network of progressively technical mountain bike trails. **www.forestryengland.uk/dalby-forest**

- Cloughton (postcode YO13 0AE) is the next village we pass through, which is smaller and more in keeping with what you might expect of the North Yorkshire Coast.
- Continue on A171 until just after Wayside Farm holiday cottages (postcode YO13 0DX).

- Turn right onto minor road (signposted: Staintondale and Ravenscar). There is also a brown tourist sign: Coastal Centre and Hotel.
- After a short distance, turn right onto Stubbs Lane (signposted Staintondale and Ravenscar). There are brown tourist signs to: Shire Horse Farm, Hotel and Coastal Centre. There is also a blue cycle route sign.

We are now into very open country, with great scenery.

- Stubbs Lane soon changes name to Gainforth Wath Road, then Rudda Road.
- At T-junction turn left onto Bloody Beck Hill (signposted Ravenscar). There are brown tourist signs to: hotel and Coastal Centre. This road appears narrower on Google Maps, but is very similar to the one we have just turned from.
- Bloody Beck Hill crosses Bloody Beck (a stream), then changes name to Scarborough Road.
- We reach a disused windmill, which has been converted to a house (postcode YO13 0ER). This is labelled Beacon Windmill on the OS map.
- The road takes a 90 degree right turn here, changing name to Raven Hall Road.
- Take the narrower straight on option, onto Scarborough Road signposted as a dead end. Ahead of you is a TV mast, where there is car parking.

Note: it is possible to continue downhill on Scarborough Road. But it is steep and single track, with few passing places.

I did drive down with my small camper van. There is some parking where a Bridleway splits left, slightly uphill, and the road (Cleveland Way) drops steeply ahead.

Parking spot (off camera to the right) at junction of Scarborough Road, the Bridleway and Cleveland Way

The road ends at Stoupe Bank Farm (postcode YO13 0NQ), where there is a turning circle, but no parking available.

Robin Hood's Butts are historic burial mounds on Brow Moor.

There are several walking options to visit them.

The easiest is a fairly flat walk from the TV mast. A well-trodden path leads north-west across the moor. Robin Hood's Butts are marked on the OS map. You can then re-trace your steps back to the TV mast, which provides an excellent landmark.

I took advantage of a friend's local knowledge and enjoyed a much steeper walk, which takes in more of the area's history and scenery.

Walking directions for a circular walk to Robin Hood's Butts

From my parking spot at the junction of Scarborough Road, the Bridleway and Cleveland Way, I walked back uphill on Scarborough Road. (You could also begin at the TV mast).

Look carefully on the right of the road, as the path is not signposted.

Look for a single car-sized parking place, just after a right hand bend, the path goes off at roughly your 1 o'clock.

Start of path up Stoupe Brow

This path is steep as it zig-zags up the hillside of Stoupe Brow. It summits at a large conical cairn at the edge of the plateau.

Look to roughly your 11 o'clock, and you will see the first of several wooden marker posts for the Stoup Brow Trail. (The spelling is different on the posts and map.)

This is post number 5. The first mound is alongside the post.

Stoup Brow Trail marker post

Mound between posts 9 & 10

Ahead of you from post 5, are posts 9 and 10, between which is the second burial mound.

Continue to follow the marker posts clockwise around the plateau, until you come to post 6.

Post 6 is taller than the others, and marks the junction with a rutted vehicle track.

Turn left, downhill on this track.

Go through a wooden pedestrian gate (alongside a larger vehicle gate) and continue along the track.

About 100 meters after the gate, step right over a low embankment, onto a less defined vehicle track across grass.

Meet the fence-line with views of Robin Hood Bay.

Follow this fence-line left, through two stone gateposts and continue to follow the fence. There are fantastic views to your right.

The fence-line curves to the left, and you come to a ruined sheep-fold on your right.

The track down is behind this sheep-fold.

100 metres after the sheep-fold, turn right through an empty set of stone gate-posts, onto a rutted track.

You soon reach the other side of the ruined sheep-fold.

Go through a wooden pedestrian gate, into a narrow sunken lane.

This track is interesting, as there are several sections of bed-rock, which have been carved to ease passage up the hill.

Carved track from Brow Moor

At the bottom of the track, meet the concrete surfaced Bridleway. Turn right, past the former Howdale School, back to the parking area.

There are great views on your walk along this Bridleway. There are several cottages, most of which are holiday lets.

Behind these cottages, a reclaimed railway line crosses over a pretty stone bridge. This is now a walking route from Ravenscar to Whitby.

Where the concrete Bridleway meets the tarmac road is where I parked. If you left your car at the TV mast, you would walk uphill on Scarborough Road – either all the way to the top, or by taking the zigzag path up Stoupe Brow onto the plateau.

Reclaimed railway line which is now a walking route from Ravenscar to Whitby

Robin Hood's Butts

Robin Hood's Butts are three Bronze Age barrows, situated on the Brow Moor plateau, on top of Stoupe Brow and over-looking Robin Hood's Bay.

Archaeological excavation in 1771 showed it to be a Bronze Age burial place. Local legends have grown around Robin Hood and his men using the low tumuli which covered the graves to place targets for archery practice.

The mounds were labelled as Robin Hood's Butts on Jeffery's 1772 Map of Yorkshire.

Ravenscar to Robin Hood's Bay: 11 miles - 25 minutes

- After leaving Robin Hood's Butts, we re-trace our route back to the A171.
- Turn right onto A171 (signposted Whitby)

Signposted to your right from the A171, is the interest-ingly-named Boggle Hole.

Boggle Hole (car-park Mill Bank, Whitby, YO22 4UQ)
Boggle Hole is a small cove with unique curved-out hollows, worn away by the sea. The hamlet lies at the foot of a wood-ed valley, with a very steep access road. The curious name comes from the Boggles, which legend says lurk on the slopes above the cove.

A Boggle is the local dialect name for a hobgoblin. They are mischievous little people who were thought to live in caves along the coast, and in remote corners of the moors. Local people used to believe that Boggles had healing powers, and sometimes took sick children to Hob-Holes, where Boggles were thought to live, in the hope that they might be cured.

In times past, smugglers used to land and hide their contraband in the caves, which fits with some of the stories I will tell you about Robin Hood's Bay.

It is a winding lane down to the parking area, and you have to walk the last bit (and carry all your stuff in and out) down a steep hill and over a bridge. Alternatively, it is just a mile on foot along the beach or over the cliffs from Robin Hood's Bay.

The YHA has a 42 bed hostel here, in a converted mill (postcode YO22 4UQ). **www.yha.org.uk/hostel/yha-boggle-hole**

The 109 mile long Cleveland Way long distance path goes through Boggle Hole. **www.nationaltrail.co.uk/en_GB/trails/cleveland-way**

- Turn right from A171, on a local road (signposted Fylingthorpe and Robin Hood's Bay) to Robin Hood's Bay.

Robin Hood's Bay (car-park on Robin Hood's Bay Road, Robin Hood's Bay, YO22 4QN)
Visitors should not drive into the harbour area, as the lanes are steep and narrow. There are two visitor car parks, one near the old rail station (postcode YO22 4RE) and one further down the hill near the Mount Pleasant Hotel (postcode YO22 4QN). It is probably best to arrive early in the morning or late in the afternoon, as it can be difficult to park during the busy daytime periods. **www.robin-hoods-bay.co.uk**

The first evidence of human habitation in this area was about 3,000 years ago when Bronze Age burial mounds were dug on the high moorland, a mile or so south of Robin Hood's Bay. We do not know what the Bronze Age builders called them, but at some point they became known as Robin Hood's Butts, when they were attributed to Robin and his men for archery targets.

The first regular settlers were probably Saxon peasants, followed by Vikings, attracted by the rich glacial soil and plentiful supply of fish, and this is how they survived by a mixture of farming and fishing.

As with all the legends, there are conflicting versions of how this part of the North Yorkshire coast became associated with Robin Hood. One version simply makes an association between sea-going pirates and our robber hero, while another has Robin fleeing Nottinghamshire to escape the King's men.

The local history society identified the first recorded reference to Robin Hood's Bay from sometime between 1322 and 1346. This was 120 years after the period commonly associated with Robin Hood and Richard the Lionheart, but slightly closer to the 1272 capture of Robert Godberd, who was linked to Codnor Castle. This reference is found in a letter to King Edward III, from Count Louis of Flanders, pleading for the return of a ship which was taken to "Robin Oode Bay", by the people of England. The historians think this was a reference to piracy in the bay, linked through literary licence to the outlaws in English ballads.

The area had certainly been notorious for piracy over several hundred years. Viking settlers were recorded as settling slightly inland, to better protect themselves from sea-going pirates. Clearly, 14th century seafarers were still at risk from pirates, as attested to by Count Louis of Flanders. By the

18th century, Robin Hood's Bay had reportedly become the busiest smuggling community on the Yorkshire coast. It sat in natural isolation, protected by marshy moorland on three sides, and cliffs on the other. Despite its dangers, smuggling must have paid better than fishing, and the sailors were supported by many others on land, who were willing to finance and transport the contraband. Fisherfolk, farmers, gentry and clergy were all involved in the illegal trade. Regular fights happened between smugglers and excise men, and Robin Hood's Bay wives were known to pour boiling water over excise men from upstairs windows in the narrow alleyways. Hiding places and secret passages were common, and it was said that a bale of silk could pass from the bottom of the village to the top without leaving the houses.

The French connection is supported by another local legend, in which Robin Hood encountered pirates while on a fishing trip, forcing the French pirates to surrender. The story goes that Robin returned from his trip and gave the pirates' loot to the poor people of the village in the bay, which is now called Robin Hood's Bay.

Another romantic attribution for the name Robin Hood's Bay came from Lionel Charlton, in his 1779 book *History of Whitby and Whitby Abbey*. In his book, Charlton gives us an 18th century perspective of how Robin Hood's name came to be associated with a place so distant from Sherwood Forest.

He tells us that at the end of the 12th century Robin "resided generally in Nottinghamshire or the southern parts of Yorkshire". But, continues Charlton, "his robberies became so flagrant and the popular outcry against him so loud, that troops were despatched from London to arrest him."

Charlton attributes Robin's journey north as being an escape from the government troops. Unable to fight the King's forces, Robin retreated north, crossing the moors to Whitby on the Yorkshire coast, where he acquired a few small fishing boats with which he could escape. Charlton credits Robin Hood's Bay as the place where Robin hid these boats.

Charlton goes on to say that the outlaws set up archery targets, or butts, nearby, which became known as Robin Hood's Butts.

Another version, for which I have not found an attribution, involves the Abbot of Whitby asking Robin Hood to help fight off an attack by Danish raiders.

These days, Whitby is a much bigger town than Robin Hood's Bay, but this was not always the case. In a set of Dutch sea charts published in 1586, Robin Hood's Bay is shown while Whitby is not.

From the early 19th century, Robin Hood's Bay began to attract tourists, something that has continued to the present day.

Robin Hood's Bay

By the mid-19th century, the fishing industry had taken over from smuggling and piracy, and a thriving fishing community existed in Robin Hood's Bay.

Robin Hood's Bay Museum (Fisherhead, Robin Hood's Bay, YO22 4TQ)
This free museum is housed in a historic 19th century building near the harbour. The building was bought in 1891 by the Vicar, Reverend Cooper, who converted the ground floor to a Coroner's Room and Mortuary. Since 1980 the Coroner's Room has been used to display historic artefacts linked to the bay, with exhibits on shipping, fishing, shipwrecks, sea rescues, smuggling, old maps and anything connected with village life. Note that the museum can only be approached via narrow cobbled pathways and steps. **www.museum.rhbay.co.uk**

Coast to Coast Path
The long-distance footpath known as the Coast to Coast Path was popularised by author Alfred Wainwright. This 192 mile long path links the east and west coasts of England. The path begins, or ends, at Robin Hood's Bay, with its western-most point at Saint Bees in Cumbria. A plaque on the harbourside Bay Hotel marks the official eastern end of the path. The hotel bar is named "Wainwright's Bar," in honour of the writer's connection with the path. **www.coasttocoast.uk**

For walking enthusiasts, the Cleveland Way long-distance path also passes through the village. **www.nationaltrail.co.uk/en_GB/trails/cleveland-way**

Fossil Hunting
The coast around Robin Hood's Bay is famous for its fossils. Large areas of limestone and blue shale are exposed when the

tide goes out, and exploring the rock pools in search of fossils and marine life is one of the most popular activities in the bay. A selection of the fossils discovered locally are displayed in the village museum.

What is a Gansey?

Researching a book like this teaches me the oddest things. While reading about the Robin Hood's Bay area, I came across reference to the Gansey.

The hardwearing fisherman's jumper known as a Guernsey was not new to me, but its North Yorkshire incar-nation as the Gansey certainly was. Hand knitted woollen jumpers have long been worn by fishermen around the coast of Britain.

A Gansey

The Yorkshire fishermen's version is a tough weather-proof jumper, intended to do more than just keep the fishermen warm and dry.

Each gansey is usually navy blue in colour, but has a unique pattern which varies from village to village and from family to family. So, if there was a shipwreck, the bodies washed up on the shore could be identified by their gansey and returned to their family for burial.

They were usually knitted by mothers, wives or sweethearts, and the patterns were passed down the generations by word of mouth. It takes around six weeks to hand knit a gansey. They are knitted without seams, in one piece, using five or more small needles and a fine, hardwearing four or five ply wool. They are knitted very tightly to make them weatherproof. The thicker parts of the pattern are concentrated on the upper body for extra warmth. The stitched-in patterns, which include anchors, cables, lightning, ropes and ladders, symbolise the everyday things in the fisherfolk's lives. It also became a tradition for the women to put in several mistakes to make the jumpers personal to each family member.

Ganseys were traditionally worn next to the skin with nothing underneath, and a silk scarf was worn around the neck to stop the wet wool chafing their skin. Fishermen wore their ganseys all the time and often kept a Sunday best version for church. The young women often knitted a wedding shirt gansey for their betrothed to get married in.

Although rarely worn by fishermen these days, the art of gansey knitting is alive and well and thriving on the East Coast, and they have become something of a fashion item worldwide.

Robin Hood's Bay to Whitby Laithes: 4 miles - 10 minutes

- After visiting Robin Hood's Bay, return along the same route, to the A171.
- Turn right onto A171 (signposted Whitby).
- Pass through the hamlet of Normanby and the village of Hawsker.
- Opposite a cycle hire centre (postcode YO22 4LB), with railway dining cars, turn right onto Hawsker Lane (signposted P, Abbey Headland, and Whitby Abbey on Brown tourist sign). This road is also a back way into Whitby.
- Pass through a delightful village, with a historic church and an old red brick barn on your right.
- Reach Manor House Farm caravan site (postcode YO22 4JZ).

Footpaths lead from opposite the caravan site, towards Whitby Lathes Farm.

Robin Hood's Stone and Little John's Stone are in fields behind Whitby Lathes Farm.

But there is no parking here, unless you are staying on one of several sites along Hawsker Lane.

Better parking is available a little further along the A171 on Enterprise Way industrial estate.

- To reach Enterprise Way, continue along the A171 until you reach the 30 MPH sign and the boundary sign for Whitby.
- Turn right into Enterprise Way (postcode YO22 4NH).

Walking directions to the stones from Enterprise Way

Walk back along the grass verge alongside the A171 (away from Whitby).

Just beyond the 30 MPH sign is a wooden finger-post. This directs you onto a Public Footpath, down some steps into a pleasant walled lane.

At the end of the lane, the FP curves left across a field. On your left you will see a metal gate, which forms an unofficial access onto Enterprise Way.

Continue around the field, towards an industrial unit at your 1 o'clock.

Where the hedge ends and a metal fence around the unit begins, use the wooden stile on your left.

After crossing the stile, turn right on a narrow footpath between the security fence and a barbed wire farmer's fence.

Cross a wooden footbridge over a deep banked stream.

Pass through a wooden gate, then right, through a hedge at a footpath finger-post.

Sight from the finger post, diagonally uphill to reach a wide gateway, with a FP roundel on the gatepost. You can now see a caravan site directly ahead of you.

Go through this gateway, continuing straight on, with a hedge on your left.

Come to another similar farm gate to the last one. Go through this gate.

In front of you is a hedge and barbed wire fence separating two fields. There is a gateway on your left, linking these two fields. These fields are Little John Field on your right and Robin Hood Field on your left.

The stones are on either side of the fence, Robin to the left, and John to the right.

They are carved with "Robin Hood Close" and "Little John Close." These curious names come from the contraction of the word "enclosure." During the 17th century, Common Land was enclosed by royal decree, preventing ordinary people from grazing their livestock on the land. Often these newly enclosed fields were given names, with the word "close" added.

On recent maps, these archaic names of Robin Hood Close and Little John Close have been replaced with the more modern Robin Hood Field and Little John Field.

Robin Hood's Stone

The Reverend George Young gave us an account of Robin Hood's activities along the North Yorkshire coast, in his 1817 book, *History of Whitby*. Reverend Young tells us that Robin and Little John were dining with the Abbot of Whitby, who asked how far each of them could shoot an arrow. The two outlaws loosed their arrows from the top of the Abbey. Their arrows travelled 1.3 miles, to the area we have now reached. At nearly a mile and a half, this must have been a superhuman feat of archery. His story goes that the arrows fell to the west of Whitby Lathes, "beside the lane leading from thence to Stainsacre." The Reverend says that Robin Hood's arrow fell on the north side of the lane, and Little John's about a hundred feet farther on the south side of the lane. He tells that on the spot where Robin's arrow fell, a stone pillar about a foot square and four feet high was erected, and that a similar pillar 24 feet high marked the spot where John's arrow fell. The fields became known as Robin Hood Closes, and Little John Closes.

**Little John's Stone (left) and
Robin Hood's Stone (right)**

Today's stones are clearly different from those described by Reverend Young.

They are much closer than 100 feet apart. They are also round, rather than square, and much smaller than 24 feet high.

Whitby Abbey can be sighted from the stones and looks a very long way for anyone to shoot an arrow.

The shot from Whitby Abbey

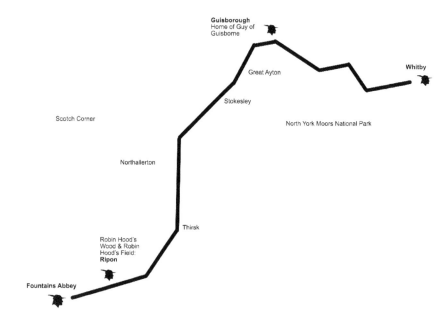

Guisborough
Home of Guy of
Guisborne

Whitby

Great Ayton

Stokesley

Scotch Corner

North York Moors National Park

Northallerton

Thirsk

Robin Hood's
Wood & Robin
Hood's Field:
Ripon

Fountains Abbey

Whitby to Fountains Abbey

Whitby Laithes to Fountains Abbey: 70 miles - 1 hour 30 minutes

- From Whitby Laithes, continue north on the A171 towards Whitby.

Whitby (Park & Ride at Cross Butts Roundabout YO21 1TL)

Robin Hood's Bay might have been the dominant settlement when the Dutch charted the coast in 1586, but Whitby is now very much the bigger sibling.

Like Robin Hood's Bay, Whitby developed as a fishing port during the Middle Ages. As the herring fleet grew, Whitby grew with it. Then, in the 18th century, it developed into a whaling port, and later into a coal port where Captain Cook learned his seamanship. **www.visitwhitby.com**

Whitby benefited from the transport of Newcastle's coal to London. Whitby provided the ships and the sailors to the coal trade, including the young James Cook.

HMS Endeavour, the ship captained by Cook on his voyage to Australia and New Zealand, also started its career in Whitby. It was built in 1764 as a coal carrier named Earl of Pembroke. She was bought by the Royal Navy in 1768, refitted, and renamed as HMS Endeavour.

It is something of a maritime superstition, that renaming a ship might invite bad luck. Legend says that when every ship is named, its name goes into the Ledger of the Deep, kept by Neptune. Renaming a ship suggests that you are trying to slip something past the gods and you will be punished for your deviousness. The Earl of Pembroke seemed to have survived the bad luck of being renamed, since Endeavour successfully carried Cook and his crew to the southern continent.

143

Cook did die a violent death in 1779, when he was struck on the head and stabbed to death in the Hawaiian surf. But he was not commanding the Endeavour at the time, and actually survived his old ship by a year.

HMS Endeavour was once again renamed, this time as the Lord Sandwich, and put into service as a British troop transport during the American War of Independence. She was finally scuttled in a blockade of Narragansett Bay, Rhode Island in 1778.

The whaling tradition is celebrated with a whalebone arch that sits at the top of the West Cliff and Captain Cook is remembered with a statue nearby.

Whitby's whaling tradition is celebrated with a whalebone arch

Today, the harbour (Pier Road, Whitby, YO21 3PU) is used by commercial, fishing and pleasure craft. This is mostly inshore fishing, for lobsters, crabs and line fish. Between May and August, salmon are found in the Esk, and small open boats are licenced to net these around the harbour entrance. There are around 40 boats licenced to take out angling parties. A fish market springs up on the quayside when the need arises, and the ready supply of fresh fish has resulted in Whitby's abundance of chip shops. The famous sea food chef Rick Stein described Whitby's Magpie Café (14 Pier Road, Whitby, YO21 3PU) as "the best fish and chip shop in Britain".

Whitby Harbour's east and west piers, each with a lighthouse and beacon, are both Grade II Listed. On the west pier is a foghorn that sounds a blast every 30 seconds during fog.

Tourism began in Whitby during the Georgian period and grew after the arrival of the railway in 1839. Its attraction as a tourist destination is helped by its proximity to the North York Moors National Park and through its association with *Dracula*.

The 35 mile stretch of coast around Whitby is known as the Dinosaur Coast, or the Fossil Coast. Dinosaur footprints can be seen on Whitby's beach, and its rock strata contain fossils and organic remains including jet. Fossil discoveries have included the bones of an almost complete crocodile and a plesiosaurus measuring 15 feet 6 inches (4.72 m) long, and 8 feet 5 inches (2.57 m) wide. Rotunda Museum in Scarborough has an extensive collection of fossils from the area.

Ammonite fossils led to folk tales of serpents having once inhabited the area. It was said that in the 7th century, Abbess Saint Hilda of Whitby rid the region of snakes by casting a spell that turned them to stone, before throwing them from the cliff tops. The spiral ammonite fossils became known as Snake Stones, and unscrupulous fossil dealers often carved heads onto the ammonites, to increase curiosity value and improve sales. In 1935 Whitby incorporated three snakestones into its Coat of Arms, in recognition of the folklore.

Whitby Jet: You will no doubt come across many shops selling Whitby Jet. However, this name is potentially misleading. Whitby is undoubtably the main marketplace for the black gemstone, but it was neither mined nor worked in Whitby itself. Different forms of Jet are found throughout the world, but local differences in geology give each area a unique version of the carbon-based mineraloid. The form known as Whitby Jet is found exclusively in the North Yorkshire Moors.

Jet is actually a form of coal, created by geological heat and pressure on fallen trees. Indeed, the experimentally minded might like to try a couple of "school" experiments. Touching Jet with a red hot needle will produce a sulphur smell, in a similar way to coal. Jet can also induce an electric charge when rubbed.

Its coal-like structure makes Jet a particularly soft gemstone, which is easy to carve. Although it is difficult to create fine details without breaking, so it takes an experienced carver to create the more elaborate pieces.

Jet has been used in Britain since the Neolithic and Bronze Age periods, where it was used for necklace beads. It went out of fashion in the Iron Age, before the Romans again used it for jewellery.

The Romans found their Jet through beachcombing rather than quarrying. They did not work the jet in Whitby itself, transporting it to York, where considerable evidence for

Jet production has been found. They used the carved Jet in rings, hair pins, beads, bracelets, bangles, necklaces, and pendants, many examples of which can be seen in the Yorkshire Museum at York. Roman Jet rings followed the design of existing metal rings, while their pendants were carved in a cameo style with Medusa's head being a popular design. Many Romans thought Jet to be a magical material, frequently using it in amulets and pendants for its supposed ability to deflect the evil eye. Pliny the Elder suggested that "the kindling of jet drives off snakes and relieves suffocation of the uterus. Its fumes detect attempts to simulate a disabling illness or a state of virginity."

The Vikings continued using jet to carve rings and miniature sculptures of animals, with snakes being a common theme.

Jet fell out of fashion as a gemstone for quite a long time after the Roman period. It once again became fashionable during the reign of Queen Victoria, after the queen wore a Jet necklace as part of mourning dress for Princess Victoria of Saxe-Coburg & Gotha. She again wore Whitby Jet as part of her mourning dress after the death of Prince Albert.

In Whitby the Victorian tradition of Jet jewellery continued until WWII. It remained out of fashion until the late 70s, when Jet beads and antique Jet jewellery started to rise in value, prompting new jewellers to start making Jet Jewellery.

Whitby has a very strong literary tradition, with authors as famous as Charles Dickens and Bram Stoker linked to the town. Some of England's earliest literature comes from Whitby, in the poetry of Caedmon. The Anglo Saxon poet was a monk at Whitby Abbey during the abbacy of Saint Hilda in the mid-7th century.

Lewis Carroll, the *Alice in Wonderland* creator, stayed at 5 East Terrace during 1854. Some of his earliest writings were published in the *Whitby Gazette*.

Charles Dickens mentioned a visit to Whitby in 1861, when he wrote about the visit in a letter to his friend Wilkie Collins.

Dracula is Whitby's most famous literary creation. Bram Stoker's 1897 novel featured Count Dracula as a large dog, which jumped ashore at the headland and ran up the 199 steps to the graveyard at Whitby Abbey. It has even been said that Stoker discovered the name *Dracula* at the town's old public library. The *Dracula* connection draws Goths to Whitby, and since 1993 the town has hosted a bi-annual Goth Weekend. Then, since 2008, an annual Bram Stoker Film Festival has been held in October.

Whitby Abbey (Abbey Lane, Whitby, YO22 4JT)
As you drove up from Whitby Laithes, I hope you were able to visualise Robin and Little John's arrows shooting towards you from Whitby Abbey. The Abbey does hold a very high position, but it would still, some might say, be a "legendary" feat of archery. **www.english-heritage.org.uk/visit/places/whitby-abbey**

Whitby Abbey has been demolished and rebuilt several times. It now stands as a ruin but does have Grade I Listing by English Heritage.

The abbey began as a 7th century Christian monastery, founded in 657 AD by the Anglo-Saxon King of Northumbria, Oswy. The settlement was then known as Streoneshalh, which is thought to signify Fort Bay or Tower Bay, in reference to an earlier Roman settlement.

Streoneshalh monastery was sacked by the Danes in successive raids between 867 and 870. The abbey remained unused for more than 200 years.

New life was breathed into Whitby Abbey by Rein-frid, a soldier of William the Conqueror, who became a monk. He approached the landowner, William de Percy, who grant-ed him the land and ruined monastery, to found a new Bene-dictine monastery. Most of the original monastery was pulled down and rebuilt on a larger scale in the 1220s.

This second monastery was destroyed by Henry VIII in 1540 during his Dissolution of the Monasteries.

If Henry VIII's efforts to destroy Whitby Abbey were not enough, Kaiser Wilhelm took his turn in 1914, when the abbey was shelled by the German battlecruisers Von der Tann and Derfflinger. The Kriegsmarine were actually aiming for the Coastguard Station at the end of the headland, but instead inflicted more damage on the remains of the abbey.

Whitby Abbey

I stayed in the adjacent YHA Youth Hostel (East Cliff, Abbey House, Whitby YO22 4JT) several years ago. This gave my children and me the opportunity to go down, and back up, the 199 steps leading from Whitby harbour. **www.yha.org.uk/hostel/yha-whitby**

- Leave Whitby on the A171 (signposted Teeside, Guisborough, Pickering and Ruswarp), skirting the northern edge of the North Yorkshire Moors National Park.
- This stretch of the A171 is a stunning road which is easy to navigate. It becomes slightly more built up around Guisborough, but is still very much North Yorkshire

North York Moors National Park

The North York Moors presents a huge range of options for tourists of all interests. Its natural beauty is possibly the area's greatest draw, and the reason for its National Park status, awarded in 1952. **www.northyorkmoors.org.uk**

Robin Hood's Bay and Whitby are both on the coastal stretch of the National Park. Our journey towards Fountains Abbey follows roads which skirt the northern and western borders of the moors. Despite being A Class roads, they are all very scenic. Detours into the heart of the National Park can be taken to visit the many natural sites and attractions the area has to offer.

Even the public transport links are noted for their beauty. In 2018, the Yorkshire Coastliner bus route from Whitby to Pickering was declared Britain's most scenic bus route by Bus Users UK.

For the history enthusiasts among us, the North York Moors National Park has 12,000 archaeological sites, of which 700 are scheduled monuments, including Wades Stone (nearest viewing point on A174, near East Barnby Outdoor Education Centre, YO21 3SA) and the Two Howes burial mounds (on Two Howes Rigg, south west of Goathland).

Driving through the moors, it is obviously a farming area. Agriculture has formed the basis of its economy for over 1,000 years and many generations of farmers have formed and maintained the landscape. The hilly terrain does not lend itself to arable farming, so most of the 1,300 plus farms keep sheep and cattle, with all holding rights to graze sheep on the moor. Grouse shooting provides another financial return, utilising the vast expanse of heather.

Agriculture shaped the landscape, but tourism is now the area's biggest source of income. Outdoor activities of some description are the reason for many visits, although the many TV and film locations also provide a draw.

Walking is probably the most popular of the outdoor pursuits, making use of the Park's 1,400 miles (2,300 km) of Rights of Way. Most of the open moorland benefits from Open Access under the Countryside and Rights of Way Act 2000.

Popular named footpaths include the Cleveland Way, White Rose Way (a long distance walk from Leeds to Scarborough) and the Lyke Wake Walk, which cuts directly through the heart of the National Park.

There are also many opportunities for cycling, mountain biking, and horse-riding. These include a circular long distance bridle route around the North York Moors. Dalby Forest has an excellent network of purpose built mountain bike trails.

Stargazers have also been drawn to the National Park since it was declared an International Dark Sky Reserve in 2020. This honour confirms that the area's low levels of light pollution provide good conditions for astronomy.

The National Park has two visitor centres which have tourist information and exhibitions. These are at: Danby (Lodge Lane, YO21 2NB) and Sutton Bank (Sutton Bank, Thirsk YO7 2EH), as well as a widespread network of village information centres throughout the park.

You will likely have come across Whitby Jet during our visit to Whitby. The North Yorkshire Moors is the only place this form of Jet can be found and has been mined in the area since prehistoric times.

The TV and film industries have made regular use of the Moors' natural beauty, which has remained unchanged for a long time. Visiting these locations provides a huge draw for tourists.

A favourite for my family of Police Officers is *Heartbeat*, which was filmed in Goathland (postcode YO22 5LX). The scenes at Hogsmeade Station in the *Harry Potter* movies were also filmed in Goathland, making it a popular destination, with a shortage of parking at peak times. Other films shot in the National Park include: *The Secret Garden*, starring Colin Firth and Julie Walters (2020) and the *Downton Abbey* film, which shot some scenes at the Pickering station on the North Yorkshire Moors Railway.

The North Yorkshire Moors Railway (NYMR) (Station Postcodes: Pickering YO18 7AJ, Levisham YO18 7NN, Goathland YO22 5NF, Grosmont YO22 5QE, Whitby YO21 1YN) **www.nymr.co.uk**

This heritage railway runs through the National Park and was first opened in 1836 as the Whitby and Pickering Railway. It was planned by George Stephenson as a means of connecting inland markets with seaport of Whitby. This closed as a commercial railway in 1965, and the section between Grosmont and Pickering was reopened by the North York Moors Historical Railway Trust Ltd in 1973.

In 2007, the railway began to run regular services over the six mile (9.7 km) section of the Esk Valley Line north of Grosmont to Whitby. In 2014, a second platform was added at Whitby, allowing the NYMR to run an enhanced service and increasing its passenger numbers to around 350,000 people.

By 2020, the Railway had 24 miles (39 km) of track. It is owned and operated by a charitable trust, with 100 full time staff, 50 seasonal staff, and over 550 volunteers.

- Continue on A171, passing north of Guisborough, to a roundabout with A173 (postcode TS14 6QS).

Guisborough

Guisborough is a pretty market town, which enters the Robin Hood legend as a possible home for Guy of Gisborne. The Lancashire town of Gisburn, in the Ribble Valley, also makes its own claim to this villain.

Second only to the Sheriff of Nottingham for his perceived villainy, Guy of Gisborne first appears in The Ballad of Robin Hood and Guy of Gisborne. This is one of the historic ballads collated by Francis Child. We will encounter the *Child Ballads* again at Fountain's Abbey, where another ballad introduces Friar Tuck.

Robin Hood and Guy of Gisborne is *Child Ballad number 118*, and both introduces and disposes of Guy of Gisborne.

This ballad survives in a single 17th century copy but is thought to be much older in content. Robin Hood and the Monk, a play with a similar plot, survives in a copy dated to 1475.

The Oxford Companion to English Literature (4th edition), describes this as the best of the Robin Hood ballads. But, along with Robin Hood and the Monk, it is also most often cited for its excessive brutality. In the ballad, Guy of Gisborne comes to Barnsdale to capture Robin Hood, but Robin kills and beheads him. Meanwhile, Little John gets captured by the Sheriff of Nottingham, and Robin rescues him by impersonating Guy of Gisborne.

Guy of Gisborne's part was built up through 19th century theatrical adaptations and 20th century cinema. At some point he picked up the "Sir" title, and is often dramatised as part of a love triangle, involving Robin, Marian and Guy. However, the original ballad paints Guy as a hired killer seeking Robin Hood.

Early in the ballad, Robin Hood and Little John are walking through the forest. Robin describes a bad dream about two men attacking him. While talking, they see a stranger leaning on a tree. Little John tells Robin to wait while he approaches the stranger, but Robin objects, imagining that John had accused him of cowardice. They argue and John storms off in a huff, and is captured by the Sheriff of Nottingham. The Sheriff's men tie John to a tree, awaiting being hanged. Meanwhile, Robin goes up to the stranger, who turns out to be Guy of Gisborne.

Guy and Robin have a shooting contest, which Robin wins with ease. Robin identifies himself as "Robin Hood of Barnsdale". The two fight, Robin trips and Guy stabs him. But Robin recovers his advantage, killing Guy with his sword.

If that was not enough to justify the ballad's alleged excessive brutality, Robin dresses himself in Guy's distinctive horsehide robe, then cuts off Guy's head, sticks it on the tip of his bow and slashes the face.

Robin then blows Guy's horn to signal victory to the Sheriff. Disguised as Guy and carrying what he passes off as Robin Hood's head, Robin sets off to rescue Little John. He convinces the Sheriff to allow him to kill Little John, but instead cuts him loose. John then took up his bow, shooting the Sheriff through the heart.

- After passing around Guisborough, at roundabout (postcode TS14 6QS), take first exit, turning left (south) on A173 (signposted Great Ayton).

Newton Under Roseberry

The car parks and tourist infrastructure for Roseberry Topping (postcode TS9 6QS) and the surrounding walks are in this pretty village. It can get very busy.

Roseberry Topping

Roseberry Topping is a very distinctive looking hill, which I climbed with my Scouts on many occasions. Its summit has a half-cone shape with a jagged cliff, which has caused it to be compared with the much higher Matterhorn in the Swiss-Italian Alps. Its image is so iconic that it features in the logo of the nearby Teesside International Airport.

At 1,049 feet (320 m), Roseberry Topping was once thought to be the highest hill on the North York Moors; however, there are actually 15 higher peaks in the National Park.

Roseberry Topping

- Continue along the A173 to drive through Great Ayton. The Cleveland Hills dominate the view to our left along the whole length of this road.

Great Ayton

Great Ayton is a pretty town with a river flowing alongside the road. I have not found any connection between Great Ayton and Robin Hood, but the village was the boyhood home of Captain Cook, who we encountered during our visit to Whitby.

The explorer and navigator was born in nearby Marton, moving to Great Ayton with his family, when he was eight years old. He lived there until he was 16. Their family home on Bridge Street was built by James' father in 1755. The cottage was dismantled in 1934 for shipping to Australia. Each stone was numbered so that the cottage could be reconstructed in its new home in Melbourne.

Great Ayton has several landmarks relating to Captain James Cook.

A granite obelisk marks the original site of the Cook family cottage (Bridge Street, Great Ayton, TS9 6NP). The obelisk is constructed from granite taken from Point Hicks, which was the first Australian land sighted by Cook.

The Captain Cook Schoolroom Museum is in a former charity school, founded in 1704. James Cook received his early education here between the years of 1736 and 1740. **www.captaincookschoolroommuseum.co.uk**

A statue on High Green depicts James Cook at the age of 16, looking towards Staithes where, according to tradition, he first felt the lure of the sea.

- At roundabout outside Stokesley (postcode TS9 5NY), take second exit (left), to join A172 south-bound (signposted Thirsk).

Lord Stones is signposted from A172 on a brown tour-ist sign.

Lord Stones Walk (Lord Stones Country Park, Carlton Bank, Chop Gate, Middlesbrough TS9 7JH)
This is a walk of just under three miles. It is described on the tourist website as "an adventure walk for all the family, with awe-inspiring views." It boasts panoramic views of Middles-brough, the Cleveland plain, Roseberry Topping and Cook's Monument. Part of the return leg follows the Cleveland Way National Trail across Cringle Moor. The start of the trail is in the privately owned Lord Stones Country Park, where there is access to the ancient stone that gives the walk its name. The

country park has parking, a café and a local produce shop.
www.nationaltrail.co.uk/app/uploads/lord-stones.pdf

- Meet junction with A19 and turn left / southbound. Be careful not to miss this Y junction, which does not look like a major A road junction.
- Take the left fork onto A19 (signposted Northallerton and Osmotherley on a white local sign before the junction) (Signposted The South A19 Thirsk on a green A road sign at the junction.)

Mount Grace Priory, House and Gardens are signposted from the A19 on a brown tourist sign.

Mount Grace Priory (Mount Bank, Northallerton, DL6 3JG) Mount Grace Priory was founded in 1398. It is the ruins of one of England's nine houses of the Carthusian Order from the Middle Ages, which were known as Charterhouses.

Unlike the monks of other orders, who live together as a community, the Carthusians (still to this day) live as hermits in their individual cells. They come together in the church only for the night-time service, and on Sundays and feast-days. All other devotions are sung by each monk separately in his cell. Carthusians are silent, and their diet is strictly vegetarian.

The monks at Mount Grace were very conscious of hygiene and sanitation. There is a reconstructed cell containing a replica toilet, and visitors can investigate the ditches used as a sewage system.

The priory was closed in 1539 during the dissolution of the monasteries by Henry VIII. The site then passed into private ownership.

Today, the property is owned by the National Trust and is under the care of English Heritage. **www.english-heritage.org.uk/visit/places/mount-grace-priory**

- On the outskirts of Thirsk, the A19 becomes the A168 without a junction.
- The A19 continues off a slip road (signposted A19). **Do not** take A19.
- We continue on the main carriageway along A168.

Thirsk

Thirsk is a popular tourist destination close to both the York-shire Dales and the North York Moors. It might not have any specific Robin Hood connection, but it does have at least two famous sons. Thirsk was the home of author James Herriot and the birthplace of Thomas Lord, after whom Lord's Crick-et Ground is named.

Thirsk's museum is in the house where Thomas Lord was born, although it does show exhibits from across the whole history of the town, not just its cricket connections.

Possibly Thirsk's most popular claim to fame is as home to James Herriot.

The author, who wrote under the pen name of James Herriot, was a Thirsk-based veterinary surgeon, whose real name was James Alfred Wight, OBE, FRCVS.

For his semi-autobiographical books *All Creatures Great and Small*, Herriot re-named Thirsk as Darrowby. Star-ring alongside him in his books about a vet's life in the York-shire Dales, was his business partner Donald Sinclair (Called Siegfried Farnon in the books). Their very real veterinary practice was at 23 Kirkgate (known as "Skeldale House" in the books), which now houses The World of James Herriot Museum (23 Kirkgate, Thirsk, YO7 1PL), dedicated to Herriot's life and works. **www.worldofjamesherriot.com**

**Statue of Alf Wight (AKA James Herriot)
at The World of James Herriot Museum**

When James Herriot died in 1995, Hambleton District Council bought the house and started a £1.4 million restoration programme. The work included recreating their original living quarters and reproducing some of the sets used in the *All Creatures Great and Small* TV series. They also have the car that Herriot drove in the TV series. In addition to the TV memorabilia, the museum has an extensive collection of veterinary apparatus from the period. At time of writing, the author's grandson and granddaughter were both on the museum's board. In an effort to give back to the veterinary profession, the museum established The James Herriot Foundation Trust in 2018 to provide bursary awards for people wishing to become veterinary nurses.

Sports fans might want to visit Thirsk Racecourse (Station Road, Thirsk, YO7 1QL), set on the western edge of town. This is a thoroughbred horse racing venue, consisting of a left-handed oval of about one mile and two furlongs. The present course opened in 1923, but racing had taken place on the old course for more than 200 years before. **www.thirskracecourse.net**

- Near the village of Dishforth, the A168 meets the A1M.
- Leave the main carriageway of the A168 at Junction 49 (signposted Ripon), to continue on A168.
- **Do not** go onto the A1M.
- The A168 now runs parallel with the motorway.
- At roundabout turn right onto B6265 towards Ripon.
- Brown tourist signs for Fountains Abbey begin here.
- Follow brown tourist signs for Fountains Abbey through Ripon, alongside the Ripon Canal.

Ripon

The cathedral city of Ripon is an attractive place to visit in its own right. It also provides an ideal base from which to visit the Robin Hood and Friar Tuck locations in the National Trust site of Studley Royal Park and Fountains Abbey.

Being less than four miles from one of Friar Tuck's homes, it should be no surprise that Ripon too has its own Robin Hood locations. Much of Robin Hood Wood and Robinhood Field have now been swallowed up by the park and housing estate at Borrage Green, but for travellers wanting to visit all of the Robin Hood locations, it too makes for a pleasant interlude.

Ripon was established at the confluence of two rivers: the Skell and the Laver. As we will learn from our forthcoming visit to Fountains Abbey, the Skell is claimed as the location for Robin Hood and Friar Tuck's first meeting.

Christianity has played a major role in Ripon's development as a city, which will account for the nearby location of Friar Tuck's legend. Whether as the setting for a fictional character, or the home of a real friar embellished by legend, it is no coincidence that Ripon and Fountains Abby are in such close proximity.

Solid evidence for the beginning of Ripon as a settlement can be traced back to the 7th century, and the Anglian kingdom of Northumbria. The first structure known to have been built in the area was the Inhrypum, a Christian church dedicated to Saint Peter in the year 658. This was founded by a Northumbrian nobleman called Wilfrid, who later became Archbishop of York. Ripon's earliest settlers were the stonemasons, glaziers, and plasterers that Wilfrid brought over from Lyon and Rome, to help build the Ripon monastery.

Northerners rebelled against the Norman conquest in 1069, even trying to bring back Viking rule. William the Conqueror hit back with a purge that became known as "the Harrying of the North." Roughly one-third of the population were killed in the North of England, with Ripon shrinking back to a small community around the church. The church lands were transferred to Saint Peter's Church at York and a grand Collegiate Church was built on top of the ruins of Wilfrid's building.

During the 14th century, Ripon and Fountains Abbey forged their closest bonds. In 1326, English people were forbidden from wearing foreign cloth, and Ripon developed a cloth industry which was third largest in Yorkshire, after York and Halifax.

The Cistercian monks at Fountains Abbey already had a long tradition of sheep farming. The substantial amount of grazing land they owned was a considerable advantage in supplying Ripon's cloth trade with wool.

The Christian church in England had a massive upheaval following Henry VIII's break from Rome in the 16th century. The pattern of Church of England dioceses created by Henry remained unchanged for around 200 years, until the Industrial Revolution boosted population during the 18th century. It soon became clear that the existing dioceses were not big enough for the much enlarged northern towns. The Church of England decided that it could not sustain a programme of building new cathedrals on a national scale, so Ripon benefited from already having a high status parish church. Ripon was the first of the new dioceses to be created, when its church was promoted to cathedral status in 1836.

Ripon Council presumed this had turned their town into a city and began referring to itself as such. However, the promotion did not become official until the passing of the City of Ripon Act in 1865.

Ripon Cathedral (Minster Rd, Ripon, HG4 1QT), or more correctly The Cathedral Church of Saint Peter and Saint Wilfrid, remains an important religious building and is also a draw for tourists. The cathedral contains a tomb which is said to contain the bones of Saint Wilfrid, who founded both the original monastery and with it the town itself.

Architectural afficionados will appreciate the cathedral for its Gothic west front in the Early English style, which is considered one of the best of its type, as well as its geometric east window. The 17th century crypt of Wilfrid's church is a significant example of early Christian architecture. The cathedral has Grade I Listed status.

In addition to its religious programme, Ripon Cathedral has a huge range of arts and cultural events throughout the year. Details of these can be found on the cathedral's website **www.riponcathedral.org.uk**

Saint Wilfrid is the focus of one of Ripon's oldest traditions. The Wilfrid Procession originated in 1108, when King Henry I granted the privilege of holding a fair for him. In the procession are many decorated floats and locals in costume.

The tradition represents the return of Wilfrid to Ripon, usually as a decorated dummy, but sometimes by a man in costume. The depiction of Wilfrid is sat on a horse, accompanied by two musicians with another man carrying Saint Wilfrid's hat. Visitors to the procession will also get to see Ripon's dancing traditions, such as the Long Sword dance and Morris dance.

The Wilfrid Procession is held on the Saturday before the first Monday in August, which can sometimes be the last Saturday in July, and begins around 2pm in the Market Place. **www.stwilfridsprocession.com**

Ripon Obelisk (Market Place, Ripon, HG4 3XX) stands in the market square. The Grade I Listed monument was erected in 1702, it is 80 ft (24 m) tall and is capped with a weathervane bearing a representation of a Wakeman's horn.

The tradition of the Ripon Hornblower began in the year 886 and continues on to this day. It began with the Wakeman of Ripon, whose job in the Middle Ages was like that of a mayor, although with additional responsibilities for keeping of law and order. Each day at 9pm the horn is blown at the four corners of the obelisk. The horn has become the symbol of the city and represents Ripon on the Harrogate borough coat of arms.

Yorkshire Law and Order Museums: Ripon has three museums, which are collectively known as the Yorkshire Law and Order Museums; these museums include: the Courthouse (Minster Road, Ripon, HG4 1QS), the Prison & Police Museum (1 Saint Marygate, Ripon, HG4 1LX) and the Workhouse Museum (Allhallowgate, Ripon, HG4 1LE) **www.riponmuseums.co.uk**

The three sites operate on a one-ticket-accesses-all basis. The Courthouse was closed for renovation during my visit, but we did enjoy visiting the Workhouse, with many costumed volunteers to aid visitor enjoyment. As a former Police Officer, I particularly enjoyed visiting the former Police Station, and seeing the range of punishments meted out to lawbreakers throughout the years.

- Continue along B6265, following Fountains Abbey signs, until just after Ripon Cathedral.
- To visit Robin Hood Wood and Robinhood Field, leave the B6265 turning left onto a weight restricted road, Low Skellgate.
- Cross the River Skell on a stone bridge.
- Low Skellgate becomes A61 Harrogate Road.

On your right, at the corner of Borrage Green Lane, is a children's' park (Harrogate Road Playground, HG4 1SW). This is all that remains of the once large Borrage Green area, of which Robin Hood Wood and Robinhood Field once formed a part.

It is possible to start a walk here, but there is very limited parking. A better place to start is the car park for Hell Wath Nature reserve.

- Continue past the park, along Harrogate Road, taking your third right into Whitcliffe Lane, which is a residential estate.
- Whitcliffe Lane is a long road. On a map, it appears to go straight on, with Hell Wath Lane turning to the right. On the ground, the opposite is true. Whitcliffe Lane narrows and is marked "Unsuitable for motors"; Hell Wath Lane is the natural continuation.
- After a short distance you will see car parking areas at the junction with Hell Wath Grove (postcode HG4 2JT).

Robin Hood Wood and Robinhood Field: Ripon

We now reach the part of Ripon that brings it into our **500RH** journey. The names have fallen out of use, but the area in which they lay can still be visited.

Walking directions to Robinhood Field

There are lots of walks in the area, and I did a short circular walk.

From the car park, walk down Hell Wath Lane to Hell Wath Cottage.

Opposite the cottage, take the narrow footpath into the woods. (**Do not** take the straight on path, unless that is the route you have planned.)

After a short distance the path forks; take the right fork, towards the old quarry. This is a less defined path. Go through the remains of a broken metal kissing gate.

In the field are a set of metal sculptures. From a distance, I thought these were Robin Hood and his merrie men. The middle two especially could be mistaken for Robin and Marian.

Up close, you can see they are WWI memorials, so I paused for a moment of reflection. This area was used as an Army training camp during WWI.

Statues in Robinhood Field

After the statues, a set of steep steps descend to your left, towards the river.

One interpretation of the Ballad of Robin Hood and the Curtal Friar puts Robin Hood and Friar Tuck's first meeting at the River Skell.

Tradition puts their battle in the Skell as it flows through Fountains Abbey, but this could just be the interpretation of the Abbey's Victorian tour guides. Their fight could just have easily been at this more remote section of the River Skell.

We can thank the Vikings for the unusual Hell Wath name, which is Old Norse for "ford with flat stones." A ford would seem a logical place for Robin and Tuck to fight over who was to be carried across the river.

Path alongside the River Skell

Follow the riverside path back to Hell Wath Cottage and the car park.

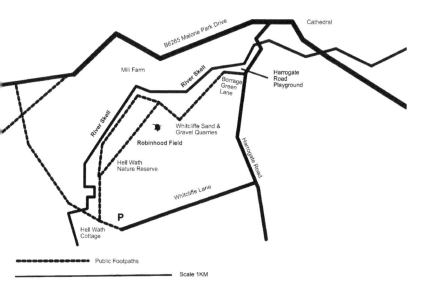

Public Footpaths

Scale 1KM

Footpaths around Robin Hood Wood and Robinhood
Field: Ripon

Robin Hood Wood was marked on the six inch O.S. map published in 1856, but is not shown as such on more recent maps. It was the name of a wooded area along the south bank of the Skell, to the eastern side of Hell Wath Nature Reserve and at the north-western end of the disused Whitcliffe Sand and Gravel Quarries.

When the 1856 map was prepared, the wood stretched in a curving arc towards the south-west into the present Hell Wath Nature Reserve.

Robinhood Field was the name of a field at the north-western end of Robin Hood Wood. The name was recorded in the 1838 tithe award for Ripon, which lists two adjacent fields under this name.

Despite being first recorded as late as 1840, it is possible that Robinhood Field is actually a much older field name. The spelling "Robinhood" is not very common for a modern Robin Hood place-name.

Of course, the key link for Ripon's Robin Hood Wood and Robinhood Field to the wider legends, is most likely through being just 4 km north-east of Fountains Abbey, and the ballad connecting it with the Curtal Friar and Friar Tuck.

From Hell Wath, we continue our journey to Fountains Abbey.

- Retrace your route along Whitcliffe Lane, and back through Ripon to re-join the B6265.
- Turn left onto the B6265 Somerset Row.
- We are once again following brown tourist signs for Fountains Abbey. All subsequent junctions are well signposted.
- Turn left onto minor road to Fountains Abbey.

- Follow National Trust signs for the main car park and Visitors' Centre (postcode HG4 3DY).

Fountains Abbey (including Robin Hood's Well & Robin Hood's Wood)

Fountains Abbey is one of the largest and best preserved ruined Cistercian monasteries in England. It was founded in 1132 and operated for 407 years, becoming one of the wealthiest monasteries in England, until its dissolution by Henry VIII in 1539. Its significance to the **500RH** comes from Robin Hood's Well & Robin Hood's Wood, which are both to be found close to the Fountains Abbey ruins.

Fountains Abbey enters the Robin Hood legends through the Ballad of Robin Hood and the Curtal Friar, which tells a version of the Friar Tuck story. In the ballad, Robin Hood tells his fellow huntsmen that "there is no match for Little John within a hundred miles." Will Scadlock (the name by which the ballad called Will Scarlet) tells Robin that a monk at Fountains Abbey could beat Little John. Robin sets out to see this monk, finding him by a riverside (thought to be the River Skell).

Although claims to the location vary, the fight between Robin Hood and Friar Tuck have been retold in many versions. Robin forces the monk to carry him across the river, and the friar throws him in halfway across. They battle until Robin asks a favour: to let him blow on his horn. When the friar agrees, Robin's men appear. The friar too asks a favour, to be allowed a whistle. When Robin agrees, a pack of fierce dogs appear.

In a later version of the ballad, Little John shoots twenty of the dogs, and the friar makes peace with Robin.

In the earlier version, Robin Hood refuses further combat. The outcome is the same in both versions, with Robin inviting Friar Tuck to join his Merrie Men.

Like many other locations on our journey, Fountains Abbey benefitted from the arrival of the railways. When passenger services came to Ripon, tourists would take horse drawn carriages to Fountains Abbey.

At the Abbey, tour guides were engaged to take groups around the ruins, and the park. Drawing on its connection to the Curtal Friar, the story of Robin Hood's Well developed, with the guides even hiding a longbow in the undergrowth, and claiming it to be Robin Hood's actual bow.

Fountains Abbey

There is an admission fee to the park. National Trust members are allowed free admission. The directions above are for the main Visitors' Centre car-park (postcode HG4 3DY). There is also a car park at the Studley Royal entrance, from which you can access the lake and Deer Park, which are free to walk around. The Studley Royal Tea Room is also outside of the abbey wall. **www.nationaltrust.org.uk/fountains-abbey-and-studley-royal-water-garden**

The 70 acre abbey site is surrounded by an 11 foot (3.4 m) wall built in the 13th century, some parts of which are still visible to the south and west of the abbey.

The site is cut into sections by the River Skell, which flows through it from west to east. The church buildings are in the centre of the precinct, on the north side of the river. The inner court, containing the domestic buildings, stretches down to the river, and the outer court, housing the industrial and agricultural buildings, is on the river's south bank.

Close proximity to the River Skell has added to the site's fragility, with extensive flood damage caused in 2007, when the 12th century ruins and water garden became submerged. A grant from the National Lottery Heritage Fund was announced in 2021, to help finance the Skell Valley Scheme, intended to minimise the risk of flooding along a 12 mile section of the river.

The original abbey church was built of wood, but was soon rebuilt in stone. The church was damaged when the abbey was attacked in 1146 and it was rebuilt in a larger scale, with building work completed around 1170.

Many additions and improvements were added by successive abbots, including a lantern tower in the late 12th century, improvements to the presbytery in the 13th century, a greatly lengthened choir was built around 1211, and a 160-foot-tall (49 m) tower was added not long before the dissolution.

During Henry VIII's Dissolution of the Monasteries in 1540, the abbey buildings and over 500 acres of land were seized by the Crown, and sold to Sir Richard Gresham, who was a Member of Parliament and a former Lord Mayor of London.

Gresham set about stripping some of the abbey's stone, timber, and lead for sale as building materials to help cover the cost of purchase. In 1597 the site was bought by Sir Stephen Proctor, who further stripped the monastic complex for stone to build Fountains Hall. The site passed through the hands of the Messenger and Aislaby families, before being merged into the Studley Royal Estate.

The abbey is now a Grade I Listed building owned by the National Trust, and the parkland and ruins became a UNESCO World Heritage Site in 1986.

It has become quite a theme for the places we visited to be used as film locations, and Fountains Abbey seems to have specialised as a moody location.

The 1965 black and white film, *Life at the Top*, about a wife killer, started the cinematic ball rolling.

During the winter of 1981 Orchestral Manoeuvres in the Dark used Fountains Abbey as a location for the music video to their single *Maid of Orleans (The Waltz Joan of Arc)*.

A year earlier in 1980, even more macabre images were filmed there, when *Omen III: The Final Conflict*, filmed its final scenes.

The abbey grounds took on a starring role in 1993, when one of several adaptations of *The Secret Garden* was filmed there. In that version, the exterior of Fountains Hall became Misselthwaite Manor, while a small doorway opposite became the secret entrance into the garden.

Several TV shows have also been filmed at Fountains Abbey, including *Flambards*, *A History of Britain*, *Terry Jones' Medieval Lives*, *Antiques Roadshow* and *Treasure Hunt*.

I used Google Street View quite extensively in planning the **500RH**, so it interested me to learn that in January 2010 Fountains Abbey became one of the first National Trust properties to be included in Street View, using their Google Trike. A look at videos of this heavy-looking tricycle will make you appreciate the hard work pedalling the camera around hilly Yorkshire locations without vehicle access.

Fountains Abbey and the River Skell

Robin Hood's Well

The well is not specifically marked on the National Trust map you are given on admission to the site. But it is drawn as a stone arch, alongside the path which runs between Number 7 (Fountains Mill) and Number 8 (De Grey's Walk).

The well itself must have existed in medieval times since an underground lead pipe was found leading from the well to the abbey. There is also evidence of it being called Robin Hood's Well from at least 1731.

The current well cover was built much more recently, though. A note found among papers at York Minster Library suggests that it was built with stones from the ruins of Fountains Abbey, after Walter Scott visited the site in the early 1800s. Scott apparently suggested to the owner of the estate that she should build a well house. Scott also wrote a poem for use as an inscription, but there is no evidence that it was ever displayed on the well. The construction of a well house during this period would have been in keeping with the craze for building follies among wealthy landowners.

Robin Hood's Well

Robin Hood's Wood
Robin Hood's Wood is a little wood adjacent to the grounds of Fountains Abbey. Like the well, it is not labelled on the National Trust Map, but it is marked on the 1:25,000 OS map of the area. It is the wooded hillside which starts behind the well, and curves around in front of you, towards Studley Royal Water Gardens.

The energetic among you can climb the paths through Robin Hood's Wood to Anne Boleyn's Seat, Surprise View, the Temple of Fame and the High Ride Path (Numbers 13, 14 and 15 on the National Trust map).

Robin Hood's Wood was first mentioned in a land deed of 1734. We know that Fountains Abbey became associated with Robin Hood, through the ballad of Robin Hood and the Curtal Friar, which appeared during the 1600s. So it seems likely that the place-name Robin Hood's Wood came into use after the abbey ruins became connected with Robin Hood through the ballad.

Robin Hood's Wood

The Robin Hood 500: 500RH

Part Four

South Yorkshire

47 Miles - 2 Hours travelling

Travelling time does not include time spent exploring the
attractions en-route

Fountains Abbey

Killinghall

York

Wetherby

Leeds

Bradford

Robin Hood village
Wakefield

Fountains Abbey to Robin Hood (Wakefield)

Fountains Abbey to Robin Hood Village (Wakefield):

35 miles - 1 hour 20 minutes

- Exit Fountains Abbey via the West Gate (postcode HG4 3EA), not the main entrance by which you arrived. National Trust signposts direct you around the estate's network of roundabouts.
- This first section of our journey is winding and rural. The roads are a little narrow, but do not present any difficulties.
- At the estate's West Gate entrance, turn right (south) onto Fountains Lane.
- After crossing a small river, reach a Y junction, with the road signs set on a triangle of grass.
- Take the left fork (signposted Markington and Harrogate)
- Continue along the same road as it changes name many times to: How Hill Road, and Watergate Road.
- At T junction with Fountains Abbey Road, turn left (signposted Ripley, Knaresborough and Harrogate).
- Continue along the same road as it changes name many times to: Oakwood Park, High Kettlespring Farm, Fountains Road, Scarah Bank, and finally Fountains Road again.
- At T junction with B6165, turn left (signposted Ripley, Knaresborough and Harrogate). Ripley Castle is also signposted from here on a brown tourist sign.

Ripley Castle (Back Lane, Ripley, Harrogate, HG3 3AY)
Ripley Castle is a Grade I Listed, 14th century country house, which has been the seat of the Ingilby Baronets since 1308.

The castle is still privately owned, now by the 6th Baronet and his wife, Lady Ingilby, but is open to the public for guided tours.

The Yorkshire TV children's series *The Flaxton Boys* (1969–1973) used Ripley Castle as the fictional Flaxton Hall. It was used in the 1976 Disney film *Escape from the Dark*, as the home of Lord Harrogate, played by Alastair Sim. The BBC Television series *Gunpowder* (2017) used the castle as a location. **www.ripleycastle.co.uk**

- Follow B6165 to roundabout junction with A61 Ripon Road.
- Take second exit from the roundabout onto A61 (signposted Knaresborough and Harrogate).
- At next roundabout, continue on A61 Ripon Road (signposted Harrogate).
- Cross the River Nidd, continuing on A61 Ripon Road.
- In the village of Killinghall, just after a pelican crossing and the Greyhound Inn (postcode HG3 2DG), turn right onto B6161 Otley Road (signposted Otley).

Killinghall

Killinghall dates back well before the Normans arrived, possibly as far back as the Celts, so it would have existed as a village during the time of Robin Hood.

The *Domesday Book* lists the village as Chenihalle. (Which translates to Kennelhall, or a place where the Lord of the Manor's hounds were kept.) The Saxon kings granted Yorkshire nobleman the right to keep Mastiff dogs for chasing wolves off their land.

After the English Civil War's Battle of Marston Moor in July 1644, Cromwell's troops were quartered at Kennel Hall Farm (postcode HG3 2AY). A plaque on the oldest of the farm buildings commemorates the event.

Today, Killinghall functions mainly as a commuter village for Harrogate, which is just three miles away.

Cycling fans might like to visit this part of the 2014 Tour de France. Stage one of the race from Leeds to Harrogate passed through Killinghall.

If a section of Le Tour is too much for you, Killinghall has a more leisurely cycling option. The Nidderdale Greenway is a cycle path that follows the route of a disused railway. The route begins in Harrogate, crossing the 93 feet high viaduct over the Nidd Gorge, built in 1848. From there the path crosses fields to reach the bridge at Killlinghall. It then continues on to Ripley Castle.

Another cycling option is The Bilton Triangle, a trio of reclaimed railway lines, which bisect the Nidderdale Greenway.

- At roundabout with A59 (Old Spring Well Pub - postcode HG3 2AP), continue straight on, following B6161 as name changes to Oaker Bank (signposted Otley).
- At Jubilee Roundabout, continue straight on, following B6161 Oaker Bank (signposted Beckwithshaw, Leathley and Otley).

We are now starting to see slightly more urban development, with military housing to the right, and the outskirts of Harrogate to the left.

A short detour into Harrogate is possible from here.

Harrogate

Harrogate is a popular spa-town, which is a tourist draw in its own right.

Harrogate spa water contains iron, sulphur and common salt. The town became known as "The English Spa" in the Georgian era, after its waters were discovered in the 16th century. During the 17th and 18th centuries its iron rich "chalybeate" waters were a popular health treatment, and the influx of wealthy but poorly visitors contributed greatly to the town's wealth. Harrogate earns over £150 million for the local economy every year and attracts more than 350,000 business visitors annually. **www.visitharrogate.co.uk**

The Royal Pump Room houses Europe's strongest sulphur well, but is now a museum showcasing the town's spa history.

Bettys Tearooms on Parliament Street is a popular, if expensive, tea-room. Bettys was established in 1919 by Bettys and Taylors of Harrogate – the same company that sell Yorkshire Tea.

Harrogate Grand Opera House opened in 1900, with a charity gala in aid of British soldiers fighting the Boer War in South Africa. You can still see a show there, as the building now houses Harrogate Theatre.

Harrogate International Centre hosted the Eurovision Song Contest in 1982.

The Royal Horticultural Society (RHS) has its main northern presence at Harlow Carr Gardens, on the western edge of Harrogate. These are award-winning themed gardens. **www.rhs.org.uk/gardens/harlow-carr**

The RHS presence likely played a part in Harrogate winning the 2003 and 2016 Britain in Bloom competition, in the category of Large Town. It was also a gold medal winner of Europe in Bloom in 2004.

Cycling fans will remember that on 5th July 2014, Harrogate was the finish town for the first stage of that year's Tour de France. The town has since hosted stages of the Tour of Yorkshire and UCI Road World Championships.

For three consecutive years (2013–2015), polls voted the town as "the happiest place to live" in Britain.

- Continue to follow B6161 as name changes to Pot Bank.
- At the beginning of Beckwithshaw village (postcode HG3 1QP), go straight on (second exit) at a roundabout, onto Otley Road (signposted Harrogate and Knaresborough).
- In Beckwithshaw turn left onto Shaw Lane (signposted North Rigton).
- We return to very rural scenery.
- Continue along same road (through crossroads with your priority) as name changes to High Moor Road.
- The road briefly changes name to Rigton Hill, as you enter the village of North Rigton, just before the next turning.
- At Square and Compass pub in North Rigton (postcode Leeds LS17 0DJ), turn left at mini-roundabout, onto Hall Green Lane (signposted Harrogate and Harewood).

North Rigton

North Rigton is another Yorkshire village which has hosted TV crews. The nearby Almscliffe Crag was used for scenery at the end of Yorkshire TV dramas, *The Beiderbecke Affair,*

The Beiderbecke Tapes and *The Beiderbecke Connection*, though the area was never referred to by name.

Until the 19th century the village was known as Rigton. North was added to distinguish it from East Rigton, 7 miles southeast. The name is from the Old English hrycg and tun, meaning "farmstead on the ridge". The village was listed in the *Domesday Book* as Riston, an Anglo-Norman spelling of the name.

- Cross the busy cross-roads junction with A658, onto Dunkeswick Lane. (Heading towards a railway level crossing).
- At T junction turn right onto A61 Harrogate Road (signposted Leeds).
- Cross the River Wharf on a historic stone bridge.
- Continue on A61 Harrogate Road (signposted Leeds).

Harewood House is signposted a short distance off the A61, with a brown tourist sign.

Harewood House (Harewood, Leeds, LS17 9LG)
Harewood House is a Grade I Listed country house, built between 1759 and 1771, for Edwin Lascelles, the 1st Baron Harewood, who was a West Indian plantation owner. The landscape was designed by the famous Lancelot "Capability" Brown.

The estate has a royal connection, as in 1922, Viscount Henry Lascelles married Princess Mary, the only daughter of George V.

The house is still home to the Lascelles family, and home of David Lascelles, the 8th Earl.

The house and grounds are managed by Harewood House Trust, and are open to the public for most of the year.

Harewood has a collection of paintings by masters of the Italian Renaissance, some modern art collected by the 7th Earl and Countess and plenty of family portraits. Artist J. M. W. Turner painted the outdoor landscape of the house in watercolours around 1797. Restaurants in the house include Michelin-starred fine dining.

As well as tours of the house and grounds, Harewood has over 100 acres of gardens, including a Himalayan Garden, with a reproduction Buddhist stupa, an educational bird garden, an adventure playground and Yorkshire's first planetarium (added in 2008).

For the walkers, The Leeds Country Way and The White Rose Way pass through the Harewood Estate.

Harewood House has also seen its share of popular culture. In 1999, Elton John held a concert in the grounds. Westlife also performed here in 2006. The house was used as a film set for the 1991 comedy film *King Ralph*. In 1996, part of the estate was turned into the village set for the ITV soap opera *Emmerdale* (which had been filmed in two different villages since it began 24 years earlier). The ITV drama *Victoria*, starring Jenna Coleman and Tom Hughes, did some of its filming here. The 2019 film version of *Downton Abbey* was also filmed here.

The house was the location for Mary Berry's 2018 show, *Mary Berry's Country House at Christmas*. **www.harewood.org**

- Opposite Lofthouse Lodge B&B (postcode LS17 9LU), turn left onto Wike Lane, which changes name to Forge Lane (signposted Wike).

- NB: this is a narrow road, along which inconsiderate parking can cause difficulties in passing.
- In Wike village, turn left onto Backstone Gill (signposted East Keswick).
- This is an unusual, triangular shaped junction, which in effect, operates as a T junction.
- After 100m, at Moor Allerton Golf Club (postcode LS17 9NH), turn left onto Coal Road (signposted Scarcroft).
- Continue through crossroads (with your priority) onto Brandon Lane.
- Bay Horse Lane merges from your left. Bear right as road name changes to Bay Horse Lane.
- Pass through crossroads (with your priority) as road name changes back to Coal Road.
- At T junction with A58, turn right onto A58 Wellington Hill, which becomes Weatherby Road.
- At roundabout, turn left onto A6120 (signposted Ring Road, M1, M62 and A1M).
- We are now entering the suburbs of Leeds, and the scenery changes accordingly.
- Continue on A6120 Ring Road Seacroft, straight across four roundabouts.
- This is an outer city ring road, but it is not as busy as some I have driven on.
- At the fifth roundabout, turn right onto Stile Hill Way (signposted Oulton, Newson Green and Colton). (If you reach the M1 roundabout, you have gone too far).
- This is a busy and complicated, traffic light controlled roundabout, with a retail park on your right (Colton Retail Park, Leeds, LS15 9JA).

- At roundabout, go straight on, onto Bullerthorpe Lane.
- This is a long stretch of road, which crosses over the M1.
- We are still in the suburbs of Leeds, but this road is more rural than the ones we have just travelled along.
- At T junction with A642 (Bridge Farm Hotel, postcode LS26 8PZ), turn right onto A642 Aberford Road.
- Cross the River Aire and the Aire & Calder Navigation, continuing on A642.

Aire & Calder Navigation

The Aire and Calder Navigation is the canalised section of the Rivers Aire and Calder. The first improvements were completed in 1704, when construction of 16 locks made the Aire navigable to Leeds and the Calder to Wakefield. **www.canalrivertrust.org.uk**

The upper sections of the navigation are now designated as leisure routes, but it does still carry commercial traffic amounting to several hundred thousand tonnes per year. Although this sounds a significant amount of freight, it is a huge drop from the 1.64 million tonnes recorded in the year 2000. Most of today's cargo is petroleum and gravel, rather than the coal which kept the canal profitable for 150 years.

The Leeds to Castleford section, and most of the Wakefield branch, are now used mainly as leisure routes. But below Castleford, the industrial heritage of the waterway is still obvious. Pleasure boats must give way to commercial traffic, since the 600 tonne vessels are not as manoeuvrable as a narrow boat.

Between Wakefield and Leeds, the Navigation is part of a circular cruising route, or "ring", formed by the Leeds & Liverpool and the Huddersfield or Rochdale canals. The Outer Pennine Ring uses the Huddersfield Canal, while the North Pennine Ring makes a southern crossing of the Pennines via the Rochdale Canal. Beyond Castleford, leisure boaters can travel on to Selby, York, Goole, Sheffield, and Keadby. The planned restoration of the Barnsley Canal and the Dearne and Dove Canal might open up a new "Yorkshire Ring".

Walkers and cyclists can also find activity in this area, since the rivers and canals run alongside sections of the Trans-Pennine Trail. Parts of the National Cycle Network are also signposted along these trails. **www.transpenninetrail.org.uk**

Cycling along the Aire & Calder Navigation

- A642 Aberford Road briefly changes name to Calverley Road, before reaching a roundabout.
- At roundabout, go straight over, onto A654 Rothwell Lane, passing Oulton Hall Golf Club (postcode LS26 8HN) (signposted Rothwell and Oulton Hall).
- Continue on A654 Aberford Road as it changes name to Oulton Lane, then Carlton Lane, then Leadwell Lane.
- The Village of Robin Hood is located off the A654, just before you cross the junction with Leeds Road, where the A654 becomes Thorpe Lower Lane.
- The Halfway House Public House is a good Sat Nav setting (postcode WF3 3AB).

The village of Robin Hood

This area seems to be having something of an identity crisis. Several villages once grew up independently of each other and separate to the cities of Leeds and Wakefield. They grew from small farming communities during the industrial revolution, when the many stone-built houses, churches and shops were constructed. Then, as Leeds and Wakefield needed dormitory villages, newer housing was built in the gaps between the villages. Today, some of the surrounding villages blend into each other along the connecting roads, but they do retain a rural character at their outer edges. There is an element of neglect on some of the buildings, which inevitably began when the coal mines and quarries ceased work. But there are still enough of the delightful stone buildings to give a feel for the industrial Yorkshire of old.

It would be easy to write off this village, but there are reasons to visit. The two local public houses are pleasant, traditional pubs. You can buy a chippy tea at Robin Hood Fisheries, and you might even see the Robin Hood Football Club play a game.

The Leeds City Council Ward containing the village does still retain a Robin Hood connection, in its name of Ardsley and Robin Hood Ward.

The general area of South Yorkshire claims its connection to Robin Hood, through many references to Barnsdale Forest in the ballads. Closer ties to this specific area are claimed through the villages of Outwoods and Stane Lea, which are both mentioned in the ballads. Like many villages around large urban centres, these were long ago swallowed up by Wakefield, to become the districts of Outwood and Stanley (both to the south of the M62).

The name Robin Hood was first given to a spring or well located near the old quarries. The original well-trough had an iron ladle chained to it, although sadly neither the well nor its trough now exist, having been covered up with quarry refuse. The well still runs underground, and feeds the local streams.

The well-dressing ceremonies that are common throughout Yorkshire and Derbyshire were once held here. Thomas Ravenscroft composed a country dance in 1609, called "Robin Hood's Dance before the Queen." It is said that this, or a similar dance, was performed at the well-dressing ceremonies.

Robin Hood, Robin Hood, said Little John,
Come dance before the queene-a:
In a red petticote, and a greene jacket,
A white hose and a greene-a.

The centre of Robin Hood is the Halfway House public house, on the junction of the A61 and A654. The pub takes its name from being half-way between Leeds and Wakefield, exactly four miles in either direction. It used to be known as "The Old Halfway House", and a public house or inn has been on this site for centuries.

Robin Hood was originally part of nearby Carlton village, where the original villagers worked as miners and quarrymen. Mining in this area dates to the late 1600s. The largest of the local mines was Robin Hood Colliery, which was opposite the Halfway House pub. The J&J Charlesworth Company opened the mine in 1854. Charlesworth owned several collieries in the area, naming most of them after his daughters. The Robin Hood Colliery was known as "Jane Pit". Several hundred local men worked underground, until the mine closed in the 1960s and was derelict until a large housing estate was built in the 1990s.

Robin Hood village also had some big stone quarries and a nearby brickworks. The main quarry was to the left of Thorpe Lower Lane, where it meets Middleton Lane. This was called Robin Hood Quarries, and was worked from the late 1800s until the 1950s. Most of this old site is now covered by the M1 Motorway, which was built in the 1960s.

The village was also the unlikely location for a GPO (General Post Office) Telegraph Repeater Station and an RAF Bunker.

The Telegraph Repeater Station sat on the corner of Sharpe Lane, where it meets the A61 Wakefield Road, and was used to boost the strength of electric telephone signals.

Just behind the GPO building was a large concrete building with blast proof doors, guarding an underground bunker, which was built as part of Britain's Cold War preparations. The GPO building was demolished around 2007, but the concrete bunker still stands today within a private garden.

Even the local football club has a connection with our hero. Robin Hood Athletic Football Club play at the Coach Ground, just behind the Coach and Horses pub on the A61, which is actually in the adjoining village of Rothwell (post-code LS26 0SF). Anyone expecting a Premier League ground should remember that this is an amateur local team, not Manchester or Liverpool.

Robin Hood Athletic Football Club

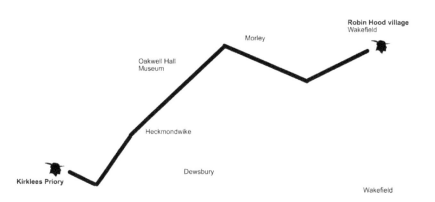

Bradford

Robin Hood village
Wakefield

Morley

Oakwell Hall
Museum

Heckmondwike

Dewsbury

Kirklees Priory

Wakefield

Robin Hood Village (Wakefield) To Kirklees Priory

Robin Hood Village (Wakefield) To Kirklees Priory: 16 miles – 40 minutes

After visiting the village of Robin Hood, we resume our journey to Kirklees Priory.

- Turn left out of the Halfway House car park and go straight through traffic light crossroads, onto A654 Thorpe Lane.

Note: for the Coach House pub and Robin Hood FC, you should turn right at this set of traffic lights, onto A61 Leeds Road / Wakefield Road (Postcode LS26 0SF).

The next village after leaving Robin Hood is Thorpe. Unlike some of the other village boundaries in the area, there is a defined green space between Robin Hood and Thorpe.

- Pass under the M1 motorway.
- At T junction turn right onto A654 Middleton Lane (There is no directional signpost, but there is a street sign for Middleton Lane). This is the village of Thorpe on the Hill (postcode WF3 3BX).

The village of Thorpe on the Hill begins very rural, with well-spaced out stone buildings and stone boundary walls. As we progress along Middleton Lane, the village has grown slightly, with the addition of a modern council estate.

We soon leave Thorpe on the Hill behind us and return to rural scenery. The urban sprawl of Leeds and Bradford are visible off to our right, but the immediate area is rural.

- Cross over M62 motorway.
- Soon after crossing motorway reach a traffic light controlled T-junction.
- Turn right onto A650 (signposted M62 Bradford and Dewsbury).

This T-junction marks the start of more urbanisation with council housing ahead of us.

- Reach the large and complicated Tingley Interchange roundabout (postcode WF3 1JX).
- We are taking the A650 Bradford Road, which is the second exit (signposted Bradford and Morley).
- Soon after Tingley interchange, Bradford Road changes name to Tingley Common.
- Reach a complicated traffic light junction, which operates almost like a roundabout.
- We are continuing straight on, along the A650 Britannia Road. This would be the second exit if it was a roundabout (signposted Bradford).

The area around Britannia Road is quite built-up, but there is still evidence of industrial revolution stone buildings.

- A650 Britannia Road changes name to Bruntcliffe Road, near another Halfway House pub (postcode LS27 0BJ). This is the Leeds suburb of Morley.
- Continue along Bruntcliffe Road, to a traffic light controlled cross-roads, just before a large public house (postcode LS27 0LY).
- Turn left at this junction onto A643 Howden Clough Road (signposted Birstall).

We leave the urban area and the view opens ahead of us.

- Cross over the M62.
- A643 Howden Clough Road changes name to Leeds Road.

After passing over the motorway we descend on a hilly road through woods, and back into countryside.

At the bottom of the hill, we enter the District of Kirklees, and are nearing our destination of Kirklees Priory.

There are speed cameras in Howden Clough village.

- Reach a traffic light controlled crossroads.
- Turn left onto A62 Huddersfield Road (signposted Huddersfield). There is also a brown tourist sign for Oakwell Hall Museum.

Oakwell Hall Museum (Nova Lane, Birstall, Batley, WF17 9LF)

Oakwell Hall is a Grade I Listed Elizabethan manor house surrounded by 110 acres of country park. A stone dated 1583 gives a good indication of its date of construction.

Oakwell Hall has been used as TV and film locations, but its greatest fame comes from Charlotte Brontë using it as the basis for Fieldhead in her novel *Shirley*. Oakwell's TV credits have included: the 2017 BBC series, *Gunpowder*, and most recently the ITV drama *Victoria*. Other location credits are *Gentleman Jack* (BBC), *Jonathan Strange and Mr Norrell* (BBC) and the 2009 adaptation of *Wuthering Heights* (ITV). **www.kirklees.gov.uk/beta/museums-and-galleries/oakwell-hall.aspx**

Legend has it that the ghost of Captain William Batt haunts Oakwell, once leaving a bloody footprint in his bedroom. A version of the story was written by Elizabeth Gaskell in her 1857 book, *The Life of Charlotte Brontë*, which said "Captain Batt was believed to be far away; when one winter evening, he came along the lane, through the hall and up the stairs, into his room, where he vanished." Mrs Gaskell went on to discuss Captain Batt's death, writing that "He was killed in a duel in London that same afternoon of December 9th 1684." Historical records do show that Batt was at the Black Swan, in Holborn, on 9th December, where he borrowed some money.

Brontë fans will visit Oakwell Hall for its connection to the 19th century author. Oakwell Hall was being used as a girls' school at the time Charlotte Brontë and her sisters were considering setting up a school of their own at Haworth. Charlotte's closest friend, Ellen Nussey, brought her to see the school, and she was inspired to use it as Fieldhead manor house, in her novel *Shirley*.

Ramblers and Brontë fans alike will find an entertaining diversion at Oakwell, as it is a trailhead on the Brontë Way. This 43-mile (69 km) long-distance footpath skirts Bradford on a 15 mile section to Haworth Parsonage. The Parsonage is where the Brontë sisters wrote most of their novels while their father was the parson. The trail then crosses the South Pennines, continuing to Gawthorpe Hall, Padiham and into Lancashire.

The A62 looks a major route on the map but in fact goes through some lovely rural scenery. We follow this road all the way to our destination at The Three Nuns.

- Take care as you approach The Three Nuns, as it is a complicated junction.
- There is a petrol station on the left.
- The Three Nuns car park entrance is in the middle of the junction, to your right.
- END POINT: Three Nuns Inn, Leeds Road, Dewsbury, WF14 0BY

Kirklees Priory & Robin Hood's Grave

The remains of Kirklees Priory are on private land, within the Kirklees Estate, at Clifton, near Brighouse. The owners open the estate to the public for a single weekend each year for guided tours, led by Calderdale Heritage Walks. These are usually towards the end of June.

Outside of this narrow window for visitors, the area still has a lot to offer to walkers. There is a vast network of footpaths surrounding the Kirklees Estate, which can be turned into circular walks. As well as taking in the open space to the east of the estate, footpaths loop round to the west, where they follow The River Calder, and its canal cuts.

There are also places of interest to fans of the Brontë sisters. Their parents once lived in nearby Hartshead, which can be reached by road, or as part of a circular walk.

Any on-line map search for Robin Hood's Grave will show you a point on the A644. This is because the grave is about 200 metres inside woodland to the north of the road. However, the A644 is a busy road, with no opportunities to park, and little can be seen from this side of the Kirklees Estate.

A check of the maps will give several parking options along the A644, either at hotels and pubs, or in the industrial areas across the River Calder to the south-west.

The better option for getting close is to use the public footpath on the east of the estate. This footpath starts just east of the Three Nuns and runs north towards the village of Hartshead, where it links to a network of paths, including The Bronte Way, The Kirklees Way, The Spen Way Heritage Trail, The Luddite Trail and The Brighouse Boundary Walk.

Walking Routes around Kirklees Priory

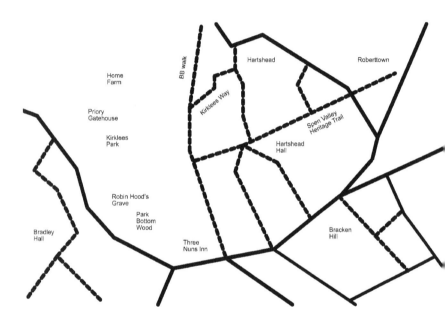

Home
Farm

BB walk

Hartshead

Roberttown

Priory
Gatehouse

Kirklees Way

Kirklees
Park

Spen Valley
Heritage Trail

Hartshead
Hall

Robin Hood's
Grave

Park
Bottom
Wood

Bradley
Hall

Bracken
Hill

Three
Nuns Inn

Walking Routes around Kirklees Priory

We start our walk with the Three Nuns on our left and a landscape gardeners to our right.

Continuing a little further along the path, the Kirklees Estate makes clear that Park Bottom Wood is private property, with a "No Public Right of Way" sign, although it is clear many feet have trod a path towards Robin Hood's Grave. A former colleague (who really should know better) did jump the fence and supplied the grave photograph shown here.

The Kirklees Estate

The footpath continues, making a very pleasant walk across fields, towards the village of Hartshead and Hartshead Hall (Hartshead Hall Lane, WF15 8AX).

Hartshead

Hartshead village has pre-Norman origins, with its Walton Cross thought to date from the 11th century.

Hartshead plays a very key part in the story of the Brontë sisters. In fact, they might never have been born without their father's connection to the village. In 1811, Patrick Brontë was Parson at the Church of Saint Peter in Hartshead (Church Street, Hartshead, WF15 8EU). Patrick met his future wife Maria Branwell at nearby Rawdon, and they married at Guiseley, just north of Bradford. Patrick and Maria became the parents of Anne, Charlotte and Emily Brontë.

Kirklees Priory

Kirklees Priory fits into the Robin Hood legends at a critical point: that of our hero's death. The estate also claims to be the location of Robin Hood's Grave.

The association originates from one of the two oldest ballads which feature Robin Hood – "A Lytell Geste of Robyn Hode." This ballad was written in Middle English, a form of our language spoken from the Norman Conquest in 1066, until the late 15th century. It is believed to have been produced in printed form between 1492 and 1534.

Towards the end of "A Lytell Geste of Robyn Hode", Little John carried Robin Hood to the Kirklees Priory nunnery for treatment of an injury. Little John hoped that the abbess would cure his friend, but the abbess betrayed him. She treated his wounds, then went on to administer bloodletting with leeches, which was a common treatment at the time. However, the abbess deliberately left the leeches in place too long, and bled Robin to death.

The story of Robin and the Abbess of Kirklees was picked up again in the 18th century, when Thomas Percy compiled his *Percy Folio*. Although Percy put his collection together in the 1700s, the collected stories were much older, with some of its material dating back well into the 12th century.

Robin Hood's Grave: Kirklees Priory

It is fair to assume that some of the ballads' original content has been lost over the centuries, since the manuscript's previous owners did not treat the documents well. Possibly because they regarded the Middle English as incomprehensible and therefore worthless, the housemaids used some of its pages to start fires. Thomas Percy had the manuscript bound, but his bookbinder lost the first or last lines on many pages through careless trimming of the pages. Neither did Percy treat the historic manuscript particularly well, since he wrote notes and comments in it and tore out some pages after binding.

The Percy Folio preserves eight Robin Hood ballads; it is Robin Hood's Death (the 120th ballad in the *Child Ballads* collection) which features the supposed events at Kirklees Priory.

In the ballad Robin Hood's Death, Robin goes to get himself bled by his cousin, the prioress of Kirklees. Robin refused the bodyguard offered by Will Scarlet and took only Little John with him. The treacherous prioress conspired with her lover, Sir Roger of Doncaster, to exact revenge for Robin's family having inherited Doncaster's land and title. The prioress let out too much blood, weakening Robin, so that her lover, could stab him while he was weak. Robin Hood does claim some consolation, by mortally wounding Sir Roger before his own death. Little John wanted to avenge him, but Robin forbade it, because he had never been responsible for harming a woman.

In the earliest version of the manuscript, Robin meets an old woman during his journey to Kirklees Priory. Sadly, this is among the sections which became fragmented by the manuscript's mistreatment.

The old woman appears to be "banning" Robin Hood, but the manuscript breaks off for half a page, while the outlaws ask why she is doing so. "Banning" is usually interpreted as "cursing" someone, but there is an alternative meaning of "lamenting," which might suggest the old woman was predicting Robin's death or grieving in advance. In the next surviving fragment of the story, Robin Hood appears to be reassuring someone who has warned that he is going to his death.

A later version of this ballad, recorded in 1786, changes some key aspects of its story. The new version omits the people who predicted Robin's death, and also misses out Roger of Doncaster. It is the 1786 version that adds the now-famous detail that Robin Hood shot one final arrow, asking to be buried where it fell. This has become the most common account of Robin Hood's death.

The 1450 version of the story, A Gest of Robyn Hode, ends with praise for Robin, saying that he "dyde pore men moch god." ("Did poor men much good.")

The Kirklees Estate has a chequered history; beginning as a Roman encampment, it was settled by Bronze and Iron Age people, because of its fertile soil. The estate also got a mention in the *Doomsday Book*.

The Cistercian nunnery, where the Robin Hood ballad is set, was founded in 1155 by Reiner le Fleming, Lord of the Manor of Wath-upon-Dearne. In the 14th century it achieved its first bout of notoriety, when the priory fell into disrepute over rumours that the nuns had entertained men in their private areas.

During Henry VIII's reformation, the priory was knocked down and its stone was used in the farm buildings and Kirklees Hall, a short distance away.

All that remains of the priory today is the 16th century gatehouse which was recently renovated and converted into a two-bedroom home. It is this gatehouse which is said to be the place of Robin Hood's death, and the location from which he fired his final arrow. The fact that it was built in the 1500s puts its existence as much later than most popular versions of the legends, so we might assume it to be a structure re-built on an older site.

The upper room of the gatehouse, in which Robin Hood is said to have breathed his last, is approached by an outside staircase and there is ornamental foliated work carved into the beams, including a hunting scene with stag and hound, which seem appropriate for the greenwood outlaw.

Our next legendary location of Robin Hood's Grave lies approximately 600 metres from the gatehouse. While considerably less than the 1.3 miles claimed for Robin and Little John's shots from Whitby Abbey, it is still quite an improbable arrow shot for a dying man, made with a medieval longbow.

Robin Hood's Grave is the name given to a monument in Kirklees Park Estate, near the now-ruined Kirklees Priory. Despite lots of compelling evidence to the contrary, it is reputed to be the burial place of Robin Hood. More recent versions of the story add Robin's final act in shooting an arrow from the window of his room, telling Little John to bury him at the spot where the arrow falls. So, following this version of the story, Robin Hood's Grave marks the place on which Robin's final arrow landed.

Rather than a traditional grave site, the monument is a rectangular stone wall, topped by iron railings, which surround the supposed grave. Lying on the earth, in the centre of the enclosure, is an irregular shaped stone, marked with several crosses. Set into the inner face of the surrounding wall, is an epitaph, which reads:

> Hear Underneath dis laitl stean
> Laz robert earl of Huntingtun
> Ne'er arcir ver az hie sa geud
> An pipl Kauld im robin heud
> Sick utlawz az hi an iz men
> Vil england nivr si agen
> Obiit 24 Kal Dekembris 1247

This can be translated into modern English as follows:

Here underneath this little stone
Lies Robert, Earl of Huntingdon
Never archer were as he so good
And people called him Robin Hood
Such outlaws as he and his men
Will England never see again
Obit: 24 December 1247AD

As with many things relating to Robin Hood, there is a considerable amount of speculation as to whether this is genuinely the grave of our legendary hero, or if it is simply a tale that has been embellished over time. There are several historical references either to the grave itself, or the inscription carved on the monument. We will read later that the current inscription is most likely a modern addition, but there may have been a grave marker on this site as early as the 16th century.

John Leland compiled his *Collectanea* collection in the 1530s. In it, he mentions the tradition that Robin Hood is buried near Kirklees Priory.

The earliest definite reference to a gravestone is found in Richard Grafton's *Chronicle at Large*, written in 1569. Grafton wrote that after Robin's death, the prioress "caused him to be buried by the highway side." His transcription goes on: "And upon his grave the sayde Prioresse did lay a very fayre stone, wherin the names of Robert Hood, William of Goldesborough and others were graven." Grafton described crosses erected at either end, saying: "And at eyther end of the sayde Tombe was erected a crosse of stone, which is to be seene there at this present." Although they might have been present in 1569, there are no crosses there today.

Probably due to his misreading of a capital K, Grafton gives the name of the priory as "Bircklies."

In 1632, Martin Parker wrote his ballad "The True Tale of Robin Hood." Attached to his manuscript is a very similar epitaph to that found on the monument today.

In 1665, Nathaniel Johnston drew a sketch of a stone bearing the same inscription as that described by Grafton.

When The Dean of York, Thomas Gale, died in 1702, an epitaph matching the one carved on the monument was found among his papers.

Philemon Holland made an English translation of William Camden's *Britannia* in 1607. In the translation, "the tombe of Robin Hood" is mentioned in passing as being situated near Kirklees Priory.

In the early 1700s, Ralph Thoresby wrote that he had seen the stone, but said that the inscription was barely legible.

In 1786, Richard Gough wrote that the gravestone was "broken and much defaced, the inscription illegible". He also reported that a former landowner had excavated the site, and found that the earth below the stone had not been disturbed. Gough's illustration of this stone does not match up with the description provided by Grafton in 1569.

The monument we see today is surrounded by a low stone wall and fence. This is thought to have been erected in the 19th century, to prevent local workers from chipping away pieces of the gravestone, which they believed to be a cure for toothache.

Returning to the present day, there has been a substantial amount of research and speculation in trying to connect the real Kirklees Priory with the legends and ballads.

The well-respected National Geographic company produced a documentary series, called *Mystery Files*, which discussed the priory's part in the legend and the validity of the grave site.

The show featured Medieval historian Graham Phillips, who has something of a chequered CV. National Geographic, the BBC and even Tony Robinson, have partnered with Phillips, but many academics dispute his higher profile claims. Phillips' previous projects have included controversial claims about the King Arthur legend, and he also claimed to have located the true Holy Grail.

Graham Phillips is sceptical about the inscription, saying: "the inscription has an olde English type inscription telling us that Robin Hood was buried here. But it is stylised in a way which 19th century romantics thought that Olde English was written."

Phillips concluded: "It's not genuine; it was put there in the 1800s, several centuries after Robin Hood was supposed to have lived (in the 13th or 14th century)." He also cast doubt on the 600 metre longbow shot claimed on Robin's behalf, saying that "even a medieval master bowman could not have fired an arrow the length of five or six football pitches."

Despite his misgivings about the inscription, Graham Phillips does think there might have been an earlier grave there, before the more modern monument was erected.

He said: "There is evidence of a grave before the current one was put there in the 1800s. In fact, as early as the 1600s people refer to a grave being there." In his argument, Philips referred to a 1665 sketch by Nathaniel Johnston, which also carried the name of Robert Hode. Phillips said that: "Robin is actually a nickname for Robert and Hode is one of the old spellings of Hood." So, he concluded, "we do know there was an early grave there belonging to a Robin Hood."

A more scientific approach was used in 2015, when the TV show *Expedition Unknown* investigated the grave's authenticity with ground-penetrating radar. They found no indications of ground disturbance which might indicate a burial.

Historian Maurice Keen cast doubt on the authenticity of the monument's inscription, describing it as "clearly spurious."

Keen appears to have impeccable credentials, with a string of appropriate qualifications after his name. He is a Fellow of the British Academy, a Fellow of the Royal Historical Society, a Fellow of the Society of Antiquaries of London, and he even featured in Frederick Forsyth's 1989 novel, *The Negotiator.*

Keen said that the language used in the inscription "is unlike any variety of English ever spoken." He also pointed out that the date format "24 Kal Dekembris" has never been used.

Local history enthusiast Richard Rutherford-Moore added his opinion to the debate. Rutherford-Moore is the author of two books about our hero: *Legend of Robin Hood* (2001) and *Robin Hood: On the Outlaw Trail Again* (2004). He claimed that the bones were dug up in the 18th century, and that the whereabouts of the bones are unknown.

The Calderdale Heritage Walks around The Kirklees Estate had been suspended for Covid during the period that I wrote this book.

But the local *Examiner* newspaper joined local historian David Nortcliffe for a pre-pandemic visit, the highlights of which I share below.

David Nortcliffe had been leading CHW's "Nuns and Outlaws" walk on the estate for over 15 years when the *Examiner* joined him on a guided tour. The reporter described entering the Kirklees Estate as "like stepping back in time to a pre-industrial world with farm animals roaming between the aged buildings."

The walk began in front of a 17th century malt house, which is a Grade I Listed building on Historic England's At Risk Register. The malt house's low ceilings had made it difficult for a modern use to be found for it, which has been a problem for many of the estate's historic buildings.

From the malt house, they moved on to a Grade II Listed 17th century cowshed, which was described as being "in a terrible state." Its gable wall and roof had partially collapsed, and they were not allowed near the building for safety reasons.

Next came a Grade I Listed, 15th century double aisled barn, which was described as "magnificent."

Opposite the barn is the last remaining part of Kirklees Priory, the gatehouse where Robin Hood is supposed to have died.

From the gatehouse, they followed David down a tree-lined driveway, up a tunnel of trees and through fields of wheat, to what is said to be Robin Hood's Grave.

They described the grave as being an 18th century folly, which is meant to represent the place where Robin's final arrow landed.

I will be joining Calderdale Heritage Walks for my own tour of Kirklees Priory, when they resume. You can find more details about the site, and also book your own tour, at **www.calderdaleheritagewalks.org.uk**

The Three Nuns Inn on Leeds Rd, Mirfield (postcode WF14 0BY), has a part in the local folk law. Although the current owners have dropped the original name in favour of their corporate identity, the pub does still have its Blue Plaque. A building that previously stood on the site was run by the priory as a hostelry and guest house. It was named after Cecilia Topclife, Joan Leverthorpe, and Katherine Grace, three nuns who sought refuge at the inn. These three nuns do appear to be different to the ones who gained Kirklees Priory its reputation as a house of ill repute. The present pub was built in 1939, and the site of the former guest house is buried under the car park.

The Three Nuns Inn

Blue Plaque at the Three Nuns Inn

Robin Hood's Cottage (Park Bottom Wood)

Robin Hood's Cottage is located very close to Robin Hood's Grave in Park Bottom Wood within the Kirklees estate. Like the grave, it cannot be seen from outside the estate's boundary.

Ordinance Survey maps between 1854 and 1949 show it as Robin Hood Malt Kiln.

Local historians did see estate agent's material from the sale of Kirklees Farm, which notes that "A repair notice has been received in respect of Robin Hood's Cottage." English Heritage has also agreed in principle to provide a £100,000 loan towards the repairs, so the cottage is still there. While we cannot see the cottage for the trees, we could wait for a bus on Wakefield Road, at a bus stop named Robin Hood's Cottage.

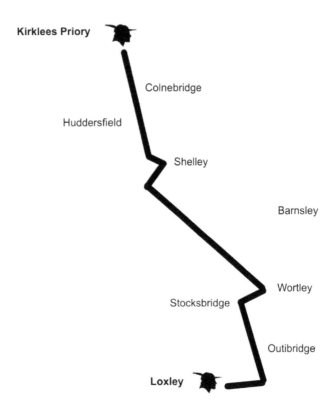

Bradford

Kirklees Priory

Colnebridge

Huddersfield

Shelley

Barnsley

Wortley

Stocksbridge

Outibridge

Loxley

Kirklees Priory to Loxley

Kirklees Priory to Loxley: 30 miles - 1 hour

- Leaving the Three Nuns car park and getting onto the A62 is not straightforward, since the exit falls inside a busy traffic light controlled junction.
- Ideally, we would turn right from the car park, but this is not possible.
- Turn left out of the car park onto A62 Leeds Road (travelling in the opposite direction to our route), then find a safe way of returning to the junction.
- A good satnav setting from here is the superstore, on Penistone Road, Waterloo, (postcode HD5 8QW). There is a petrol station here and the onward navigation is straightforward.
- Pass the Three Nuns on your right, continuing straight on to the traffic island.
- Take first exit onto A62 Cooper Bridge Road, which soon becomes Leeds Road.
- At traffic lights (postcode HD5 0RP), turn left on B6118 Colne Bridge Road.
- Go straight across a traffic island at an industrial estate, continuing on B6118 Colne Bridge Road.
- Just after crossing a stone built road bridge, turn right onto Dalton Bank Road (signposted Dalton).
- Continue on Dalton Bank Road, passing Dalton Bank Nature Reserve on your left.
- Dalton Bank Road becomes Nettleton Road.
- At a roundabout on a housing estate, take first exit, onto Sutton Avenue. This might look like a wrong turn into the housing estate, but it makes for an easier left turn at the next junction.
- At T junction, turn left onto Crossley Lane.

- At roundabout, take second exit, turning right onto School Lane. Entering village of Kirkheaton.
- At mini roundabout, take second exit onto Waterloo Road.
- At the end of Waterloo Road, we reach a complicated series of junctions. We are going onto A629 Penistone Road.
- Care needs to be taken at this junction. The A629 turning is give way, but all other parts of the junction are traffic light controlled.
- The superstore (postcode HD5 8QW) is on your left soon after this junction.
- The next waypoint for your satnav is: The Bridge Inn, Cote Lane, Thurgoland, Sheffield, (postcode S35 7AE).
- If you have stopped at the superstore leave the car park turning left onto A629.

This long stretch of the A629 provides easy navigation. It is a good class road, allowing reasonable progress, yet still affording pleasant views.

The Trans-Pennine Trail criss-crosses our route all along the A629.

Signposted off to our right is Almondbury Castle Hill (Car park: Castle Hill Side, Almondbury, HD4 6TA).

Almondbury Castle Hill
Almondbury Castle Hill is a scheduled ancient monument. The hilltop has been settled for at least 4,000 years. The site has the remains of a late-Bronze Age or early Iron Age hill-fort, a later Iron Age hill-fort, a 12th century motte-and-bailey castle, and the site of a deserted medieval village.

In more modern times, Castle Hill's flat top was used for many political and religious meetings. At least four Chart-ist rallies were held during 1843 and 1848. During the great weavers' strike of 1883, 2,000 to 3,000 people braved bitter weather to listen to their union leaders' speeches.

The hill's most prominent landmark is The Victoria Tower. It was completed in 1899, to commemorate Queen Victoria's 60 years on the throne. It cost £3,298 to build.

The 106 feet high tower increased the height of Castle Hill to an impressive 1,000 feet above sea level. **www.castlesfortsbattles.co.uk**

- The A629 passes through several villages on the way to our next turning, including: Shelley village, Shepley village, Birds Edge and High Flatts.

Shepley village

The name Shepley comes from Old English sceap (sheep) and leah (clearing), which translates to a clearing where sheep are kept. But there are several villages in the area with the suffix "ley": Crossley, Longley, Shelley, Emley, Midgley, Coxley, Stanley, Scholey, Methley and Astley. In 1925, historian Al-fred Watkins suggested a reason for this in his book *The Old Straight Track*. He suggested that ancient British people used hill tops as sighting points to help them navigate, and that the suffixes of ley actually means "a grassy track across country".

Today, Shepley is the home to one of Britain's largest bottled water companies, named Shepley Spring. But in Vic-torian times, the villagers bottled something a little stronger. In 1829, Seth Senior established a brewery at the Royal Sov-ereign Inn (172-174 Penistone Road, Shepley, HD8 8BE), pay-ing a single Gold Sovereign for the pub. The Seniors built up their estate, taking on several other local pubs, including the Railway (now the Cask and Spindle, 112 Abbey Rd, Shepley, HD8 8EL), The Black Bull (1 Marsh Lane, Shepley, HD8 8AE), the Stagg's Head (the building still stands on Abbey Road), and the Farmer's Boy (44 Marsh Lane, Shepley, HD8 8AP). In 1946, their business was taken over by Hammonds Brewery.

Note: the pub information was correct in late 2021, but pubs do close. The postcodes will take you to where they were.

It is a Yorkshire tradition to commemorate any builder killed during building work by carving his face into the building. One such face is carved into the eastern gable of the Sovereign Inn, although some speculate this carving actually represents Seth Senior himself.

Driving through Shepley, I spotted Whitby Court industrial Park on my right, which was a welcome reminder of our time on the North Yorkshire Coast. I have not found any reason for its use of the Whitby name.

Holmfirth

Fans of the TV series *Last of the Summer Wine* might wish to take a five mile detour to see one of its main filming locations.

I have visited Holmfirth several times, finding something new on each visit. Sid's café (4A Town Gate, Holmfirth, HD9 1HA) is there, although only the outside is used as a location. The TV café is much bigger than the small café is in real life. Nora Batty's house is a tearoom, named The Wrinkled Stocking (30 Huddersfield Road, Holmfirth, HD9 2JS). The surrounding hillsides are instantly recognisable from the characters' walks around their village.

High Flatts

The hamlet of High Flatts is most famous for its part in the history of The Quakers, or The Society of Friends. In 1652, the new church was just establishing itself, and locals began holding meetings in a barn. The Quakers continued to meet in their barn until 1697, when they converted a building on Firth Lane. The Meeting House was re-built in 1754, and the area became known as Quaker Bottom. It is still there and has been Grade II Listed (9 Quaker Bottom, High Flatts, HD8 8XU).

You can also visit the earthwork remains of an Iron Age hill fort. A selection of flint arrow heads, tools and stone axe head fragments found at the site, can be viewed at Tolson Museum in Huddersfield.

- At Hoylandswaine roundabout, take second exit, continuing straight on, along A629 (signposted Rotherham).
- At the village of Thurgoland turn right just after the Green Dragon pub (postcode S35 7AE), onto Cote Lane (there is no signpost).
- The road heads downhill into a valley and becomes more rural.
- We soon reach the Bridge Inn, which we used as a satnav way-point (postcode S35 7AE).
- Our next satnav way-point is the Co-op on Langsett Road South, at Oughtibridge, S35 0GY.
- Leaving the Bridge Inn, continue on Cote Lane, which becomes Forge Lane just after a very narrow stone bridge.

- Cross the River Don on another old stone bridge. Forge Lane bends to the right and loosely follows the line of the river.
- Just before you would pass under an arched railway bridge, turn right onto Soughley Lane.
- Soughley Lane winds through woodland area, interspersed with the remains of its former industrial past.
- At T junction, turn right on A6102 Wortley Road (signposted Oughtibridge, Stocksbridge and Deepcar)
- A6102 Wortley Road becomes Manchester Road. The road winds through a mix of rural and industrial areas, on its way to the outskirts of Sheffield.
- The A6102 passes through the villages of Deepcar and Wharncliff Side.

Wharncliff Side

The village of Wharncliff Side is famous for a legend based at nearby Wharncliffe Crags.

The Dragon of Wantley tells of a local Knight slaying a dragon on Wharncliffe Crags. The story is told in a 1685 ballad, which was included in Thomas Percy's 1767 *Reliques of Ancient English Poetry.* We have met Thomas Percy though his *Child Ballad* collection, which features much about the Robin Hood legend.

The ballad tells of a huge dragon, almost as big as the Trojan Horse, who eats everything it comes across, including trees and buildings.

More of More Hall is the Knight who slayed the dragon. He bought a suit of spiked Sheffield armour and delivered a fatal kick to the dragon's "arse-gut", which the dragon explained with its dying breath was its only vulnerable spot.

The Grade II Listed More Hall is still there, on the opposite side of the valley to Wharncliffe Crags. The 16th Century house has been restored, and when last on the market, the seven bedroomed house was listed at £1,500,000. The house, at the southern edge of Bitholmes Wood, is surrounded by a snaking stone wall, which ends with a carved dragon's head (off More Hall Lane postcode S35 0BN).

The Dragon of Wantley

- We soon reach the village of Oughtibridge.
- The White Hart Inn on Langsett Road (postcode S35 0GX) sits in the fork of a one-way system of roads. Take the left side of the pub, onto Orchard Street.
- If you are looking on a map, we need to turn right onto Bridge Hill, but we are prevented from doing so, by the one-way system.

- Where the two roads re-join, double back onto the opposite carriageway. The turn is not signposted, but you drive around a pretty, stone-walled park area.
- At a zebra crossing, with a parade of stone-built shops on your right, turn left onto Church Street (signposted Worrell & Bradfield).
- Pass the Hare & Hounds pub (postcode S35 oFW) on your right.
- Drive uphill through Oughtibridge village. Take care in larger vehicles, as cars park on both sides of the hill, narrowing the road.

Oughtibridge

Oughtibridge dates back to the early 12th century, when a ford in the area crossed the River Don. The crossing was managed by a man named Oughtred, who lived in a nearby cottage. When a bridge was built in 1150 it became known as Oughtred's Bridge, which was often shortened to Oughty's Bridge. The small settlement around the bridge adopted the same name.

For over 500 years, Oughtibridge remained a small isolated rural hamlet. Even by 1747 it had only five families. The population started to rise in the late 18th century because of the Industrial Revolution and an expansion in farming. Oughtibridge's position in the Don valley made it a good location for the river's waterpower to drive the machinery of the Industrial Revolution.

By 1841 the population had risen to 1,005 with Oughtibridge Forge becoming its main industry. The forge still stands on Forge Lane and is Grade II Listed. It has now been renovated and turned into apartments.

The modern-day Oughtibridge is a commuter village for nearby Sheffield, with most of the local industry having given way to housing developments.

- Opposite number 128 Church Street, turn left onto Haggstones Road (signposted Worrall and Sheffield).
- Enter the village of Worrall, which is still quite built up.

Worrall

Road names such as Towngate Road and Lund Road indicate Viking origins for Worrall. Although the village's name comes from a Saxon word Hrivfull, meaning "top," in reference to Worrall's high position above the Don and Loxley valleys.

Worrall developed some small-scale industry at the start of the Industrial Revolution in the late 18th and early 19th centuries. It was one of many villages that adopted the Little Mester system, which became the backbone of Sheffield's cutlery and tool making industries. The Little Mesters were a network of craftspeople working out of small workshops or from their own homes. The self-employed craftsmen were specialised, performing part of the manufacturing process for goods ordered and sold by Master Manufacturers. They concentrated on individual aspects of forging, grinding or finishing. They tended to specialise in particular products, such as razors, penknives, or surgical instruments. Only a handful of Little Mesters remain in Sheffield today, most working in reconstructed museum workshops.

Ganister mining and quarrying developed in Worrall during the mid-17th century. Ganister is a hard siliceous rock used for furnace linings, so it was greatly in demand by Sheffield's growing steel industry.

- At the end of Worrell village, and just after a zebra crossing, turn right onto Kirk Edge Road (signposted Loxley & Bradfield).
- After a short distance on Kirk Edge Road, turn left onto Long Lane (signposted Loxley & Stannington).
- Hillsborough Golf Course (postcode S6 4BE) is on both sides of the road as you drive down Long Lane.
- At the end of Long Lane, reach the T-junction with B6077 Loxley Road.
- Turn left (signposted Sheffield & Wadsley). A view into the Loxley River valley opens up ahead of you.
- Turn left onto B6077 Loxley Road.
- Soon after turning onto Loxley Road, the Admiral Rodney public house (postcode S6 6RU) is on your left. Just after the pub is a row of stone troughs, presumably placed there to refresh horses coming up the steep hill from Sheffield.
- Just after these stone troughs, turn left uphill onto Rodney Hill.
- Look for Loxley Primary School on your left (postcode: S6 6SG).

There is a long parking layby opposite the school and in front of a row of houses (probably best to avoid the school's drop-off and pick-up times).

Loxley Primary School

Loxley

Three miles northwest of Sheffield city centre, Loxley is now a suburb of the city, and has been a Ward of Sheffield City Council since 1974. Before being merged with Sheffield, Loxley was a village in its own right, as part of the West Riding of Yorkshire. The name Loxley derives from the Old English words "lox", meaning lynx and "leah", meaning glade. So, Glade of the Lynx seems quite an appropriate name for our cunning hero's possible birthplace.

Historically, Loxley Chase, upon which the village sat, was a large expanse of high moorland set aside for hunting by the Norman lords in the 11th century. The Loxley valley, beneath the village, was an extensive woodland which would have been far better suited to Robin Hood.

In the 12th century, the forest of Loxley Chase extended as far south as Nottinghamshire where it joined up with Sherwood Forest, so it is not inconceivable that Robin Hood and his Merrie Men roamed between the two. Yorkshire claims that Robin of Locksley, or Robert Locksley, was born in the area sometime around 1160.

There have been many references linking Loxley to the Robin Hood legend. The earliest was a pardon held in the Public Record Office, which was awarded to Robin Hood one year after the riots of the Peasant's Revolt. Robin's pardon reads, "Robert Dore, also known as Robert Hood of Wadsley in the County of Yorkshire, received the king's pardon on 22nd May 1382." Many of the rioters of the Peasant's Revolt were hung, but it appears that Robin paid a massive fine to save his life.

During the early 1600s, Yorkshire antiquarian Roger Dodsworth wrote about a Robert Locksley, born in Bradfield Parish, who killed his father and became friends with a man called Little John.

A few decades later the *Sloane manuscript* refers to Robin as being born in "Locksley" around 1160. The *Sloane manuscripts* do have some academic credibility. The collection was put together by Sir Hans Sloane, who was physician to the English Governor of Jamaica in the late 1600s. Sloane married a sugar plantation heiress, whose fortune greatly aided his collecting of historic manuscripts. Sloane's collection was bought from his executors through the Act of Parliament which established the British Museum. It represents one of the British Library's three foundation collections, and has been described as the greatest collection assembled by a single person, not just in quantity but in the exceptional quality of the items.

In his *Exact and Perfect Survey and View of the Mannor of Sheffield*, written in 1637, John Harrison wrote "Little

Haggas Croft wherein is ye founacion of a house or cottage where Robin Hood was borne."

Little Haggas Croft was in the area of present-day Normandale House on Rodney Hill. Harrison claimed to have found remnants of the cottage, said to have been the birth-place and childhood home of Robin Hood. The 1637 date of his writings precluded any photographs, but a photograph in a local newspaper from 1937 showed a wooden beam that was purportedly from this house.

In March 2020, the local *Star* newspaper reported that a teacher at Loxley Primary School had discovered the birth-place of Robin Hood, in an ancient woodland at the back of the school. The school uses the archer as its logo and has a statue of Robin Hood in the playground.

Dan Eaton, a teacher and local historian, is a lifelong Robin Hood fan, who joined the school in 2017. Mr Eaton came across a large marker stone with a cross carved into it. The stone was in the middle of woodland, a few steps away from a dense area of ancient holly bushes, which reminded him of early drawings of the outlaw.

Other researchers have pinpointed the general area as the birthplace of Robin Hood, but Mr Eaton claimed to be the first researcher to have access to the site, allowing him to shed new light on the mystery of who the folk hero really was. He said: "Everyone knows the legends and there is a massive amount of scholarly work, but virtually no one has set foot in Loxley to try and do this."

After more investigation, his headteacher asked him to put together an educational package, using the Robin Hood legend to teach pupils about maths, science, history, English, geography and art. Mr Eaton told *The Star*: "It's been amazing to see the kids getting their heads into it and really motivating for me as a teacher to pass on local history knowledge."

The school has since received funding from Bradfield Parish Council for a Robin Hood storytelling hut to be built near the woodland.

Local MP Olivia Blake, even got in on the Robin Hood action in her 2020 maiden speech to Parliament. Ms Blake said that her Sheffield Hallam constituency had a "very long history of social justice", alluding to the idea that Loxley was the birthplace of Robin Hood.

Rodney Hill will look very different today in comparison to how it appeared in a more agricultural economy. Residential development of Loxley started around 1905, accelerating towards the start of WWI. Rodney Hill and Loxley Road near the village green saw most of this pre-war building boom. Then, between the wars, building moved to the Normandale area and, after WWII, a large Council House building programme began in the area.

Robin Wood (postcode S6 6SS)

Robin Wood is an area of ancient woodland, which is owned by Loxley Primary School. This is where teacher Dan Eaton found the lost marker stone, which he believes marks the location of Robin Hood's birth. The woods are open to the public, with a nature trail and information about the flora and fauna you will find there.

Robin Wood is only a short walk from the school, and you are best to remain parked on Rodney Hill.

- With your back to Loxley Primary School start walking downhill, to your right. Take the first right turn into Chase Road, uphill. Then the next right into Philips Road.

- Turn right at number 28 Philips Road, at a hilly lawned area. Follow the footpath in front of houses to the entrance of Robin Wood.

- Go through the entrance and follow the rough paths anti-clockwise around the wood.

Within the wood is evidence of historic occupation. There are dry stone walls and the remains of stone enclosures. Standing on a high point in the wood, just before finishing your circuit, is the marker stone with its cross found by Mr Eaton.

**The marker stone in Robin Wood,
found by Dan Eaton**

Robin of Loxley

Traditionally, the Robin Hood legends are placed within the
reign of King Richard I (The Lionheart), between 1189 and
1199. According to a document in the Public Records Office,
Loxley's claim to Robin Hood sits within the reign of The
Lionheart's successor, King Richard II, in 1382.

A pardon granted by King Richard II read: "Robert
Hode (Hood), also known as Robert Dore of Wadsley, received the King's pardon on 22nd May 1382". Under the medieval feudal system, Loxley was a subordinate village to nearby
Wadsley.

The records show that this particular claimant to the
mantel of Robin Hood was born in 1399. His mother was the

granddaughter of John de Balliol, King of Scots, a descendant of King David, the Earl of Huntingdon. His cousin provides a link to the legends concerning Kirklees Priory, when she became the Prioress of Kirklees in 1402, shortly before her cousin died.

In his *Exact and Perfect Survey of the Manor of Sheffield and other Lands*, published in 1637, John Harrison wrote, "William Green held these parcels of land; Great Haggas Croft, near Robin Hood's Bower, is surrounded by the Loxley Firth, Little Haggas Croft wherein is the foundation of a cottage where Robin Hood was born."

In 1618, the antiquarian Roger Dodsworth wrote, "Robert Locksley, born in Bradfield Parish, wounded his stepfather to death while ploughing and fled into the woods. When discovered, he fled to Clifton-upon-Calder (Kirklees) where he met Little John, who kept the kine (an archaic plural of cow)".

Loxley also provides a link to a noble title, somewhat belatedly accorded to our hero. Some 127 years after the death of Loxley's Robin Hood, one of his descendants became Earl of Huntingdon. Since then, many generations have continued a family tradition by naming their firstborn after Robin Hood. The current Earl is William Edward Robin Hood Hastings-Bass, the 17th Earl of Huntingdon.

The Loxley Valley Trail

I remember studying The Great Sheffield Flood of 1864 for my Master's degree. Loxley suffered terribly when the dam wall of the Dale Dike Reservoir, four miles east of Loxley, failed, killing 17 villagers. Most of the industrial mills in the area were either destroyed or badly damaged, but they were quickly rebuilt with compensation from the Water Company.

Running parallel, and to the south, of Loxley Road is the Loxley River. The river would no doubt have provided water for our medieval hero and his family, but in the mid-17th century it was the catalyst for industrial expansion at Loxley. Mills were set up on the fast-flowing River Loxley, and small pocket businesses, including steel and iron forging, and rolling mills were established. These developed the Loxley Steel Works, the Green Wheel Steel Works, the Little Matlock Rolling Mill and the Olive Rolling Mill. The industry is all but gone, but many of the mill ponds are still there, providing havens for fish and wildlife.

Walkers can enjoy a six mile circular walk along the River Loxley and the villages south of the river. The Loxley Valley Trail starts and ends at the junction of Hanson Road with Loxley Road, opposite the Admiral Rodney public house. A route guide can be downloaded from the Bradfield Walkers website. **www.bradfield-walkers.org.uk**

The Robin Hood 500: 500RH

Part Five

Derbyshire & Nottingham

80 Miles - 3 Hours travelling

Travelling time does not include time spent exploring the
attractions en-route

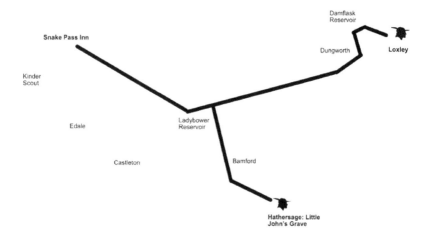

Snake Pass Inn

Kinder
Scout

Edale

Castleton

Ladybower
Reservoir

Bamford

Damflask
Reservoir

Dungworth

Loxley

Hathersage: Little
John's Grave

Loxley to Hathersage

Loxley to Hathersage: 16 miles - 30 minutes

- Re-trace your route down Rodney Hill, to the junction with B6077 Loxley Rd.
- Turn right, to leave Loxley heading west on B6077 Loxley Rd.
- At the start of Damflask Reservoir, turn left on B6076 New Road, driving along the top of the dam. (signposted: Dungworth, Low Bradfield & Stannington).

Damflask Reservoir (New Road/Oaks Lane, Sheffield, S6 6SQ)
Damflask is one of four reservoirs in the Bradfield area, built to supply water for the population and industries of Sheffield. It was completed in 1896, with the dam walls built from local stone. Its original purpose was to ensure a continuous flow of water to the River Loxley. It takes its name from Damflask village, which was destroyed in the Great Sheffield flood of 11th March 1864. The village stood near the site of the current dam wall and had a public house, corn mill, paper mill, wire mill, blacksmith's shop and a few cottages. The village was never rebuilt, because plans were already underway to build Damflask Reservoir.

The reservoir is owned by Yorkshire Water, who have opened it to various recreational groups. Three rowing clubs and a sailing club train on the reservoir. Anglers also fish for Bream, Pike, Roach and European Perch.

The woodlands around the reservoir are popular with walkers. A £60,000 project was completed by Yorkshire Water in 2015, providing better access for disabled people onto the circular walking route around the reservoir. The Peak

District Boundary Walk also runs along the south-western edge of the reservoir from Low Bradfield.

- Begin driving along the opposite side of Damflask Reservoir.
- Turn left from B6076 New Road onto B6076 Briers House Lane (signposted Dungworth & Stannington).
- Take care with navigation, as the map gives the impression that this is a natural continuation of New Road. It is actually a very tight left turn, onto a distinctly different road.
- Briers House Lane is very steeply uphill, with several tight corners. It is not suitable for caravans.
- Continue to follow B6076 through Dungworth Village (postcode S6 6HF), as the road name changes to Yewes Lane and Cliffe Hill.

Dungworth

Like many villagers in this area, the people of Dungworth and nearby Sykehouse, were involved in the manufacture of knives during the 17th and 18th centuries. Syke House farm has hearths and a workshop dating from this period. The 1861 census shows most men in the Dungworth area combined farming with the production of knives in small workshops attached to their cottages.

There are several historic buildings within the village dating from the 18th century: a cruck barn at Briers House Farm dates from the 16th century. Green Fold Farm dates from the early 18th century, and Padley Farmhouse dates from the mid-18th century. The village pub dates to 1813, and parts of the village primary school from the 1840s.

- At a point where Cliffe Hill bends to the left, take a right turn onto Skye House Lane, just before a detached stone house.
- At a T junction, turn right onto Game Lane (signposted Glossop).
- Game Lane changes name to Beaton Green.
- At T junction, turn right onto Rod Side. You are on quite a remote road, with a stone built farm on your right.
- After a long stretch of straight road through open country, Rod Side takes a series of sweeping S bends, before reaching a T junction with A57 Manchester Road.
- Turn right onto A57 (signposted Glossop).
- This road twists and undulates through moorland, eventually reaching Ladybower Reservoir.
- Soon after this turning we enter the Derbyshire Peak District. The A57 may sound like a major road classification, but it is a delightful stretch of road.

Peak District National Park
The Peak District National Park covers 555 square miles, including most of Derbyshire, and extends into Staffordshire, Cheshire, Greater Manchester and South & West Yorkshire.
www.peakdistrict.gov.uk
    The Peak District became the UK's first National Park on 17th April 1951.
    Theories about the area's name include the Pecsaetan or Peaklanders, an Anglo-Saxon tribe who lived in the area during the 6th century, when it was part of the Anglian kingdom of Mercia.

As with all of Britain's National Parks, land within the park is a mix of public and private ownership. The National Trust owns about 12% of the land. Its three estates (High Peak, White Peak and Longshaw) include ecologically significant areas at Bleaklow, Derwent Edge, Hope Woodlands, Kinder Scout, the Manifold valley, Mam Tor, Dovedale, Milldale and Winnats Pass. The National Park Authority owns around 5%. Other major landowners include several water companies, with the remainder in mostly private hands.

Walking is a hugely popular pastime in the Peak District, with a single political event securing its place in history. The Kinder Trespass of 1932 was a landmark in the campaign for open access to British moorland, and eventually led to the creation of Britain's national parks. Before the trespass, open moorland was owned by the landed gentry, who used them for 12 days of shooting each year. Access to the moors was jealously guarded by their gamekeepers.

Since it became a National Park in 1951, several long distance routes have been created through the area. Britain's first long-distance footpath was the Pennine Way, which opened in 1965 and starts at the Nags Head Inn, in Edale village. **www.nationaltrail.co.uk/en_GB/trails/pennine-way**

The Peak District's gritstone outcrops are recognised as some of the finest rock climbing sites in the world. Cavers explore the natural caves, potholes and old mine workings within the limestone of the White Peak. Its reservoirs have become centres for water sports, including sailing, fishing and canoeing. Other activities include sports like hang gliding and paragliding, birdwatching, fell running, off-roading, and orienteering.

The landscape of the Peak has inspired writers for centuries. Various places have been identified as locations in the

14th century poem *Sir Gawain and the Green Knight;* Lud's Church, at Gradbach in Staffordshire (postcode SK17 0SU), is thought to be the Green Chapel.

Key scenes in Jane Austen's 1813 novel *Pride and Prejudice* are set in the Peak District. William Wordsworth was a frequent visitor to Matlock, with the area inspiring several of his poems, including an 1830 sonnet to Chatsworth House.

The village of Morton in Charlotte Brontë's 1847 novel *Jane Eyre*, is based on Hathersage (where we soon visit Little John's grave), where Charlotte stayed in 1845.

Beatrix Potter, author of *Peter Rabbit*, visited her uncle at his printworks in Dinting Vale (near Glossop). She copied cloth samples from his pattern book, and based Mrs Tiggywinkle's shawl on one of these patterns.

Cutthroat Bridge (A57, Hope Valley, S6 6JA)

Before reaching the reservoirs, though, we can stop and admire the interestingly named Cutthroat Bridge. There is a tarmac layby on the left, although it is often quite full of walkers and mountain bikers.

You might think the bridge's lurid name is something to do with our legendary outlaws. However, the tales are more recent. About 400 years ago a man was discovered nearby with his throat cut. The man was still alive and was taken to Bamford Hall, where he died two days later.

Then more recently, in 1995, perhaps inspired by a 400 year old spirit, a Sheffield man beheaded his own stepfather with a samurai sword and dumped the body at Cutthroat Bridge. This tale has a celebrity twist, as the murderer, Anthony Antoniou, was once the lover of pop singer Gabrielle.

Cutthroat Bridge

- At the bottom of the hill, we reach a set of traffic lights at Ladybower Reservoir and Ladybower Inn (postcode S33 0AX).
- We will be turning left at these lights, onto the A6013 towards Bamford, but there is lots to explore in this area first.
- Continuing on the A57 towards Glossop will take us up Snake Pass.

Snake Pass

The highest, and probably most famous, of Derbyshire high passes, Thomas Telford built the Snake Pass in 1821, to link Sheffield to Manchester. Topping out at 510 metres above sea level, the high point of the pass is crossed by the Pennine Way, long distance footpath and is a draw for many ramblers.

It is easy to assume that the name Snake describes the twisting nature of the road. However, the name was actually taken from the Snake Inn (Snake Road, S33 oAB), which in turn was named for the serpent logo on the Cavendish arms.

William Cavendish, 6th Duke of Devonshire, was one of the two main financiers of what was originally called the Sheffield to Glossop Turnpike, which cost £18,625 to build. The toll road was run by the Sheffield and Glossop Turnpike Trust and as the highest toll road in England, it proved a very popular route.

A note of caution is worthwhile here. Even in summer, the Snake Pass has a poor accident record. In winter it can be even more tricky, as I remember from a November crossing in 2005. I chose the route for a Sunday evening motorcycle journey to Manchester's Police Training Centre. The road had not been officially closed, but I rode the highest section using my feet as outriders.

The road is very popular with drivers. Caterham Cars voted the Snake Pass their Best Driving Road in the UK, in a 2008 survey. The following year, *Auto Trader* magazine listed it as one of the best driving roads in Britain, saying it "offered unparalleled views over Manchester."

Cyclists might like to join the many people taking on the Snake Pass as an interesting challenge. In 1902, the *Lancashire Evening Post* described the downhill journey as "nine miles unbroken freewheeling," through "magnificent" scenery. Serious cyclists compare the uphill climb with those encountered in continental races. The steepest three mile section has a gradient of 7%, and has featured several times in the Tour of Britain route.

There are also regular cycling time trials, organised by the local Glossop Kinder Velo cycling club. Tejvan Pettinger set the record time of 11 minutes 51 seconds (current in 2021).

Fans of New Romantic band, The Human League, may recognise the road from their 2001 song, *The Snake*.

Ladybower Reservoir

The three reservoirs of the Upper Derwent Valley are almost universally, if incorrectly, known as Ladybower Dam. The Y shaped Ladybower Reservoir, in front of you, is the lowest of the three reservoirs, which feed into the River Derwent. The other two are Howden Reservoir and Derwent Reservoir, which both sit higher up the valley to your right. The three reservoirs between them cover almost 200 square kilometres and have a combined capacity of 464 billion litres.

A workforce of over 1,000 workers took 14 years to build the dams between 1912 and 1916. It was such a huge undertaking that a temporary town, called Birchinlee or Tin Town, was built for the workers and their families. The town had a school, a pub, shops, a hospital and a police station. The remains of Birchinlee, and sections of the railway that serviced it, can still be seen on the banks of Derwent Reservoir today.

Many of Ashopton's buildings were demolished before the reservoir was filled in 1946, but parts of Derwent village re-appear in times of drought. The water level dropped sufficiently in 1976, 1995 and 2018. I was among the many who visited in 2018, although I was not among those who daubed graffiti on the remains or needed Mountain Rescue to get them out of the mud.

A stone packhorse bridge over the River Derwent was removed and rebuilt at the top of the Howden reservoir, which I have cycled across many times. The bridge is now a Scheduled Ancient Monument. The church tower was originally left visible above the water level, until it was deemed a hazard in 1947 and was blown up.

As with many such locations, it is the movie industry which brought Ladybower its fame.

The reservoir was used in 1943 by the RAF 617 Squadron, better known as the *Dambusters*, to train for their raid on Germany's Ruhr Valley. The Lancaster Bombers returned in 1955 to recreate Operation Chastise for the movie cameras. There are still regular flypasts by The Battle of Britain Memorial Flight, which I have been privileged to see on several occasions.

Hollywood returned in 2015, to film scenes for Tom Cruise's *Mission Impossible: Rogue Nation*. The dam is unusual in having two bellmouth overflows, which are known locally as the "plugholes." These stone-built overflows are 80 feet (24 m) in diameter. Each plughole discharges through hydro-turbines, which generate electricity. You might not immediately recognise the plugholes in the film, as their Gothic splendour is made to look much more futuristic as Tom Cruise dives into one.

The Fairholmes Visitor Centre (postcode S33 0AQ) sits at the north end of the Ladybower Reservoir and has a gift shop, a takeaway food kiosk and toilets, as well as information boards about the area.

- Returning to our official route, we leave the A57 at the traffic light controlled junction, turning left on A6013 towards Bamford, entering Derbyshire's Peak District.

Bamford

Bamford is a pretty Peak District village, with an entry in the *Domesday Book*, when it was called Banford. The name comes from the Anglo-Saxon Bēamford, meaning tree-trunk ford.

For those visiting the churches around our route, the parish church of Saint John the Baptist was built around 1860, and its graveyard hosts the re-interred graves from Derwent and Ashopton, which were flooded by Ladybower Reservoir.

Bamford's growth as a village came as a result of its water mill, which pre-dates the Industrial Revolution. Christopher Kirk, a local farmer and miller, built a water-powered corn mill in 1782. Kirk's mill lasted only until 1791, when it was destroyed by fire and was replaced by a cotton mill.

In the early 19th century, a 60 horsepower steam engine was fitted, although this was supplemented with waterpower. The isolated mill also had its own gasworks until 1951.

The mill closed permanently in the 1990s, and has now been converted into flats. The steam engine remains on site, but is no longer operational.

In testament to its working heritage, Bamford once had four public houses. The Ladybower Inn and the Yorkshire Bridge Inn (Ashopton Rd, Bamford, Hope Valley S33 0AZ), which was the childhood home of *Blue Peter's* Peter Purvis, remain open as traditional pubs. The Derwent Hotel is now converted to self-catering accommodation.

It is the Anglers Rest (Taggs Knoll, Bamford, S33 0DY), though, which demonstrates the true community spirit of the villagers. In 2013, 300 people from the local area bought the Anglers Rest from the brewery, turning it into Derbyshire's first community-owned pub. As well as a pub, the building also houses a café and post office.

Until quite recently, Bamford had a very busy July Carnival, with fell race, pet show, parade and all the other trappings of a Derbyshire Carnival. The villagers still keep up the tradition of Well Dressing and the making of scarecrows during July.

- After passing through Bamford, we reach the traffic light controlled T junction with the A6187.
- We will be turning left towards Hathersage and Little John's grave, but a five mile detour to your right, towards Castleton, is worth taking.

Castleton (Castleton Visitor Centre, Buxton Road, Castleton, S33 8WN)
Castleton is also mentioned in the *Domesday Book*, when it went by the name Pechesers. It was re-named Castleton, in honour of the castle built by William Peverel to secure William the Conqueror's new lands.

Mineral wealth drew the Normans to Derbyshire, and Castleton's contribution was predominantly its lead.

Victorian England's Industrial Revolution became notorious for its air pollution, but Derbyshire's lead mines were ahead of the Victorians, during the two centuries following the Norman Conquest. Scientists studying ice cores from a Swiss glacier found that levels of lead pollution in the air between 1170 and 1216 was as high as those from the Industrial Revolution, with the main source being Peak District mines.

Lead is no longer mined in Castleton, but it did create the town's biggest tourist draw: its spectacular caverns. Four of these show caves are now open to the public: Peak Cavern, Blue John Cavern, Speedwell Cavern and Treak Cliff Cavern.

Possibly the most unusual is Speedwell Cavern, which is visited by boat, along its flooded tunnels.

The only mineral now mined in Castleton, albeit on a very small scale, is Blue John. This semi-precious mineral is a type of fluorite with bands of blue or yellow colour. It is found only in Castleton's Blue John Cavern and Treak Cliff Cavern, from where it is said to have been exported to France in the 1700s, earning its name, which is a corruption of "bleu-jaune", meaning "blue-yellow". Working the mineral into something resembling a gemstone is complex. The stones are first air dried for a year, before being heated in an oven. They are then placed in a bowl of hot resin – originally pine resin, but now substituted with epoxy resin – before being heated in a vacuum oven. This drives out air from the stone's minute pores, replacing it with the resin, which binds the crystal structure, allowing it to be cut and polished.

Blue John also has a literary reference, when it featured in a short story by Sir Arthur Conan Doyle. In 1910 *The Strand Magazine* published *The Terror of Blue John Gap*, about a doctor investigating mysterious goings-on in a cavern mined for Blue John.

Castleton draws outdoor enthusiasts with a huge range of activities. The area's network of footpaths and bridleways is fantastic. The start of the Pennine Way at Edale is just a short walk away. Here you can visit the site of the 1932 Mass Trespass of Kinder Scout, which pioneered the modern Right to Roam. Caving and pot-holing are very popular for those with the necessary skills and equipment. Paragliders often launch themselves from the hills surrounding the town. In the right winter conditions, the face of Mam Tor freezes, permitting an ice-axe climb, which I completed many years ago.

Visitors on 29th May, which is Oak Apple Day, will experience the Castleton Garland Day, when a Garland King is paraded around the streets wearing an extremely large garland of flowers, followed by local girls dressed in white with flowers.

The film industry has visited many parts of the beautiful Peak District, with Castleton also featuring several times. The caverns represented Narnia's underworld in in the 1990 BBC adaptation of *The Silver Chair*. The impressive valley of Cave Dale featured in both *The Princess Bride* (1987) and *The Other Boleyn Girl* (2008).

In a book about a road trip, it would be remiss not to discuss Castleton's unique road network.

We enter and leave Castleton on the A6187, but the routes out of Castleton to the west are the more interesting.

Castleton was once on the A625 road between Sheffield and Chapel-en-le-Frith. This route towards Manchester left Castleton to the north-west, flanking the lower slopes of Mam Tor. The hill's loose shales gained it the name "Shivering Mountain," and the constant landslides caused the road to be abandoned. Today it makes an entertaining mountain bike route, but is impassable for vehicles.

Castleton's only remaining westbound exit is now the unclassified road through the narrow Winnats Pass. This steep and narrow road is unsuitable for large vehicles or caravans, and road signs discourage through traffic by showing only local destinations. Thus, most traffic enters and leaves Castleton the same way as we have done.

- Having exhausted all that Castleton has to offer, we re-join the A6187 towards Hathersage, resuming our search for Robin Hood locations.

Robin Hood's Cross: Abney Moor

Off to our right, in the hills above the A6187 Hope Road, once sat Robin Hood's Cross. It was about 1.25 km south east of Bradwell, on an old track to Shatton.

A list of Derbyshire monuments published in 1934, notes it as being "on Abney Moor; built into wall near an old track to Shatton; behind a stile".

The Ordinance Survey maps from the years 1883 to 1923 show Robin Hood's Cross, but it has disappeared from modern editions. I have not personally been able to find it on my walks in the area.

Between Hope and Castleton, we pass Jagger's Lane on our left. There are several lanes in Derbyshire with similar names. This interesting northern word referred to someone who owned or managed a team of packhorses, and was adopted as a surname. The most famous holder of the surname is Rolling Stone, Mick Jagger, who grew up in Kent, but presumably has some northern ancestry.

Hathersage (Main Road, Hathersage, S32 1BB)

Hathersage too was around when the *Domesday Book* was written, recording its name as Hereseige. The last part of the name almost certainly derives from the Old English word "ecg," meaning "edge," and referring to the gritstone edges that overlook the town. Habitation of the area began long before the Normans, with a Bronze Age stone circle located on Bamford Moor and prehistoric microliths being discovered below Stanage Edge.

Industrial development caused the growth of many Derbyshire towns, and Hathersage is no exception. The gritstone edges overlooking the town are of a hard sandstone, known as Millstone Grit. These cliffs were the source of building stones and millstones, which were exported to North America, Russia and Scandinavia for wood-pulping. More locally, the millstones were also used to crush lead ore. The gritstone tended to discolour bread, so it was not generally used to grind wheat.

Today, the gritstone edges are a draw for rock climbers.

Hathersage has also played a role in the history of metalworking and factory safety. In 1566, Christopher Schutz, a German immigrant, invented a process for drawing wire. His Hathersage workshop made sieves used by miners, and later diversified into pin and needle production.

Inhalation of grinding dust in the wire works resulted in a workers' life expectancy of just 30 years, leading to one of the first Factory Acts.

Hathersage vicarage has a literary connection to Charlotte Brontë, who stayed there with her friend Ellen Nussey in 1845. Several locations in *Jane Eyre* match places she visited during her stay, with her "Thornfield Hall" being based on nearby North Lees Hall (1 Birley Lane, Hathersage, S32 1BR). The name Eyre itself is borrowed from a family of local gentry (who we visit at Highlow Hall).

- We continue through the town, in search of Little John's Grave.
- Soon after passing the last of the shops, we turn left onto School Lane, which becomes Church Lane.
- These roads are narrow, with limited parking.
- The pretty Church of Saint Michael the Archangel is 200 metres along Church Lane in Hathersage.

Little John's Grave: The Church of Saint Michael the Archangel (Church Bank, Hathersage, S32 1AJ)

Stones in the churchyard mark the grave of Little John, where a thigh bone measuring 28 inches (72 cm) was said to have been unearthed. This would have made Little John eight feet (2.46 m) tall.

Little John was supposedly born in East Yorkshire, but local tradition says that he retired to Hathersage and was buried in the churchyard. No other place has claimed Little John's grave, unlike Robin Hood's resting place, for which there are several claims. We are only eight miles from the village of Loxley, across the moors on the edge of Sheffield, fitting with the geography of some legends.

There are several documentary references to Hathersage's claim as Little John's resting place.

In the late 1600s astronomer, alchemist and intellectual, Elias Ashmole discussed Little John's grave. He wrote that Little John's bow hung in the church chancel and that he was buried at Hathersage, with a stone set at each end, with a large distance between.

In 1784 the vicar, Charles Spencer-Stanhope, wrote that the Squire's brother, William Shuttleworth, hung a thigh bone from Little John's grave in his room. However, as it was feared to be bringing bad luck, Shuttleworth ordered it to be reburied by his clerk. But the clerk kept the labelled bone, charging sixpence to view the curio. The bone was allegedly stolen by Sir George Strickland, during a visit to Hathersage, and has never been rediscovered.

In 1944, J.W. Walker, President of the Yorkshire Archaeological Society, gave some ratification to the claim, when he reported the inheritance of the Hathersage estate by James Shuttleworth in 1780. Then, four years after his inheritance, Shuttleworth opened the grave of Little John, which was marked by two stones, each lettered J.L. (thought to mean

John Little). The stones were 13 feet four inches apart, one at the head the other at the foot, suggesting a very tall man. J.W. Walker also recorded the story of the thigh bone's exhumation, and its theft by Sir William Strickland, who he claims buried it under a tree at his home at Boynton, near Bridlington, on the North Yorkshire coast.

Little John's Grave

Little John's Grave

Eagle eyed readers might have spotted a parking meter alongside the grave. This is a novel way in which funds are raised to maintain Little John's Grave.

Even without the Little John connection, Saint Michael the Archangel is worthy of a visit.

The earliest recorded church was built during the reign of Henry I. The present Grade I Listed building dates mainly from the late 14th and early 15th centuries. The church also has a more recent connection to the flooding of Ladybower, when a stained glass window was removed from Derwent Chapel before it was submerged. The window was by the renowned Victorian artist Charles Kempe, who contributed to over 4,000 churches during his career.

Church of Saint Michael the Archangel in Hathersage

Robin Hood's Cave: Stanage Edge (Hooks Carr car park, Hope Valley, S32 1BR)

Stanage Edge is the cliff face that towers over Hathersage to the north. During industrial times, it was a quarry for the Millstone Grit from which the area's famed mill stones were carved.

Today, it is one of England's most popular rock climbing venues. Stanage has particular significance for me, as it was where I gained my Rock Climbing Instructor's qualification. The assessment criteria to demonstrate skills "with the ease of long practice" necessitated many long days and summer evenings on the rock face. I actually used Robin Hood's Cave as a picnic spot for the role-playing trainees during my assessment.

Like many of the places that bear his name, it is hard to say whether Robin Hood actually used the cave, especially since Little John is supposed to have come to Hathersage after his retirement from being an outlaw. But it is a beautiful spot to visit on a walk.

The film industry recognised the dramatic impact of Stanage Edge when Keira Knightley stood on the Edge, playing Elizabeth Bennet in *Pride and Prejudice*.

Robin Hood's Cave is first named as such, on the 1880 edition of the Ordinance Survey map.

Robin Hood's Cave: Stanage Edge

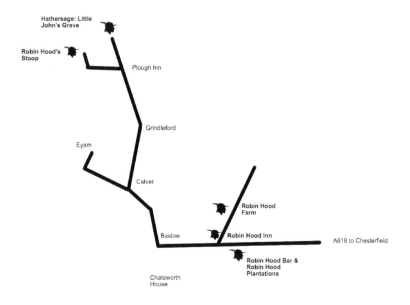

Hathersage: Little John's Grave

Robin Hood's Stoop

Plough Inn

Grindleford

Eyam

Calver

Robin Hood Farm

Robin Hood Inn

Baslow

A619 to Chesterfield

Robin Hood Bar & Robin Hood Plantations

Chatsworth House

Hathersage to The Hamlet of Robin Hood (Baslow)

Hathersage to Baslow: 7 miles - 15 minutes

- Retrace your route into the centre of Hathersage.
- Then, turn left onto B6001 Station Rd, passing the Little John Pub (postcode S32 1DD).

Hathersage Lido (Oddfellows Road, Hathersage, S32 1DU)
Up Oddfellows Road, on your left, is Hathersage Lido, one of very few open air swimming pools left in the country. **www.hathersageswimmingpool.co.uk**

The swimming pool opened in 1936, as part of a bigger development which included tennis courts, a band stand, playing fields, a sand pit and a large paddling pool. All of this, except the swimming pool, is now gone.

A grand opening was held on Saturday 25th July 1936, with water polo, swimming and diving displays from groups including Sheffield City Police. The pool was unheated at its opening, but today's Derbyshire chill is removed by a gas boiler.

The King George V Memorial development, as it was formerly known, was funded through Hathersage's industrial connections. George Lawrence, a Sheffield manufacturer of razor blades, paid for the entire project. Sadly, Mr Lawrence was killed in 1940, when his razor blade factory took a direct hit from a German bomb.

- We detour from the B6001 on narrow and steep roads, to visit Robin Hood's Stoop, on Offerton Moor.

This Robin Hood location is not easy to reach; in fact, it is really only practical on foot or by cycle. The area is very well serviced by foot and cycle rights of way.

The road up from the Plough Inn is driveable and is used by the gliding club to access their airfield. But from High-low Hall, our route turns off the public road, onto single track lanes which link the local farms. These are White Roads marked with green dots on the OS maps (other undefined rights of way). In theory they are passable by motor vehicles, but they are steep and narrow, with very few passing places, making a cycle a good option.

Parking is in short supply around Highlow Hall too. There are a small number of rutted pull off spaces, but they are tiny and widely spaced. I parked in a layby near the Plough Inn. There is a pay car park at Hathersage Railway Station.

Walking / cycling directions to Robin Hood's Stoop
From the Plough Inn (postcode S32 1BA), turn uphill onto minor road (signposted Abney, Gliding Club, Great Huck-low).

At Highlow Hall (postcode S32 1AX), turn right onto narrow lane towards Callow House Farm and Offerton Hall (Robin Hoods Stoop is before we reach Offerton Hall).

This narrow single track tarmac road drops steeply downhill to cross a stream.

After crossing the stream, the tarmac turns sharply right, before climbing steeply to reach and exceed the height you started at Highlow Hall.

Reach a left hand bend and the driveway to Callow House Farm. (The farm access is a public footpath.)

Continue around the left hand bend to climb the tarmac road.

The climb becomes steeper after this bend, but it is a very short climb.

As soon as the road flattens out, pass a vehicle gateway on your left. On the verge, after the gate, are three rather old looking small trees.

Robin Hood Stoop is just inside the field to your left, immediately after these trees.

It is possible to continue along the road towards Shatton and make a circular ride, either back through Hathersage, or on one of the many Bridleways.

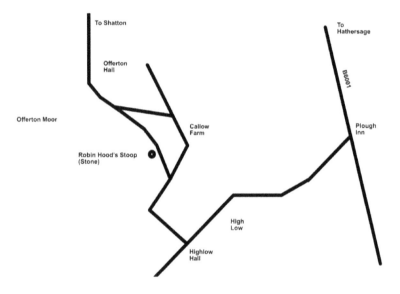

To Shatton

Offerton
Hall

Offerton Moor

Callow
Farm

Robin Hood's Stoop
(Stone)

To
Hathersage

B6001

Plough
Inn

High
Low

Highlow
Hall

Directions to Robin Hood's Stoop (Offerton Moor)

Highlow Hall (postcode S32 1AX) is a Grade II Listed Elizabethan manor house which dates back to the late 16th century. Highlow Hall is associated with the White Lady, the ghost of a woman named Elizabeth Archer, said to haunt the estate. The story goes that in 1344, Nicholas Eyre, the owner of Highlow Hall, rejected Elizabeth and married her younger sister. Elizabeth cursed the Eyre family and haunts them forever as the White Lady.

Charlotte Brontë borrowed the family name of Eyre for her novel *Jane Eyre*. Brontë visited her friend Ellen Nussey in Hathersage during 1845, when she visited several of the places that featured in her famous novel.

Highlow Hall

Robin Hood's Stoop: Offerton Moor

Offerton Moor is on the south side of the Hope Valley, slightly east of Abney Moor.

Robin Hood's Stoop is an old boundary stone which may once have formed part of a medieval wayside cross. Along with Whitby Abbey and Kirklees Priory, it features in a legend about a highly improbable longbow shot. According to local legend, Robin Hood shot an arrow from the Stoop all the way to Hathersage Churchyard, about 2 km to the NE.

Church of St Michael the Archangel in Hathersage

Arrow flight from Robin Hood's Stoop to the Church of Saint Michael the Archangel in Hathersage

Hathersage Churchyard features in the legends as a possible grave site for Little John. So, it seems unsurprising that Robin Hood's Stoop has an alternative name linked to Robin's second in command. Local historians found an early postcard showing a view of "Hathersage from Little John's Flight, Highlow". The stone in the picture's foreground looks very much like Robin Hood's Stoop.

The earliest source I have found for this place-name is the 1880 OS map of the area.

Robin Hood's Stoop

- After visiting Robin Hood's Stoop, we re-trace our route to the Plough Inn (Leadmill Bridge, Hathersage, S32 1BA) and turn right onto the B6001.
- Cross over the River Derwent, from where the B6001 runs parallel with the river and is sheltered by a canopy of trees.
- At T junction turn right on B6521 Main Road.

A short detour to the left takes us to Grindleford Station Café (Upper Padley, Grindleford, S32 2JA), which is well visited by Peak District outdoor enthusiasts. The café, in the former station house, is a little notorious for its (slightly tongue in cheek) signs, giving instructions on how to order black tea or coffee, and how to control unruly children.

- The B6521 merges with the A625 and continues to traffic lights near Calver Sough (postcode S32 3WY).

Calver

Calver began as a lead mining village. The sough, from which the junction takes its name, is a mine drainage tunnel which emerges south east of the junction.

During the 18th century, Calver became a centre for cotton spinning. The impressive seven storey Calver Mill operated from 1785 to 1920. The building still stands on the River Derwent to the east of the village at Calver Bridge (Old Mill Lane, S32 3YU). The mill's austere appearance allowed it to stand in for Colditz Castle in the *Colditz* TV series. The mill has since been turned into apartments, and its appearance gentrified.

- A short detour up the A623 to our right, brings us to the villages of Stoney Middleton and Eyam.

Stoney Middleton

Our road was blasted through Middleton Dale in 1830, and in 1840 an octagonal toll house was built, which is now a fish and chip shop (The Bank, Stoney Middleton, S32 4TF).

The village of Stoney Middleton grew up as a lead mining settlement, and its limestone cliffs became a draw for rock climbers.

The village's strangest story is that of Hannah Baddeley, who is said to have jumped from the cliffs in 1762 after losing her lover. Her billowing skirts acted as a parachute, saving her life, and earning the name Lover's Leap for the cliff above the village. A commemorative board on the side of the restaurant (The Dale, Stoney Middleton, S32 4TF) tells Hannah's story.

During 2021, a disused quarry above the village was used as a location for *Mission Impossible 7*, where a train was run off its rails into the quarry.

Eyam: the plague village (Eyam Museum, Hawkhill Road, Eyam, S32 5QP)
Eyam's main claim to fame is the way the village chose to go into isolation to prevent infection spreading when Bubonic Plague was discovered there in 1665. The local economy now relies heavily on the tourist trade, with Eyam being promoted as "The Plague Village".

The Plague reached Eyam in 1665 when the local tailor received a flea-infested bundle of cloth from London. His assistant noticed the bundle was damp and opened it up. Before long he was dead and others in his household began dying soon after.

The villagers turned to the Reverend William Mompesson for leadership. He introduced several precautions to slow the spread of The Plague. These included families burying their own dead and moving his church services to the natural amphitheatre of Cucklett Delph. The villagers also put themselves into complete isolation from the surrounding towns and villages. Merchants left supplies on marked rocks, where Eyam's villagers had left payment in holes filled with vinegar, to disinfect the money.

It took 14 months for the plague to run its course. Mortality estimates differ, but it is said to have killed at least 260 villagers, with only 83 surviving out of a population of 350.

I began writing this book during one of the 2021 Covid lockdowns. Re-reading about Eyam's experience made me consider what a terrifying experience The Plague must have been for superstitious 17th century people.

Plague Sunday has been celebrated in Eyam since The Plague's bicentenary in 1866. It was originally held in mid-August, but now takes place in Cucklett Delph on the last Sunday in August. This date coincides with the more ancient Wakes Week and Well Dressings.

Eyam Museum was opened in 1994 and, besides its focus on The Plague, includes exhibits on the village's history in general. **www.eyamvillage.org.uk**

- We return to the traffic lights at Calver Sough going straight across, and continuing on the A623 Kingsgate, towards Baslow.

Baslow (postcode DE45 1RY)

Nestling on the northern edge of Chatsworth Park, Baslow is an attractive village, close to some of the Dark Peak's most dramatic scenery. It sits on the bank of the River Derwent and is overlooked by gritstone edges.

Sights to look out for within the village include Goose Green, Baslow's pretty village green, which is bright with daffodils every spring. Beside Goose Green, a narrow packhorse bridge leads towards Chatsworth House, past thatched cottages, which are a rare sight in the Peak District.

The 17th century bridge at Bridge End has a small toll house. The Church of Saint Anne boasts an unusual clock face, with the inscription "VICTORIA 1897" instead of the usual numbers. Inside the church, you can still find the whip once used to clear the church of dogs.

Hill walkers and rock climbers come to the area for its famous gritstone edges, including Baslow, Gardom's, Curbar and Froggatt, all of which have breath-taking views across the surrounding hills, valleys and moorland. There are also plenty of easier walking routes along the Derwent valley. These include the Derwent Valley Heritage Trail (a 55 mile walking route linking Ladybower Reservoir with the river Trent in south Derbyshire), which passes through Baslow.

Local men began climbing on Baslow Edge, long before rock climbing became a sport. The natural weathering of the gritstone produced a six metre high block, known as the Eagle Stone. Traditionally, local men had to climb the Eagle Stone to become worthy of marriage. Just behind the Eagle Stone is a monument to the Duke of Wellington, commemorating a visit by Wellington to the moor. It was also intended as a balance to the nearby Nelson's Monument, which we shall visit at our next stop on the **500RH**.

Baslow village is composed of five distinct areas, or "Ends," as they are known to locals.

Bridge End is the original settlement, which grew around the church, ancient ford and bridge across the River Derwent.

Nether End, at the eastern end of the village, is what you might now consider the village centre. It has several pubs, restaurants and tea rooms. It also has a caravan site and a pedestrian entrance to Chatsworth Park. (We visit Chatsworth on the next section of our journey).

Over End is now the village's main residential area, sitting on the hillside to the north. Over End contains Baslow Hall, which is now a Restaurant.

The other "Ends" are: Bubnell, to the west of the river; Bridge End, which is alongside the river crossings); Over End, to the north of the main road; and Nether End, which is adjacent to Chatsworth Park.

Just outside Baslow are the so-called "Golden Gates", dating from the 1st Duke's rebuilding of Chatsworth in the 17th century. They were moved here in the 19th century by Sir Joseph Paxton (designer of London's Crystal Palace) for the 6th Duke of Devonshire, to make a new entrance to the park. Today, the gates are rarely used, opened only for large public events in the park.

- We leave Baslow on the A619, turning left at a roundabout, passing through Nether End and past Chatsworth's Golden Gates.
- At a much larger roundabout, we continue on the A619, towards Chesterfield.
- After a very short distance, we see a minor road on our left and the Robin Hood public house.

The Hamlet of Robin Hood (Chesterfield Rd, Baslow, DE45 1PQ)

There is no definitive record of how this hamlet gained the name of Robin Hood, but it is thought to have been given first to the inn, with the hamlet later adopting the name. The first written evidence of habitation is in Parish records from 1733, when the whole area below Birchen Edge was known as Moorside. Today, Moorside refers only to the farm of the same name. The small area of houses nearest the Inn became the hamlet of Robin Hood.

The Robin Hood Inn (postcode DE45 1PQ) is first recorded on a one inch to the mile Ordinance Survey map published in 1840. Earlier maps show a building in the same location, but with no sign that it was an Inn.

Records show the land to have been occupied by John Savage, who died in 1842. It seems that Thomas Savage, helped by his brother, who was a baker, created an inn on the site. John Savage ran the Inn from his homestead next door. The 1851 census records him as an Innkeeper and Farmer.

Robin Hood Bar was the name of a strip of land between the A619 and Heathy Lea Brook, which runs parallel and to the south of the A619.

The 1847 tithe award for Baslow lists five plots of land under the collective name of Robin Hood Bar. It records The Duke of Devonshire as landowner and Thomas Savage as occupier. The plots are listed as being cultivated with: Rough Pasture, Meadow, or Oats. The Bar in the name refers to the Toll House, or Toll Bar, which once stood here to collect tolls for passage through the Duke of Devonshire's estate.

Robin Hood Farm is on Old Brampton Road, just past the Inn and car parks. It is now a B&B.

The Robin Hood Plantations are clusters of woodland, just south of the A619 and near the Emperor Stream. They are named on a 1922 Ordinance Survey map. The woods can be seen on a map dating from 1883, but do not show the name Robin Hood. The current edition once again bears our hero's name.

You will have gathered that I am a keen rock climber, and the hamlet of Robin Hood is the starting point to reach the popular walking and climbing area of Birchen Edge. The path to the edge begins just after Robin Hood Farm.

During our visit to Baslow, we encountered a monument to the Duke of Wellington, which was built as a balance to the nearby Nelson's Monument. We visit Nelson's Monument and his Three Ships during our walk to Birchen Edge.

Nelson's famous victory in 1805 prompted celebrations around the country, with a monument on Birchen Edge being erected five years later in 1810. It was carved and erected by two stonemasons from the hamlet of Robin Hood: Sampson Savage and George Herrington. Only Herrington left his mark on the monument, with his initials "G H" at its base.

Millstone Grit may be a particularly hard form of sandstone, but it is still susceptible to weathering. A quirk of geology left three large rocks standing atop Birchen Edge, when the surrounding ground was eroded away. After Nelson's victory, these rocks were named The Three Ships. They complement the adjacent monument by having carved onto them the names of three of Nelson's ships: Victory, Defiance and Royal Soverin (sic).

The Three Ships: Birchen Edge

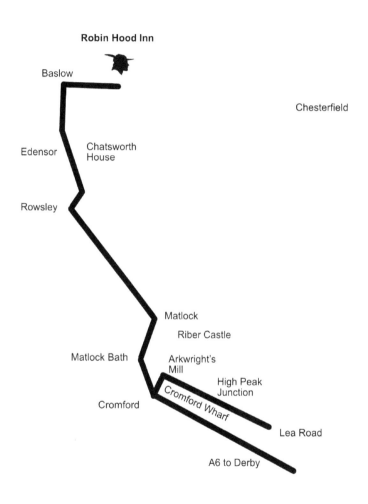

Robin Hood Inn

Baslow

Chesterfield

Edensor

Chatsworth
House

Rowsley

Matlock

Riber Castle

Matlock Bath

Arkwright's
Mill

High Peak
Junction

Cromford Wharf

Cromford

Lea Road

A6 to Derby

The Hamlet of Robin Hood (Baslow) to Cromford

Baslow to Annesley: (including the Whatstandwell hamlet of Robin Hood)
26 miles - 40 minutes

- After visiting Baslow's hamlet of Robin Hood, we retrace our route back along the A619 to the roundabout adjacent to Baslow sports field (postcode DE45 1SP).
- At the roundabout, we turn left, continuing on the A619 (signposted for Chatsworth House) for a short distance.
- On a map, you appear to reach a road junction, with the B6012 turning off to your left. On the ground, it is the continuation of the A619 which is marked as a right turn, with the B6012 continuing straight on.
- We continue onto the B6012 Bakewell Road, heading for Chatsworth.
- At the next minor road junction, continue left on the B6012 to Edensor.

Edensor (postcode DE45 1PH)
The tiny, gated village of Edensor is well worth a visit. It was specially commissioned by the 6th Duke of Devonshire, and features a delightful mix of house designs, from mock Tudor to Swiss cottage.

The 6th Duke demolished the original estate village and rebuilt it in the 19th century, because it spoiled his view from Chatsworth House.

Saint Peter's church spire dominates the village skyline, and many monuments to the Cavendish family can be found inside the church. In the churchyard, an area is reserved for the family's graves.

The churchyard has the graves of several interesting people.

There is a link to US President Kennedy, through his sister Kathleen. She married William Cavendish, the Marquess of Hartington, who was killed in action during WWII. JFK visited his sister's grave in the early 1960s, before his assassination.

Sir Joseph Paxton, who designed London's Crystal Palace, is buried here. Paxton was head gardener to the 6th Duke of Devonshire, and built the Golden Gates that we passed earlier. He also cultivated the Cavendish banana, named after the duke, and still eaten around the world.

Chatsworth House & Estate (postcode DE45 1PP)
Chatsworth House is the seat of the Duke of Devonshire, and has belonged to the Cavendish family since 1549. It is Grade I Listed and has been chosen several times as Britain's favourite country house. There are many detailed sources of information about Chatsworth, so I seek only to give an overview here. **www.chatsworth.org**

The name Chatsworth is a corruption of Chetel's-worth, meaning "the Court of Chetel". This dates the Estate's history to a Viking Chieftain named Chetel, who held lands during the reign of Edward the Confessor.

After the Norman conquest, Chatsworth passed into the hands of William de Peverel, who we met before, in Castleton.

Building of the modern estate began in earnest during the 15th century when it was bought by the Leche family who owned property nearby. They enclosed the first park at Chatsworth and built a house on high ground, in what is now part of the garden. In 1549 they sold the estate to Sir William

Cavendish, who was Treasurer of the King's Chamber and the husband of Bess of Hardwick. Bess originated from Derbyshire and convinced her Suffolk born husband to settle here. She became influential in creating Nottinghamshire's Dukeries area, which is right in the heartland of the Robin Hood legends.

During WWII, most of Britain's country houses were sequestered for the war effort. The 10th Duke thought schoolgirls would make better tenants than soldiers, and allowed Chatsworth to be occupied by Penrhos College, a girls' school in Wales. In September 1939, 300 girls and their mistresses moved in for a six-year stay. The whole house was used, including the state rooms, which became dormitories. Condensation from the sleeping girls' breath caused fungus to grow on some of the pictures. The girls grew vegetables on the Chatsworth Estate, as their contribution to the war effort.

The 11th Duke died in 2004 and was succeeded by his son, the current Duke, Peregrine Cavendish, 12th Duke of Devonshire. A structural survey in 2004 showed that major renovation was needed, so a 10 year programme of work, costing £32 million was undertaken, including restoration of stonework, statues, paintings, tapestries and water features.

Chatsworth Park's 1,000 acres (4 km²) are free to enter all year round, except for the Old Park, which is used to breed herds of deer. The house and gardens do charge an admission fee. The 105 acre garden alone attracts 300,000 visitors a year. A staff of 20 full time gardeners look after the garden, which is surrounded by a 1.75 mile long wall.

It should be no surprise that Chatsworth has appeared many times in literature, film and TV.

The house is named in the 1813 novel *Pride and Prejudice*, as one of the estates Elizabeth Bennet visits before arriving at Pemberley. It then featured in TV and film versions, including the 2005 adaptation, where Chatsworth starred as Mr Darcey's home of Pemberley.

Two rooms in Chatsworth House represented interiors of Admiralty House in the 1984 adaptation of *The Bounty*.

In 2016, Chatsworth doubled for Buckingham Palace, in a scene from TV's *The Crown*, where the Queen Mother and a courtier discuss Princess Margaret's affair with Pete Townsend.

Some scenes from series two of *Peaky Blinders* were filmed at Chatsworth.

The real life Chatsworth was showcased in a 2012 BBC TV documentary, which was also shown in the United States.

- After driving through Chatsworth Park and enjoying views of Chatsworth House, the B6012 winds its way over a hump-back bridge, before meeting the A6 at Rowsley (postcode DE4 2EH).
- Turn left onto the A6, towards Matlock. Beware, this stretch of road between Rowsley and Matlock has several static speed cameras.

There is also a lot to capture our interest on the route into the Victorian town of Matlock.

Peak Rail (Rowsley South Station, off Harrison Way, Darley Dale, DE4 2LF)
Peak Rail is a preserved railway which operates steam and heritage diesel trains for tourists. The preserved line is over three and a half miles (5.6 km) in length and its trains run between Darley Dale and Matlock. The line forms part of the

old Midland Railway line between Manchester and London Saint Pancras, which was closed in 1968.

As well as heritage train journeys, they also offer luxury dining in their Palatine Restaurant Car, with Sunday Lunches, Christmas Lunches, and Afternoon or Cream Teas. There are also special events taking place throughout the year, including Steam Experience Driving Courses, for anyone harbouring childhood dreams of becoming a Train Driver. **www.peakrail.co.uk**

Darley Dale (Postcode DE4 2EQ)
Apart from the constantly running DFS furniture sale, the village of Darley Dale's biggest claim to fame comes thanks to Sir Joseph Whitworth. The Victorian engineer developed the British Standard Whitworth System, which standardised measurements of nuts and bolts, and invented the Whitworth sniper rifle.

Whitworth was a 19th century engineer, who lived at Stancliffe Hall in Darley Dale for the last 13 years of his life. He died at Monte Carlo in 1887, aged 83, and was brought home to be buried at Darley Dale's Saint Helen's Church. Whitworth drew up grand plans for the village, which were mostly fulfilled thanks to generous endowments from his estate. One of his plans, however, was changed by his wife. Whitworth dreamed of building a comprehensive village college but his wife, Louisa, preferred a social centre. The Whitworth Institute and Park was the result of her endeavours.

The Whitworth Institute opened in 1890, with an indoor swimming pool, an assembly hall, several reading and committee rooms, a library, a billiard room and a museum of natural history. It also has a hotel, originally named The

Whitworth Hotel, but since re-named Barrington's, within a landscaped park. The Whitworth Institute was given to the people of Darley Dale and has continued to provide public amenity to the present day. I attended a Local Authority seminar there a few years ago, and I was mightily impressed by the preserved Victorian interior of the building. **www.thewhitworth.org**

The centrepiece of Whitworth Park is an obelisk commemorating Sir Joseph Whitworth.

Saint Elphins Park (Dale Road South, Darley Dale, DE4 2RH)
I first visited Saint Elphins boarding school in the 1990s, when they donated a large amount of furniture to a charity I once volunteered for. The politeness and discipline of its children was a world away from what I experienced in Nottingham's Comprehensive Schools as a 21st Century Police Officer. The school hit financial problems in 2005, when it was turned into a luxury retirement village, but it does have an interesting history, dating back to 1697.

Saint Elphins School was a boarding school for the daughters of Church of England clergy. It re-located from Warrington, in Lancashire, to Darley Dale in 1904, because the Warrington area had become very industrialised. The Darley Dale building had previously been a health spa, called the Darley Dale Hydro.

The school's famous alumni include Richmal Crompton (1890–1969), the author of *Just William*.

The story of the Invicta Stone provides an interesting postscript to the story of Saint Elphins.

After the school's closure in March 2005, the owners organised an auction on site to sell off as many assets as possible. This included the Invicta Stone, which was originally located at the top of a turret above the main front door. During the 1960s the turret and Invicta Stone were removed for safety reasons and hidden in the rose gardens. The Invicta Stone was bought by an architectural salvage company in Oxfordshire. In 2011 a former pupil tracked the Stone down and negotiated its purchase. The retirement village agreed to have the Invicta Stone returned to its rightful home and kindly paid for it. The Old Elphinians paid for a plaque to be made. The stone was professionally cleaned and returned to Saint Elphins, where it now sits on the terrace, at the top of steps leading to the croquet lawn.

Matlock (postcode DE4 3AR)

Matlock, as we see it today, grew from the Victorian fashion of spa towns. Over the years, it has prospered from the hydrotherapy industry and cloth mills built along the River Derwent and its tributary Bentley Brook. There has been a settlement there for much longer though, as the town featured in the *Domesday Book,* and its name dates to Old English. Many towns have a Moot, or meeting place of some description. Matlock comes from the Old English mæthel, meaning assembly or speech, and āc, meaning oak tree; so, Matlock means moot-oak, or an oak tree where meetings were held.

The population grew rapidly in the 1800s, because of its spas, or hydros. At the height of their popularity, there were 20 hydros in Matlock. The largest of them was built in 1853, closed as a Spa in 1955, then re-opened in 1956 as the headquarters of Derbyshire County Council. Anyone visiting Matlock with an interest in Victorian history should tour the remaining hydro buildings. None are still in use as spas, but they all retain their exterior grandeur.

The Town Hall is now home to Derbyshire Dales District Council. It was built in 1861 as a hydro called Bridge House.

The former Matlock House Hydro stands prominently on Rutland Street, and is today an apartment building called Rutland Court. The hydro was built in 1863, and an engraving of 1870 shows it to be largely unaltered.

Elmtree House, on Rufford Street, opened as a hydro in 1862. It can be found just to the north of the dominant Rutland Court.

Rockside Hydro is an imposing Grade II Listed Building with views across Matlock.

It is distinctive for its two octagonal corner turrets with conical roofs topped by lanterns. Rockside was built around 1860 but was significantly extended during the early 20th century. Rockside Hall was once used as an RAF psychiatric hospital, where mentally-scarred aircrew were rehabilitated. It became somewhat unkindly known by locals as "Hatters Castle". After the RAF moved out, it became a hall of residence for Matlock College and is now residential apartments.

Hall Leys Park, in the centre of Matlock, is a well preserved example of a Victorian public park, which first opened in 1898. It has the town's war memorial and a wishing well. A shelter from the former cable tramway was moved to the park after the tramway closed in 1927.

In the centre of the park is a Victorian bandstand, which is still used regularly by local brass bands, and for events such as the Victorian Christmas Weekend (held on the first weekend of December).

Beside the bandstand is a footbridge over the River Derwent, which has markings showing the flood levels that hit the town in the 1960s and 1970s. The café, on the opposite side of the bandstand, has markings from other floods.

The park's boating lake, with several small islands, is home to the longest running pleasure boats in the country. A miniature railway also runs alongside the river.

There are plenty more historic locations in Matlock. Many of them date from the Victorian period, although its central bridge has much older origins. Matlock Bridge is still one of the road crossings over the River Derwent. The first stone bridge was built at the site of a ford in the mid-13th century. It was narrow, allowing only a single file of traffic to cross. It remained so for 550 years until, in the 1890s, they discussed demolishing the bridge to rebuild something more suited to increased traffic. Luckily, a decision was made to double the width of the existing bridge, rather than start from scratch. Matlock Bridge is now listed as Grade II by English Heritage.

The railway station and station house were designed by Joseph Paxton in 1850, as part of the Midland Railway's Derby to Buxton route. The station house is largely unaltered and is Grade II Listed, although the station itself is unlisted.

Artists Corner is a collection of houses built along a sharp bend on Dale Road. It has been a favourite spot through the centuries for artists to admire the scenery and paint High Tor, which overlooks it from the south. Artists Corner was also the location of a toll house on the Wirksworth-Moor-to-Longstone Turnpike, which opened in 1759.

Like many scenic Peak District locations, Matlock has featured in many film and television productions. The two most famous are Ken Russell's Oscar winning 1969 film, *Women in Love*, and the medical drama *Peak Practice*.

Women in Love used number 80 New Street as the Brangwen sisters' home. It is now a B&B, so fans of the film could spend a night there. Saint Giles' Church in Church Street was also the setting for the wedding of Laura Crich.

The ITV series *Peak Practice* used locations including Highfields School, Victoria Hall Gardens and Henry Avenue, although the series' main village locations are at the nearby villages of Crich and Fritchley.

Riber Castle (Riber Road, Matlock, DE4 5JU)
Overlooking Matlock to the south-east is Riber Castle. You can get a good view up towards the castle from Matlock town centre, near the football ground.

Despite being called a castle, it was built in 1862 as a family home for the industrialist John Smedley, who also built the Matlock Hydro, which is now occupied by Derbyshire County Council. It must have been quite a project to build in such a remote location, as gritstone from a local quarry had to be pulled up the 200 metre hill with a series of pulleys. The builders also had great difficulty getting a water supply to the hill-top location, earning it the name "Smedley's Folly". Riber Castle cost Smedley £60,000, but he died just six years after its completion.

On several sections of the **500RH** I have recommended that sections of road are unsuitable for caravans or large motor homes. The roads up to Riber village exceed this description.

The road up from Tansley is steep and winding, but little worse than you found on other minor roads around the Peak District's hills. I would still not recommend driving a larger vehicle, unless you are very confident.

The road from Starkholmes is on another level entirely, and not for the faint-hearted. It is on a par with many backwoods mountain roads I have driven on. The hairpin bends are very steep and tight. I am a confident motorcyclist and I consider it a challenge.

After the death of Smedley's wife in 1892, the castle became a boys' preparatory school. Architectural historian John Summerson attended the school in the early 20th century. He was not very appreciative of the builders' efforts, describing the castle as "an object of indecipherable bastardy, a true monster."

Later generations placed more value on the castle, giving it a Grade II Listing.

The school moved out in the 1930s and, on the outbreak of WWII, the Ministry of Defence took over the castle for food storage.

Riber Castle sat empty until the 1960s, when a group of zoologists set up a nature reserve for British and European animals. I took my own children to see the zoo on several occasions during the 1980s. Riber Castle Wildlife Park specialised in breeding lynx, which they released to boost populations in the European mountains.

The zoo's original owners ran a very well-thought-of zoo, but the zoologists sold it to a commercial company who were heavily criticised for their treatment of the animals. Activists released several lynxes into the wild and sightings of the animals by the locals were referred to as the "Beast of Lumsdale", after a nearby rocky dale. The zoo closed in 2000 and has been subject to on-and-off plans for apartments ever since.

- From Matlock, we follow the A6, alongside the River Derwent, to Matlock Bath.

Matlock Bath (Main car park: postcode DE4 3AL)
Our next location along the A6 is the village of Matlock Bath. The village began as a lead mining community; it was developed into a spa town by the Victorians, and remains very much a tourist destination today.

Matlock Bath was originally built at the head of a dead-end dirt road running alongside the River Derwent from Matlock. After the discovery of warm springs, the dirt road was upgraded into what eventually became the A6. The road's improvement allowed coaches to avoid the previous coach road between Matlock and Cromford, which crossed very steep hills near Riber.

A bath house was built in 1698 to capitalise on the warm springs. As the waters became more popular, access was improved by building the bridge into Matlock and, in 1783, a new entrance was blasted at the south of the valley.

Princess Victoria of Kent visited Matlock Bath in 1832, increasing its popularity as a society destination. Poets John Ruskin and Lord Byron followed Princess Victoria. Lord Byron compared it with the Swiss Alps, coining a nickname of Little Switzerland, which survives to this day.

Rock climbing became very popular on Matlock Bath's steep limestone cliffs. I enjoyed many summer's evenings on the limestone cliffs overlooking the Derwent. One famous climb that defeated me was the imposing High Tor, which overlooks the approach from Matlock. Despite not being able to complete the difficult rock climb, I did take my children on the cable car to The Heights of Abraham and Gulliver's Kingdom theme park. The fairground rides and show caves make an entertaining day out, with access to exhilarating clifftop walks.

Even the River Derwent helps draw tourists to Matlock Bath. This section of the Derwent is a location for white water canoeing. Matlock Canoe Club hosts national wildwater racing and slalom events here, and it is also an assessment location for the tough BCU 4 Star award.

If wild water is too adventurous for you, each autumn Matlock Bath holds its Venetian Nights festival, with illuminations along the river and illuminated boats.

As well as the climbing, Matlock Bath has drawn me over the years with its popularity as a motorcycling destination. On Sundays and Bank Holidays, many hundreds of motorcyclists gather along the single row of shops, enjoying fish and chips. Do watch the time limit for free on-street parking though, as the Parking Attendants are very keen.

- Following the A6 towards Cromford, we encounter the imposing Masson Mill, on the left of the road. This is the start of the 15 mile long, Derwent Valley Mills: UNESCO World Heritage site.

We will leave the Derwent Valley corridor at Ambergate, but those who have an interest in our industrial heritage can follow the trail which leads into Derby. **www.derwentvalleymills.org**

Masson Mill (130 Derby Road, Matlock, DE4 3PY)
Sir Richard Arkwright built this water-powered, cotton spinning mill in 1783. Invention of the flying shuttle in 1733 had improved the process of weaving cotton, which had in turn increased the demand for spun cotton.

Machines for carding and spinning cotton were in use, but the quantity and quality of the yarn did not meet the weavers' needs. Arkwright patented his water frame in 1769, to utilise the extra power of water mills.

He opened Cromford Mill in 1771, which is the next stop on our journey. Masson Mill was his third mill, built to take advantage of the fast flowing River Derwent.

The five floor, 21 bay, brick-built building is an impressive site today. So, in the 19th century, it must have seemed a marvel of the modern age. In his 1840 book *Gem of the Peak*, Adams described the night-time view as "exceedingly imposing, its hundred lights reflecting on the river and the thick foliage, mingling the din of wheels with the noise of the waterfall."

Masson Mill continued to be used as a textile factory, well into the 20th century. It then became a retail outlet, which was one of many businesses to close during the Covid pandemic. At time of writing, it was rumoured to be under consideration for conversion into apartments.

- Continuing along the A6, we soon reach the mill town of Cromford.

Cromford (The Promenade, Cromford, DE4 3QF)
The village of Cromford is of sufficient historical significance to have been designated as a World Heritage Site. It is also surrounded by some glorious scenery.

Through its association with Sir Richard Arkwright, Cromford is considered by some to be the birthplace of the Industrial Revolution. Arkwright built the world's first water powered cotton mills here, and he was an early pioneer of the factory system. Victorian industrialists often developed purpose-built communities around their factories, to draw in workers and their families. Saltair and New Lanark are among the most famous, with Cromford being a village built for a very similar purpose.

We visit Arkwright's Cromford Mill next on our journey, so in this segment, I will concentrate on the village itself.

When Arkwright built Cromford village, his mill was very much a part of the isolated community he created. A rock wall, known as Scarthin Nick, prevented easy access from Matlock. This rock wall left Cromford isolated at the head of a rough valley road, accessed from the south. Then, in the early 1800s, Scarthin Nick was dynamited through, making way for what became the A6 which was, for a time, the main road between London and Manchester. This separated the mill and its industrial complex from Cromford's marketplace, shops and cottages. In this segment, I concentrate on the main village, to the west of the A6.

Some of Cromford's cottages and farm buildings predate Arkwright's time, but most of the village was built to house Arkwright's mill workers. As previously mentioned, it was not unusual for Victorian industrialists to create Model Villages to attract workers for their factories. New Lanark and Saltair have become more famous, but Cromford was certainly among the first of such factory housing developments in the world. Arkwright provided his employees with shops, pubs, chapels and a school.

North Street was constructed by Arkwright, and was rescued from dereliction in the 1970s by the Ancient Monument Society, who have since sold off the houses. One house in North Street is now a Landmark Trust holiday cottage.

Some of Cromford's workers' cottages still have Weavers' Windows visible on the top floors. These were to provide natural light for the homeworkers to work with.

Scattered around the marketplace, Cromford village has a good selection of shops, restaurants and pubs, including some specialising in minerals and second-hand books.

Behind the Greyhound Hotel is a tranquil-looking mill pond. Alongside the 15th century bridge are the ruins of an ancient chapel and an interesting old fishing pavilion.

The Via Gellia valley joins the Derwent at Cromford; however, the stream which runs through that valley is called the Ivonbrook and historically the valley was called the Ivonbrook Valley. The Via Gellia is simply the name of the road which runs along it, which – despite its Roman-sounding name – was actually named after the Gell family. The Gells were local landowners, who owned several lead mines in the area. They had the Via Gellia Road built in the late 18th century, to connect Cromford with Grangemill.

This being Derbyshire's Peak District, there is a lot to interest the outdoor enthusiasts.

There are some excellent walks, especially along the Cromford Canal from Cromford Wharf to High Peak Junction, where there is a Visitor Centre.

The High Peak Trail is a reclaimed railway line, which starts at High Peak Junction. Unlike most reclaimed railway footpaths, the High Peak Trail is steep in places. Static winding engines were provided to pull waggons up the steepest inclines. You can still see some of the winding infrastructure at Middleton Incline and Hopton Incline. **www.peakdistrict.gov.uk/visiting/places-to-visit/trails/high-peak-trail**

At the top of Cromford Hill, we find Black Rocks, with its picnic site and craggy tors set high above the village. The High Peak Trail passes close by Black Rocks, and I spent many happy summer evenings climbing on the dark Gritstone tor.

Cromford's influence reached as far as the German town of Ratingen, where an industrial site was named Textilfabrik Cromford. This is where the industrial pioneer Johann Gottfried Brügelmann built the first factory outside England, in 1783. Brügelmann used Arkwright's factory as a template for his factory, which today forms part of the Rheinisches Industriemuseum. **www.industriemuseum-lvr-de**

Like many of Derbyshire's beautiful locations, Cromford has of course attracted the film industry. Possibly the most famous of Cromford's film roles was in the 2006 film, *When Did You Last See Your Father?* This biopic about Blake Morrison starred Colin Firth as Blake, and Jim Broadbent as his father. As well as general locations around Cromford, key scenes were filmed at the village's historic bookshop.

Willersley Castle dominates the hill on the east side of the River Derwent, opposite the main village.

The grand house was commissioned by Richard Arkwright in 1790, but building work was delayed by a fire in 1791. Arkwright died in 1792, and the house was occupied by his son, also named Richard, in 1796. The Arkwright family moved out in 1922, and the building was bought by some Methodist businessmen, and opened as a Methodist Guild hotel in 1928. During WWII the building was used as a maternity hospital by the Salvation Army, when they were evacuated from their hospital in the East End of London.

Arkwright's Mill (Mill Road, Cromford, DE4 3RQ)
Cromford Mill is the world's first water-powered cotton spinning mill, and is considered to be one of the catalyst developments which started Britain's Industrial Revolution. The mill was built by Richard Arkwright in 1771 and is now a Grade I Listed building, and centrepiece of the Derwent Valley Mills UNESCO World Heritage Site. It has a popular visitor centre with shops, galleries, a restaurant and a cafe. Arkwright was so ahead of others that he has earned titles such as "Britain's first industrial tycoon" and "Father of the Factory System." **www.cromfordmills.org.uk**

Industrialisation of the textile industry gained pace in 1733, with the invention of the flying shuttle for weaving cotton. Faster weaving increased demand for spun cotton, and although machines for carding and spinning had been developed, they were inefficient. In 1769, Richard Arkwright patented a water frame, to use the power of his water mill.

Arkwright chose the site at Cromford for his five-storey mill, because it had a constant supply of warm water from Cromford Sough, which drained water from nearby lead mines. Fully operational from 1772, Arkwright ran the mills day and night over two 12-hour shifts.

He started with 200 workers, which was more than the local area could provide, and so he developed the village of Cromford, which we visited above. Despite being ahead of his time with the welfare of his workers, conditions were poor by modern standards. Most of his workers were women and children, with the youngest being just seven years old. Later, the minimum age was raised to 10 and the children received six hours of education a week. Even their schooling had benefits for Arkwright, as it enabled the children to do the record-keeping their illiterate parents could not.

Arkwright's employees had to be punctual, since the mill gates were shut at precisely 6am and 6pm every day. Any worker who was late not only lost that day's pay but were also fined another day's pay.

Many readers will be familiar with the concept of a "Company Store" from the Johnny Cash song, where workers get "another day older and deeper in debt." Arkwright embraced this concept through paying his workers in Cromford Dollars. These were produced by over-stamping Spanish coins, during a period when there was a national shortage of silver.

The cotton mill ceased operation in the 19th century and was used for a variety of purposes, including as a dyeing plant. In 1979, the Grade I Listed site was bought by the Arkwright Society, who began the long task of restoring it.

The scale of the project is demonstrated by the size of the staff and the cost of renovation. By 2019, the Arkwright Society was employing 100 people, and the restoration expenditure had reached £48 million.

The site is important, because it was the first successful cotton spinning factory. It showed unequivocally the way ahead, and Arkwright's model was copied widely.

Historic England have described the site as "one of the country's 100 irreplaceable sites".

In 1775, Arkwright took out a patent for a water-powered carding machine which led to increased output, and the fame of his factory rapidly spread. He was soon building more mills, and eventually employed 1,000 workers at Cromford alone. Many other mills were built under licence, including ones in Lancashire, Scotland and Germany. Samuel Slater, an apprentice of Jedediah Strutt (who had a mill further along the Derwent Valley at Milford), took the secrets of Arkwright's machines to Pawtucket in the USA, where he founded a cotton industry. By the time of his death in 1792 Arkwright was the wealthiest untitled person in Britain.

Arkwright's mill and other buildings are open to the public every day.

The Cromford Canal

In its heyday, the Cromford Canal ran 14.5 miles (23.3 km) from Arkwright's Mill in Cromford to join the Erewash Canal near the Derbyshire / Nottinghamshire border. It was built by William Jessop and Benjamin Outram, who went on to found the incredibly successful Butterley Company in Ripley. From Cromford, the canal ran south, following the 275-foot (84 m) contour line along the east side of the Derwent Valley to Ambergate, where it turned eastwards along the Amber Valley. Along the way, it passed through four tunnels and 18 locks, the construction of which provided plenty of work for Jessop and Outram's employees. **www.cromfordcanal.org**

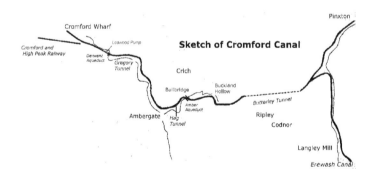

Large stretches of the Cromford Canal have fallen into disrepair, although much of it can be walked along and some is still navigable. The six mile section between Cromford and

Ambergate is listed as a Biological Site of Special Scientific Interest (SSSI) and a Local Nature Reserve.

Industrialisation of the Cromford area at the end of the 18th century prompted building the Cromford Canal. The factories needed coal from the south of the county, and the mills and quarries of Cromford needed to send their goods to customers in the south. The Erewash Canal Company refused to fund an extension to Cromford, so local businessmen engaged Jessop and Outram to build it for them.

The Butterley Tunnel, near Ripley, provided several income streams for the shrewd Jessop and Outram. The Canal Company had to pay for passage through Butterley Company land. Jessop and Outram provided engineers and labour for the complicated tunnel, which required 33 shafts to be dug, before they could be joined up by tunnelling. Jessop had planned for an underground wharf to service Butterley iron furnaces above, via the construction shafts. But they got a huge bonus when coal and iron ore were discovered under their land, which could be easily extracted through the tunnel.

Jessop was a major shareholder in the canal, which proved more profitable than expected by encouraging new enterprises. Expected to carry mainly limestone from Cromford and Crich and coal from Pinxton, narrowboats were soon transporting lead, iron ore and copper from as far away as Ecton Hill in Staffordshire. Chert from Bakewell was taken to the Staffordshire Potteries. Butterley's cast iron and Arkwright's spun cotton soon found their way onto the Derby and the Nottingham Canals, which were added in 1796.

Arkwright wanted the canal to draw water from the Derwent, necessitating improvements to his weir at Masson Mill. Jessop found a cheaper solution, which still benefited Arkwright. A connection was made to Cromford sough, the drainage tunnel for local lead mines. They paid Arkwright £1,000 to cross the garden of his house. An unexpected benefit of using mine water was that coming from underground, it was slightly warm and never froze.

By 1802 the canal had carried over 150,000 tons of freight and by 1842 nearly 300,000 tons. Then in 1849 the railway arrived, providing serious competition to the canal. By 1888 canal trade had shrunk to 45,000 tons a year.

Subsidence, which permanently closed the Butterley Tunnel in 1900, dealt the final blow to the canal. Most of the canal was abandoned in 1944 except for a half-mile stretch to Langley Mill, which was closed in 1962.

Restoration began in 1968, with the five miles between Cromford and Ambergate at least partially restored by the Cromford Canal Society (CCS). They also restored the Leawood pump beam engine, allowing it once again to pump water from the River Derwent to the Canal above. CCS carried around 15,000 passengers a year on horse-drawn passenger boats along the 1½ mile section from Cromford to Leawood, and regularly steamed the beam engine. Sadly, CCS ceased to exist in 1990 and this part of the canal began to deteriorate.

Restoration work began again in 2013, dredging the section between Leawood Pumphouse and Cromford Wharf, which is once again open for narrowboats.

Cromford Wharf (2 Mill Road, Cromford, DE4 3RQ)
This is the northern terminus of the Cromford Canal, and is opposite Arkwright's Mill on Mill Lane. There is a good sized car park, and the surviving buildings include two warehouses (one of which is now a café), an office or counting house, and two cottages.

The warehouse was built in 1794, soon after the canal opened, and is known as the Gothic Warehouse after its Gothic castellations. The Gothic decorations were probably added at the insistence of Sir Richard Arkwright, who would have seen them from Willersley Castle. Today the Arkwright Society manages the warehouse, where two rooms are used as classrooms, and exhibitions are sometimes held inside.

A second warehouse was built in 1824, to store goods awaiting carriage by boat. It was built with a large awning to overhang the canal, which still survives. Today a café and wildlife shop are housed on the ground floor of this building. The Wharf Cottages were built in 1796 for administrative staff.

The canal towpath can be followed via High Peak Junction and as far as Whatstandwell and Ambergate. This six mile section is a SSSI, and is part of the Derwent Valley Heritage Way.

High Peak Junction (Lea Road, Matlock, DE4 5AE)
This is where the former Cromford and High Peak Railway (C&HPR) meets the Cromford Canal. In strictest terms, High Peak Junction is actually the site of the signal box, a little further east, at the end of what was a siding and where the Midland Railway eventually met the C&HPR. There is a car park here, along with some remains of railway infrastructure. There is a public footpath linking the two car parks, but High Peak Junction and Cromford Wharf are generally thought of as one and the same. Today, the former railway forms the southern end of the High Peak Trail, a 17 mile (27 km) trail for walkers, cyclists and horse riders. The Derwent Valley Heritage Way also passes High Peak Junction, and

walks lead along the canal towpath in both directions from here.

The railway was originally planned as a canal, to link into the network created by the Cromford Canal. But as railway technology improved, tracks were laid along the intended canal route.

The interchange performed precisely the function the new route was intended for: that of transferring freight between Cromford Canal and the C&HPR. The only difference was that, instead of negotiating another series of locks, freight was transferred between canal barges and railway wagons.

The large wharf-side transit shed, with its awning over the canal, was the first stop for goods on and off the barges. From here a double-tracked railway line ran beside the workshops and up the steep Sheep Pasture incline.

The workshops (built between 1826 and 1830) are important in the history of Britain's railways, since they are the second oldest railway workshops in the world. Among the engineers' many jobs, was to join up chains supplied by Pritt & Co of Liverpool, into the endless loops needed to take wagons up and down the steep inclines.

This first section of the C&HPR, from Cromford to Hurdlow, which opened in 1830, started out as an oddity in railway construction, since it was isolated from any other railway lines. Rather than being part of the nascent railway network, the C&HPR connected only with canals at either end: namely the Cromford Canal in the south, and the Peak Forest Canal at Whaley Bridge in the north.

For the first three years of its life, C&HPR were hauled by horses along the flat sections, with static steam engines powering the inclines. Then, in 1833, the first locomotive arrived, making it one of the country's earliest railways, just seven years after George Stephenson's Stockton and Darlington railway opened. It was another 30 years before all the horses were replaced by steam engines.

Even after the arrival of steam locomotives, the static steam engines were still needed for the very steep pulls up the Peak District inclines. Despite the area's heavy rainfall, water was in short supply at the static engines' locations, and up to 100 wagons of water per month were transported up and down the C&HPR.

The inclines were every bit as dangerous as you might imagine. The closest incline to High Peak Junction is Sheep Pasture, which is 1,320 yards long, and has a gradient which varies between 1:8 and 1:9. The Catch Pit at the bottom was built in 1888 following a runaway accident involving a gunpowder train.

In this accident, a wagon loaded with lime and a brake van containing gunpowder broke free from a train and hurtled down the incline at speeds of up to 120 mph. Failing to negotiate the bend at the bottom, they jumped across both the canal and the tracks of the Midland Railway, before exploding in the adjacent field. Bad as this accident was, it could have been much worse, as just minutes later a London passenger train passed through. Wreckage can be seen in the catch pit today, although this is from another runaway in the 1950s.

Passenger services along the C&HPR ended even before the accident in 1888. When passenger services began in 1855, passengers were expected to get off and walk up and down the inclines, but many risked staying aboard. A fatality in 1877 provided a reason to discontinue what was already proving to be an unprofitable service.

The railway closed in 1967, but there is plenty of history to be seen around the site today.

In 1971, the Peak Park Planning Board and Derbyshire County Council bought a section of the track bed for £1. The section from the High Peak Junction workshops to Parsley Hay was turned into the High Peak Trail. At Parsley Hay, the High Peak Trail is joined by the former Ashbourne branch line, which is now the Tissington Trail. The trail continues north to Dowlow near Buxton; a total distance of 17½ miles. Visitors' Centres, with cafes and cycle hire, are located at Middleton Top (postcode DE4 4LS) and Parsley Hay (postcode SK17 0DG).

If you visit High Peak Junction today, you will still see the foundations of the old signal box (which closed in 1967). There are a few other remnants of metal and timber, but these deteriorate as time marches on. The signal box foundation is practically all that remains around the High Peak Junction car park. Following the foot / cycleway to Cromford Wharf provides the wealth of historic infrastructure described above.

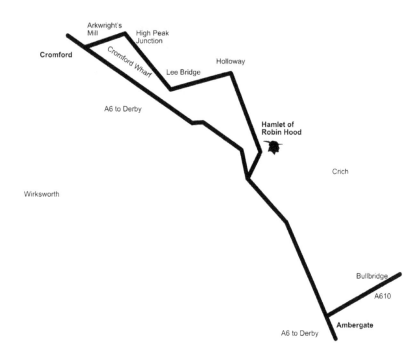

Matlock Bath

Arkwright's
Mill

High Peak
Junction

Cromford Wharf

Cromford

Lee Bridge

Holloway

A6 to Derby

Hamlet of
Robin Hood

Crich

Wirksworth

Bullbridge

A610

Ambergate

A6 to Derby

Cromford to Ambergate

Leawood Pump House (5 High Peak Trail, Whatstandwell, DE4 5HN) can still be seen, a little further along the towpath from Cromford Wharf. It was built to pump water from the Derwent to maintain the canal's water level. The need was identified in 1844 after a very dry summer, and the Pumphouse became operational in 1849.

It is now well over 150 years old, but remains in working condition thanks to volunteers. The Pumphouse has regular steaming dates throughout the year, from Easter until October. Details can be found on the Derbyshire County Council website, or from Middleton Top Visitors' Centre.

Leawood Pump House

Aqueduct Cottage (5 High Peak Trail, Whatstandwell, DE4 5HN). This cottage, near Lea Wood Nature Reserve, is a short walk from Leawood Pumphouse. It was built in 1802 as accommodation for a lengthsman (someone who maintained a length of canal) and a lock-keeper. It is Grade II Listed and sits within the Derwent Valley Mills World Heritage Site.

It was a condition of building the Lea Wood Arm that its water level should be maintained at least 12 inches above that of the Cromford Canal, to ensure that no water was taken from the main canal. To achieve this, a stop-lock was added at the entrance to the arm, which explains the construction of the cottage in this location.

Initially the cottage was built as a single, one-up one-down cottage. Then, at some point, a second cottage was added, forming a pair of semi-detached cottages. At a later date the two cottages were combined to create a single, detached, two bedroom cottage with a parlour and kitchen on the ground floor.

The cottage was occupied until 1968, despite the canal having closed 24 years earlier. For a while, it was used as a shelter by walkers, before being gifted to Derbyshire Wildlife Trust in 2012, as part of the adjacent Lea Wood.

Our next stop after leaving Cromford puts us back on the Robin Hood trail. Close to the village of Whatstandwell, there is a hamlet known as Robin Hood.

We have a choice of routes to get there, dependent on the size of your vehicle.

Option 1:

- The simplest route is to follow the A6 south, through the Derwent Valley, until the A6 takes two right angle turns across the River Derwent.
- Immediately after the road bridge and Family Tree public house (postcode DE4 5HG), turn left onto B5035.

- After a short distance uphill, cross the Cromford Canal and reach one of the Cromford Canal car parks (2 Stoney Wood Drive, DE4 5EE), which is ideal for a walk or cycle along the canal.
- Turn left onto Robin Hood Road, signposted Holloway. (Narrow and unsuited to larger vehicles).
- After approximately 600m, Robin Hood Road becomes Leashaw Road, and you have reached the hamlet of Robin Hood (postcode DE4 5HF).
- The old sawmill, which is now a B&B called Robin Hood Tower is on your left, looking downhill, towards the canal and river.

Option 2: (Unsuited to larger vehicles)

- Leave Cromford Mill on Mill Lane, crossing the River Derwent and passing the junction with Willersley Lane, which leads uphill to Willersley Castle.
- After the bridge, Mill Lane becomes Lea Road, which we follow to the hamlet of Lea Bridge.
- Here, we take the right fork, onto Mill Lane.
- Where Mill Lane becomes a steeper uphill road, it changes name to Yew Tree Hill. Follow this into Holloway.
- In Holloway, turn right, downhill, onto Bracken Lane.
- Bracken Lane becomes Leashaw Road, which soon reaches the hamlet of Robin Hood (postcode DE4 5HF).

The old sawmill, which is now a B&B called Robin Hood Tower, is on your right, looking downhill, towards the canal and river.

Whatstandwell: Hamlet of Robin Hood (postcode DE4 5HF).
Robin Hood is a hamlet in Whatstandwell. The earliest reference I found is on the six inch OS map of the area published in 1884. Appropriately, there is a Robin Hood Cottage in the hamlet of Robin Hood.

The hamlet also has a historic sawmill, part of which has been converted into a B&B called Robin Hood Tower.

Robin Hood Tower was once part of a row of buildings associated with the stone-cutting sawmill. Today, the tower stands alone on the eastern bank of the Cromford canal.

Our journey back in time starts outside Robin Hood Tower, where the brook falls dramatically through the garden of the Old Sawmill, where it once powered a turbine. The stone-lined chamber was built at the same time as the canal, long before the hamlet of Robin Hood developed.

Research by the B&B owners at Derbyshire Records Office, and visible evidence around the hamlet, suggest that stone was quarried and dressed here, providing an explanation for the hamlet's development.

Quarrying and dressing the stone so close to the new canal allowed it to be shipped to Simms' canal wharf, near High Peak Junction, and over Simms' Bridge to be moved out via their railway wharf. These two landmarks are just a few hundred metres from Robin Hood Tower.

George and Robert Stephenson were regular customers for stone quarried at Robin Hood, which they used to build railway infrastructure such as bridges and stations.

Local gritstone was also used to build London's Waterloo bridge 1817, Euston station in 1835, and the Derby and Leicester Gaols in 1823 and 1825.

Whatstandwell: The Hamlet of Robin Hood

- After visiting the hamlet of Robin Hood and Robin Hood Tower, we retrace our route to the A6 and the Family Tree public house (postcode DE4 5HG), turning left towards Ambergate.

Ambergate (postcode DE56 2EJ)
We find Ambergate at the point where the River Amber joins the River Derwent, and where the A610 road from Rip-

ley and Nottingham joins the A6 that runs along the Derwent Valley. Its position alongside the River Derwent brings the village within the Derwent Valley Mills UNESCO World Heritage site. In addition to its industrial connections with textiles, Ambergate also has historical connections with George Stephenson, and is notable for its railway heritage. It also has an unusual connection to the telecommunications industry, which I will pick up at the relevant point in the village's history.

Until the early 19th century Ambergate was known as Toadmoor, from the Derbyshire dialect "t'owd moor" or "Old Moor." The southern half of the village is still shown as Toadmoor on the current OS map. The name Amber Gate was first applied to the tollgate on the Nottingham turnpike road, but the name was adopted by the North Midland Railway for Ambergate railway station.

The burning of lime added another industry to Ambergate in 1791, when Benjamin Outram and Samuel Beresford, built kilns at nearby Bullbridge, to process limestone from their quarry at Crich. Then George Stephenson joined them, when he discovered deposits of coal at Clay Cross and started burning lime, using the slack which would otherwise have gone to waste. Stephenson leased Cliff Quarry at Crich and built eight limekilns alongside the railway. Within a year, the eight had grown to 20. Stephenson connected his kilns to the railway by a wagonway known as "The Steep", a 550-yard incline at a slope of 1 in 5.

As the Derwent Valley industrialised, its transport links improved. Initially, all the cotton from Arkwright's Mill at Cromford had to be taken a rather hilly route through Wirksworth towards Belper.

Then, in 1794, the Cromford Canal opened, with much of the valley's freight moving onto the waterway.

In 1818 the turnpike to Matlock opened, bringing with it the toll gate which gave Ambergate its name.

The North Midland Railway arrived in 1840, opening its "Amber Gate" station.

Matlock was becoming a fashionable spa town, and the arriving tourists brought trade for the new Omnibus and Posting Conveyance.

By 1867 there was a through line from London Saint Pancras to Manchester, as well as to Leeds, making Ambergate an important interchange. The main railway line runs through the elliptical Toadmoor Tunnel, which was designed by George Stephenson.

Ambergate's largest public house is the Hurt Arms, which I have visited frequently as both a customer and in my role as a Registrar, conducting wedding ceremonies inside the historic inn. Francis Hurt built the Hurt Arms in 1876, to replace the former Thatched House Tavern and Posting House, which the Midland Railway had converted into cottages.

In 1876, Richard Johnson opened a wireworks by the river. This, and the village's other industries, brought the population to 901 by 1931, and to 1,794 in 1951.

The quarry and the wagonway closed in 1957 but the limeworks carried on until 1965, when closure was forced by the Clean Air Act.

Now we reach Ambergate's part in the history of telecommunications. In 1966 a telephone exchange opened in a house on the Ripley Road. This might not seem like huge news, but it was the first fully operational electronic telephone exchange, not just in England, but in the whole of Europe. The automated exchange replaced the old manual system and provided a faster and quieter service.

Distillery: (Derwent Works, Ambergate DE56 2HE) the former Johnson & Nephew Wire Works complex has been redeveloped as a collective of small businesses, one of which is the White Peak Distillery.

Despite establishing the business in 2016, it was 2020 before they could sell their first whisky. The first two years were spent getting the buildings operational again.

White Peak keep as much as possible of their supply chain local, with the fresh, live yeast used in their 96-hour fermentations collected each week from a brewery in the Peak District.

The first malt out of the stills could only be marketed as "spirit", since at least three years of ageing are required to be called "whisky". In 2020, the first barrels passed this landmark birthday, and were sampled by judges of the Wizards of Whisky Awards, who awarded double gold in both 2020 and 2021.

The White Peak Distillery soon added a Shining Cliff Gin to their catalogue. Visitors can visit the on-site shop and book distillery tours. **www.whitepeakdistillery.co.uk**

Car Museum: (Derwent Works, Ambergate DE56 2HE) Also within the former Richard Johnson & Nephew Wire Works is The Great British Car Journey. Both a museum and an experience day location, they have around 150 historic and classic vehicles housed within the old wire-making buildings.

Their cars from a bygone age include Austin Sevens, Morris Minors, the original Mini, Ford Cortina and Vauxhall Cavalier. As well as looking at the classic cars, visitors can also take them for a spin, by booking a "Drive Dad's Car experience", where visitors drive around a freshly laid tarmac circuit with an instructor, in a selection of more than 30 British cars. **www.greatbritishcarjourney.com**

Outdoor Opportunities: I could not leave a Peak District location without mentioning the outdoor opportunities. The Cromford Canal towpath can be followed from here, all the way to Cromford Wharf, passing High Peak Junction, which is the start of the High Peak Trail. This six mile section of the canal is listed as a Biological Site of Special Scientific Interest (SSSI) and is also part of the Derwent Valley Heritage Way.

Shining Cliff Woods, on the hill behind the Hurt Arms, has been another of my outdoor favourites, as regular fell races were held there when I was a younger and fitter man.

In medieval times "Schymynde-cliffe" was one of the seven royal parks within Duffield Frith, a feudal estate set up by William the Conqueror.

Like many parts of the Derwent Valley, Shining Cliff Woods include an SSSI.

The Eastern side of the woods are owned by the National Trust and are on a long lease to the Forestry Commission. But the section of novel interest is that which is owned and managed by Grith Fyrd Pioneers, who might be thought of as carrying on the woodsman traditions of Robin Hood and his Merrie Men.

Grith Fyrd, which means "Peace Army" in Old English, was launched in 1931. Its founders belonged to the Order of Woodcraft Chivalry, an English group influenced by North American Indian bushcraft.

The movement's aim was to create an outdoor environment that would allow boys, girls, men and women to work and learn together.

The Order launched Grith Fyrd to combat the "three evils of the day", which they thought were: "monstrous labour, with its occasional relief by quick, aimless excitement; the state of passivity and absorption; and the loss of the incentive for self-expression and creativeness". The first Grith Fyrd camp opened in 1932 at Hampshire, and a year later at Shining Cliff. Their camps were intended to be a self-sufficient community that would exchange goods and services, and combat the decadence of society by training young men in self-reliance, communal living and service.

The Grith Fyrd Pioneers were a mix of young unemployed men, and idealists from middle-class backgrounds. The Pioneers built the camp buildings and furniture themselves and produced their own food.

Aldous Huxley (English writer and philosopher, noted for his opposition to organised religion) wrote in the *Sunday Chronicle* that the camp was "almost a replica of an American backwoods settlement of a century ago." He thought the primitive conditions were "an admirable counterblow against the standardisation of modern society." He also admired the leisure activities of Morris Dancing, wood-carving, folk-singing and adult education.

The present-day Grith Pioneers still provide a similar environment with woodland camping, which is intended to give people scope for self-realisation, development of personal and social responsibility, wider educational opportunities, and a sense of responsibility towards the protection of the natural environment.

Bull Bridge Aqueduct: sadly, this interesting aspect of the Cromford Canal was demolished in 1968, when the single lane road could no longer cope with traffic volumes.

It was built in 1794, where the canal turned sharply to cross the Amber Valley and the Ambergate to Nottingham road (now the A610).

Known officially as the "Amber Aqueduct", it was a 30 feet high earthwork bank, topped by masonry walls. Three arches cut through the embankment, one for the river, a second to access the small village of Bullbridge, and the main road passed through the third arch, which was the original Bull Bridge.

In 1840, George Stephenson engineered his North Midland Railway to intersect the canal at this point. He laid his tracks in the space between river and road, but put them on an embankment over the side road leading to Bullbridge. A Victorian commentator wrote "river, road, railway and canal were thus piled up, four stories high". It must have been quite a sight when all three modes of transport were travelling along the Amber Valley.

Bull Bridge Aqueduct

- At the Hurt Arms, we leave the A6 and the Derwent Valley, turning left onto the A610 and entering the Amber Valley.
- A short (1.6 mile) detour from the A610 allows us to visit Heage Windmill (unsuitable for large vehicles).

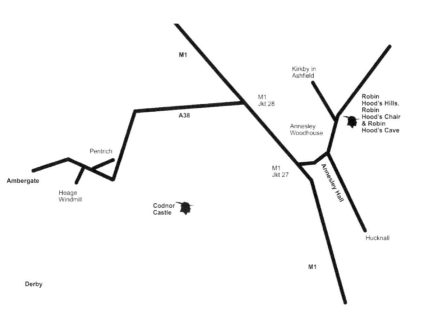

Ambergate to Robin Hood Hills (Annesley)

Heage Windmill

Built in 1797 and restored in 2002, Heage Windmill, a Grade II Listed building, is the only fully working, stone-towered, six-sailed windmill in England. It is set on a high outlook, providing spectacular views over the Derwent Valley. Car parking is available on site, with wheelchair access to the Interpretation Centre, shop, toilets and the ground floor of the mill. A Virtual Reality tour is available for those unable to climb the stairs.

The adjacent drying kiln has been rebuilt and serves as a Visitor Centre and shop selling souvenirs, light refreshments and the windmill's own flour. There are hands-on activities for children to take part in.

Flour milling takes place when the wind is favourable. The flour is stone ground on site using organic wheat from Suffolk. The flour types available are wholemeal, white, coarse brown, bran and middlings. Wheat middlings are the product of the milling process that is not flour. It is a good source of protein, fibre, phosphorus and other nutrients. They are used to produce pasta, breakfast cereals and puddings, as well as fodder for livestock and pets. They are also being re-searched for use as a biofuel. **www.heagewindmill.org.uk**

Also in Heage, at Morley Park, are the remains of two coke-fired blast furnaces for smelting iron. The first, built in 1780, was the earliest in Derbyshire. The other was built in 1818. Both represent very early examples of coke-fired blast furnaces. They closed in 1874, and most of the site is being reclaimed by nature, but the furnace towers still exist and can be seen next to the A38.

- If you have visited Heage Windmill, retrace your route back to the A610, turning right.

We pass the rather interestingly-named Excavator public house. For many years, this was instantly recognisable from the yellow JCB digger parked on the pub's flat roof. The weight was becoming too much for the structure, and it was removed several years ago to stand in front of the pub.

The Excavator is in the equally interestingly-named hamlet of Buckland Hollow. The hamlet sits within what is now known as the Starven Valley, but on the 1921 OS map it is spelt Starvehimvalley. The nearby bridge over the Cromford Canal is still known as Starvehim Bridge. Despite lots of looking, I have not found any reference to anyone actually starving in Starvehimvalley.

Buckland Hollow was the site of one of the Ambergate Brick Works' three, long since closed, brick factories.

- Another short detour away from the A610 allows a visit to the site of England's last revolution, which happened on 9th June 1817. It is a story that might well have involved Robin Hood, had he still been around during the 19th century.

Pentrich and The Pentrich Revolution
Even without its revolution, Pentrich is a village full of history. There is evidence that Pentrich was already settled when the Romans arrived in 200AD. A Roman camp, at what is now Coney Grey Farm, was named after the village. The name "Pentrich" might be of Celtic origin, possibly translating as "Boar's Hill".

It remained an agricultural community for many generations, with the medieval field system changing little over the years. If we had approached Pentrich along the A38 from

Derby, we might have seen the parallel hedges which show where the former crofts had been.

Today, it is the village's part in England's last revolution which provides a reason for walkers to visit. The Pentrich Revolution Heritage Trail is a four-mile walk, taking about two hours. For anyone wishing to avoid the steep canal steps, there is a shorter two-mile version of the walk.

Ten information plaques take you through the revolution's story. Plaque number one is near the Dog Inn.

A leaflet detailing the walk, along with a sketch map, can be downloaded from the Amber Valley Council website. **www.info.ambervalley.gov.uk**

The Industrial Revolution began to change Pentrich, and indirectly led to its part in the uprising of 1817.

The turnpike road arrived in the late 18th century (plaque no 5 is at an old turnpike milestone). At about the same time, in 1790, The Butterley Company was founded at Ripley, to develop the coal and iron deposits in the Butterley area. This company became a huge local employer, and remained in business through to the early 21st century.

The Industrial Revolution brought the Cromford Canal to Pentrich in 1790, dividing Pentrich from Ripley. The trail takes walkers along a half mile section of the towpath.

Even before the Butterley Company, Pentrich Colliery had employed Pentrich men since 1750. Mining took place here in medieval times, with evidence of bell pits uncovered when the land was reclaimed in the 1980s.

The walk takes you past the former colliery site, which is now a scrap yard and still uses some of the colliery buildings. Coal mining continued in Pentrich for centuries, the pits only being closed in 1946 when the rest of the industry was

nationalised. Animal lovers will be pleased to know that Pentrich was one of the first pits to stop using pit ponies.

One of the village's other large employers was the cotton spinners Messrs J. Towlson and Co., whose old red brick
building can still be seen on Asher Lane.

The site was taken over by Stevenson's Dyers in the
1940s. Dye working had been important in Pentrich before
the 1830s, when damson trees were originally grown as a crop
for dyeing, before chemical dyes were developed. The trees
are still enjoyed by villagers for their fruit.

The list of revolutionaries shows that many of those
involved were iron workers, miners, labourers, framework
knitters and farmers. This was a thriving village in the process
of change from an agricultural to an industrial economy. It
was against this background that the seeds of revolution were
sown.

Walking through the village of Pentrich today, the visitor could easily miss evidence of the Revolution, and the
plaques explain significant points before, during and after the
Revolution. The village landscape was very different, with
few of the original cottages remaining. The Dog Inn is one
building that does remain, and its Revolution Bar bears wit-
ness to the events of the time.

At the centre of the village, the large stone houses near
the junction of Asher Lane and Main Road were all built after 1825, on empty plots where revolutionaries used to live.

The Village Hall was once a school, and before that,
was the home of revolution leader Thomas Bacon. The school
was endowed by the Duke of Devonshire immediately after
the Revolution, and remained open until 1958.

The end of the Napoleonic Wars, with victory at the
Battle of Waterloo in 1815, brought a recession which hit Pen-

trich and Butterley particularly hard. The Butterley Company had been providing munitions to British forces, and the textile manufactures had supplied uniforms.

To help the unemployed, a Parish Relief Tax was raised. But as more people claimed relief, the tax on working families increased, in some cases bankrupting small farmers and other working people.

There was also some political turmoil, with the distri-bution of MPs still weighted heavily towards older centres of population. Neither did the Prince Regent's extravagant life-style endear the monarchy to the people, at a time when they were suffering unbelievable hardship.

In Nottingham, Derby and Ripley, reformers met as "Hampden Clubs."

In 1816 the weather added to their misery, when the Tambora Volcano disrupted global weather patterns, bringing snow to Derbyshire in June. Crops failed, and bad weather meant crops went unharvested. Starvation threatened and violent disturbances broke out throughout England over the price of food.

The French and American Revolutions were both within recent memory, and the government – fearing wide-spread revolt – adopted panic measures. Meetings of more than 50 people were forbidden, which prevented reform meet-ings like the Hampden clubs. Spies were sent out to report back on unrest, and in Pentrich, one spy took on the unau-thorised role of Agent Provocateur.

Thomas Bacon was both a war veteran and Framework Knitter. He lived in Pentrich (plaque no 10) and was active in reform meetings. He reported that an insurrection was planned, with men from Yorkshire and Nottingham planning to march on London to overthrow the government. Unknown to local people, a government spy named Oliver was reporting all that went on.

By May 1817 meetings throughout the north were broken up and ringleaders imprisoned. Oliver overstepped his role by persuading the poorly-educated local men to go ahead with their uprising. Thomas Bacon feared arrest and went to ground at Booth's Hovel (plaque no 6).

Replacing Bacon as leader was Jeremiah Brandreth, an unemployed Stockinger from Sutton-in-Ashfield. On 5th June he arrived in Pentrich and took part in meetings at Asherfields Barn (plaque no 2) and the White Horse Public House (plaque no 8).

Brandreth declared that the rising would set off for Nottingham on 9th June, collecting men and arms en-route. When they reached Nottingham, Brandreth said, they would all get 100 guineas, bread, beef and ale.

At 10pm the revolutionaries assembled at Hunts Barn in South Wingfield, setting off in two groups to knock on farm doors and force men to join them. They encountered resistance, with many men and women putting up an argument or trying to hide. During one such argument with Widow Hepworth, her servant Robert Walters was fatally shot (plaque no 4), becoming the only man to die that night.

The men reassembled at Pentrich Lane End (plaque no 5) and marched to Butterley Ironworks (plaque no 3). Here Brandreth demanded arms and cannon shot, but the Butterley men stood their ground and the marchers left empty-handed.

Marching on through pouring rain, the revolutionaries stopped at three public houses, promising to pay for their drinks after the government had fallen. Drunk, wet and demoralised, many would be revolutionaries defected, but a small group made it across the border into Nottinghamshire, to meet a detachment of the King's Hussars. There was a fight, where several were arrested, and others fled into the night.

Over the next few weeks, the revolutionaries went into hiding (plaque no 7), but many were eventually arrested. A show trial in October became a national sensation, when the ringleaders were sentenced to be hanged, drawn and quartered. The three men were the last men in England to receive that sentence. Fourteen men were transported to Australia, and six others were jailed.

Pentrich almost ceased to exist after the revolution. Houses where guilty men had lived were pulled down (plaques no 10 & 8) and their wives and children were put out of their tenancies. Land taken from guilty men was redistributed to loyal tenants, some of whom had given evidence at the trial (plaque no 9). The village became smaller and less important in the following years.

The judge at the trial commented on Pentrich men's ill-education, and in 1818 The Duke of Devonshire visited the village and endowed the school (plaque 10).

One of several Pentrich Revolution plaques

- Continuing along the A610, we reach a large roundabout and join the A38 Trunk Road turning left, towards the M1.
- Take M1 South for one junction, leaving at J27.
- Take A608 towards Mansfield (best avoided at peak times, as the business estates on your left cause congestion).
- On your right is Annesley Hall.

Annesley Hall

Annesley Hall is a Grade II Listed building, which dates from the 13th century. I have read several references to Robin Hood's boots once being kept at the Hall, but none of the references tell what has happened to them today.

- At traffic lights, turn left on A611 Derby Rd, signposted Mansfield.

Within a short distance, you are back among rural scenery.

- Robin Hood's Hills, Chair & Cave are all in the vicinity of the junction with B6021 Nottingham Rd. An Ordinance Survey map shows the wooded hills to the east of Derby Road and the right of way around the site.

Robin Hood's Hills

During his 1824 visit, Washington Irving rode to Robin Hood's Hills. Here, leaving his horse at the foot of the crags, he scaled their rugged sides, and sat in a niche of the rocks, called Robin Hood's Chair. Irving said, "it commands a wide prospect over the valley of Newstead, and here the bold out-law is said to have taken his seat, and kept a look-out upon the roads below, watching for merchants, bishops, and other wealthy travellers, upon whom to pounce down, like an eagle from his eyrie".

Descending from the cliffs and remounting his horse, Irving rode along a narrow "robber path," as it was called, which wound up into the hills to an artificial cavern cut in the face of a cliff, with a door and window cut through the stone. In Irving's time, this cave bore the name of Friar Tuck's cell, although it is now known as Robin Hood's Cave.

Robin Hood's Hills are accessed from Derby Road, Annesley. There is a network of Public Footpath rights of way around the area, but dog walkers have trodden many more unofficial paths around and over the hills.

The official Public Footpath access begins within the traffic light controlled junction of Derby Road and Shoulder of Mutton Hill.

- There is a limited amount of parking on a wide grass verge, along the south side of Derby Road. There is also plenty of roadside parking down Shoulder of Mutton Hill, after its name changes to Nottingham Road.

After passing through a metal kissing gate, The public footpath heads quite steeply downhill. Towards the bottom of the hill, the path splits left and right.

I first headed right (west), looking for Robin Hood's Cave. I had read accounts saying that the cave was now filled in, which seemed correct from my visit. Contouring around

the hillside brings you to a broad gully. The cave site is on the
south face of this gully, on the bracken covered hillside.

**Robin Hood's Cave
(no longer visible in the hillside)**

After looking at the former cave site, I retraced my
steps and followed the left (east) path towards Robin Hood's
Hills.

**Robin Hood's Hills
(looking from below Robin Hood's Cave)**

It is necessary to climb again, to cross the railway line. The path crosses the line across the opening of a railway tunnel. This gives us the opportunity to see one of the area's more modern Robin Hood locations. The Nottingham to Worksop railway is called the Robin Hood Line. For anyone wanting a journey on our hero's namesake railway, the nearest stations are in Newstead Village and Kirkby in Ashfield.

Robin Hood Line (railway)

The Robin Hood Railway Line runs passenger services from Nottingham to Worksop.

After the Beeching cuts of the 1960s, the line carried freight-only, and was re-opened to passengers in stages between 1993 and 1998.

The majority of the Robin Hood Line re-uses the former Midland Railway. However, due to some loss of infrastructure, the re-opened line uses small sections of the former Great Northern Railway and Great Central Railway.

The Robin Hood Line – looking from above the tunnel exit

At Annesley, both the Great Central Railway and the Midland Railway had driven tunnels through the Robin Hood Hills, but after the lines closed, both tunnels were filled in. The Great Central Railway tunnel had been much longer than that of the Midland Railway, so it proved cheaper to re-excavate the Midland Railway tunnel, over which you have just climbed.

After crossing the railway, the path descends to the base of Robin Hood's Hills. Unofficial paths lead up a broad gully to your left, which lead onto the flat-topped hill. Although the paths are not official rights of way, a very official looking bench on the summit suggests that access is not a problem.

It is possible to leave the hills at the high point, along an unofficial path leading across a field towards Derby Road.

There are several fenced areas, which should be respected. Robin Hood's Chair is a promontory which falls within one of these enclosures, but we can see the location by backtracking to the base of the hill.

Once back on flat ground, contour around the base of Robin Hood's Hills. On the east side of the hill, a broad gully cuts through the hillside. Robin Hood's Chair is the left-hand promontory, at the top of this gully. There was once a significant rock outcrop, on which legend has our hero looking out from. There is no longer anything noticeable, but you do get a feeling for the view afforded from the spot in medieval times.

Just beyond this gully, the tree cover on the hillside changes from deciduous old growth to evergreens. Walks continue along the base of the hills, and also up into the evergreen covered hillside.

Robin Hood's Chair

I retraced my route back to my van. It is not necessary to climb the steep path and re-cross the Robin Hood railway line, because a broad vehicle width track climbs more gently towards Derby Road. The track emerges on Derby Road, opposite the end of a row of terraced houses.

Following the row of houses back towards Shoulder of Mutton Hill shows us something of an anomaly. If you look on the upstairs level of number 109 Derby Road, you will see a sign declaring it to have been the highest point in Nottinghamshire during 1904. Number 109 is the lowest in the row of 20 houses, all of which are in Nottinghamshire. This suggests the other 19 were all built more recently than 1904.

Highest Point in Nottinghamshire (1904)

Highest Point in Nottinghamshire
(The plaque is just above the white truck cab)

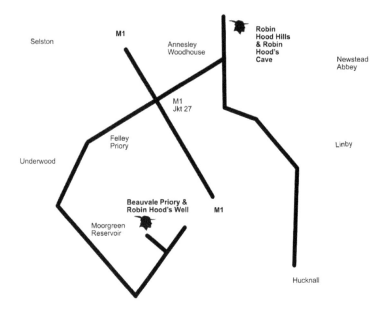

Robin Hood Hills (Annesley) to Beauvale Priory

Annesley to Beauvale Priory: 7 miles ~ 15 minutes

- Retrace your route along the A611 and A608 back to M1 J27.
- Cross the motorway, continuing on A608, passing Felley Priory on your left.

Felley Priory (Underwood, Nottingham, NG16 5FJ)
Felley Priory was founded as a hermitage by the Augustinian Order in 1156, and gradually developed into a more impressive priory. Following the Dissolution of the Monasteries in 1535, the priory was partially destroyed, and a grand residential house built on the site during the 16th and 17th centuries. Much of the priory and church was recycled into the new buildings. The pillars at the entrance to the garden were originally part of the Priory Church, and date from the late 12th Century. The house became a royalist army garrison during the Civil War. The Chaworth-Musters family, who also owned Annesley Hall, bought the property in 1822. They still occupy Felly Priory as their family home, and operate a tea-room and garden centre in the attractive grounds.

- At a T junction, turn left onto B600 Willey Lane, passing Moorgreen Reservoir (Willey Lane, Nottingham, NG16 3QS), built originally to feed the Nottingham Canal, but now a carp fishery. There are several walks and cycle rides in the hills around the reservoir.
- Just after Horse & Groom pub (Moorgreen, Newthorpe, Nottingham NG16 2FE), turn left onto

minor road, New Road, signposted with a brown tourist sign for Beauvale Priory.

- New Road is quite narrow, and perhaps not suitable for larger motorhomes or caravans.
- Beauvale Priory is off New Road to your left, down an even narrower lane (Beauvale Abbey Farm, New Road, Moorgreen, Nottingham, NG16 2AA).

Felley Priory

Beauvale Priory

Beauvale Priory was founded in 1343 by the Carthusian Order of monks. The monks lived a silent life here for 200 years, un-til the Dissolution of the Monasteries. English Heritage is working to preserve the priory ruins, which are a scheduled ancient monument. The Prior's House and Gatehouse are still in use, with the Gatehouse serving as a tearoom.

Beauvale Priory features in two of D.H. Lawrence's novels as The Abbey, and he based a short story here called *A Fragment of Stained Glass.* **www.beauvalepriory.co.uk**

Ruins of Beauvale Priory

Robin Hood's Well (Beauvale Priory)

Robin Hood's Well sits in the private High Park Wood, over-looking Beauvale Priory from the north. Sadly, public access is not allowed into the woods.

Its waters were thought to be curative and an aphrodis-iac, suggesting an earlier religious or possible pagan associa-tion. The water was used by the priory, to which it flowed via open streams round the outside wall of the cloister gar-dens, feeding a fishpond near the gate-house. Water was then run through lead pipes to each cell.

It was once the custom for local people to dance on lawns around the well on Midsummer Eve, providing further suggestion of a pagan past. However, when the woods were turned into a pheasant reserve, the dancing ceased.

D.H. Lawrence used the well as a location for two of his novels. In *Sons and Lovers* (1913) it featured as Robin Hood's Well. Whereas, in *Lady Chatterley's Lover* (1928), it appears under the name John's Well. The well still flows but is now a sluggish spring running into a mossy oval basin, reached by steps down one side.

The surrounding woods have a greater significance in *Lady Chatterley's Lover*, since Lawrence used a summerhouse that once stood there as his Gamekeeper's Hut. It was in this hut that Lady Chatterley held her passionate trysts with gamekeeper Oliver Mellors. In the early part of the 20th century the hut was a tourist attraction, but today only the foundations remain.

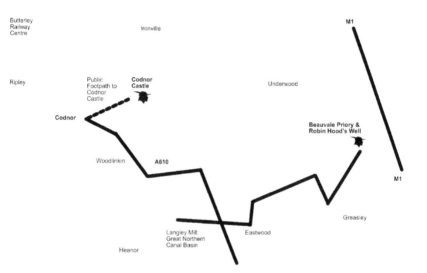

Butterley
Railway
Centre

Ironville

M1

Ripley

Public
Footpath to
Codnor
Castle

**Codnor
Castle**

Underwood

Codnor

**Beauvale Priory &
Robin Hood's Well**

Woodlinkin

A610

M1

Langley Mill:
Great Northern
Canal Basin

Eastwood

Greasley

Heanor

Beauvale Priory to Codnor Castle

Beauvale Priory to Codnor Castle: 7 miles ⁓ 25 minutes

- Retrace your route along New Road to the Horse &
  Groom pub.
- Opposite the pub, take B6010 Moorgreen.
- At T junction in Eastwood turn right on Nottingham
  Rd.

We are now entering the birthplace of D.H Lawrence, the
writer most famous for the scandal around his 1928 novel,
Lady Chatterley's Lover.

In 1928, a heavily censored version of *Lady Chatterley's
Lover* was published in the United States, but it was Penguin's publication of an unabridged version in 1960 which
caused the furore.

Penguin was prosecuted under the Obscene Publica-
tions Act of 1959, and the trial became a major public event
and a test of the new obscenity law. The chief prosecutor was
ridiculed for being out of touch, when he asked if it was the
kind of book "you would wish your wife or servants to read."
The jury delivered a not guilty verdict, resulting in greater
freedom to publish explicit material in Britain.

There is much more to D.H Lawrence than the infamous Old Bailey trial, and his somewhat unjustified reputation as a pornographer. Despite being the son of a barely lit-
erate coal miner, David Herbert Lawrence went on to be an
artist, poet and writer of several well respected novels.

Travelers wanting to learn more about D.H. Lawrence
should visit his Birthplace Museum (8a Victoria Street,
Eastwood, NG16 3AW), at the house in which he was born
in 1885.

The house is laid out in the style of a late 19th century miner's house. There are some original items from the writer's family, and everything is as authentic to the period as possible. The significance of each room is described either by interpretation boards, or by your guide on a guided tour. Lawrence was also an artist, and the museum has an exhibition of his original watercolour paintings. A slightly macabre exhibit is Lawrence's original gravestone, which was put on display on 11th September 2009, the anniversary of his birth.

- After passing through Eastwood town centre, at traffic lights take A608 Derby Road.
- At the roundabout turn right on A610 (A short detour ahead takes us to Langley Mill and The Great Northern Canal Basin).

If you choose to visit Langley Mill and the Great Northern Canal Basin, you can soak up more of this area's rich waterways history.

The canal basin and marina sit at the junction of the Erewash, Cromford and Nottingham Canals, and was once the main transport route through this region's industrial towns. Today, it makes a great family day out with plenty to remind visitors of the canals' heyday.

This area has family significance for me, as my Great Grandparents once kept the Great Northern public house (134 Derby Road, Langley Mill, NG16 4AA), built to serve the canal traffic. My Grandfather's brother drowned in the basin when he was just 10 years old, leading to all members of my family learning to swim.

The Great Northern Canal Basin & public house

- Just before reaching the village of Codnor, you will see the Codnor Castle Inn and golf course on your right (Nottingham Road, Codnor, DE5 9RL).

One of the fields surrounding the golf course is known as "Scarlet Closes." This was the site of a 1467 battle in the Wars of the Roses.

Baron Grey of Codnor supported the house of Lancaster, while most of the local barons supported the house of York. The Vernons of Haddon Hall were Yorkists, and had long been at odds with the Greys. Their dispute escalated in 1467 when Henry Grey's men murdered Roger Vernon, and a battle took place between the households of Grey and Vernon. So much blood was spilled that the field to the west of Codnor Castle became known as Scarlet Closes (closes being a contraction for the act of enclosure).

- At the traffic light controlled T junction in Codnor, turn right, remaining on A610.
- Parking is available on the former marketplace, for a walk to Codnor Castle. (Note: there is a height restriction barrier on the car park.)

The only vehicle access to Codnor Castle is along private farm roads, but there are a choice of several walking and cycling routes to the castle.

The most direct walking route starts on the left of the Poet and Castle pub (2 Alfreton Road, Codnor, DE5 9QY), taking just over a kilometre along Public Footpaths to reach the castle remains.

Other tracks, which can be easily found on the OS maps, include a longer route, which is legal for cyclists. This starts at Saint John's Church in Aldercar (269 Cromford Road, Langley Mill, Nottingham NG16 4HA), approaching the castle from the south, along Aldercar Lane.

Another interesting route, for both walkers and cyclists, starts at Codnor Park Reservoir (Coach Road, Ironville, NG16 5PL).

Positioned further along the Cromford Canal from The Great Northern Basin, this was built as a feeder reservoir for the canal and is now popular with anglers and dog walkers.

Codnor Park was originally a deer park for the castle, then became a Victorian Model Village when the Butterley Company expanded its operations away from nearby Ripley.

The route from Codnor Park Reservoir, up Monument Lane is quite steep, but does take in the Monument to William Jessop.

The 70 feet high tower was built in 1854, to the memory of William Jessop Junior. (1784-1852). Jessop had been the driving force behind the Butterley Company, and his father was one of the company's founding members. The monument was funded by public subscription at a cost of £700. Situated on high ground, its spiral staircase of 150 steps leads to a viewing platform, offering extensive views over the Erewash Valley and Codnor Park.

Canal bridge at Codnor Park Reservoir

Codnor Castle itself is a relic of Norman Britain. There is evidence of ancient British settlement here, linked to a chieftain named Cod, but significant development on the castle site came when William the Conqueror established his dominance.

Henry de Grey (1155-1219) is credited for building the first stone castle on the site. It is Henry's grandson, Reynold de Grey (c.1240-1308), who provides the castle's link with Robin Hood. Reynold is considered as a strong contender for the bad Sheriff of Nottingham, based on his tenure as Governor of Nottingham Castle from 1267.

This period also saw activity by Roger Godberd, an outlaw who lived in Sherwood Forest. Some local historians combine these factors, to establish Godberd as the basis for the Robin Hood legends.

Local historian Brian Benison, spent many years researching Reynold de Grey and Roger Godberd, and their connection to the Robin Hood legends. He published his findings in his 2015 book, *Robin Hood in Sherwood Stood: The Real Story.*

Benison thought that Robin Hood was most likely a nickname, just like Billy the Kid referred to a real person, William H. Bonney. Using this as a basis, he studied public records to see what the historians of the day wrote about outlaws who lived like the Robin of legend.

Benison's most likely candidate for Robin Hood was Roger Godberd, who served under Simon de Montfort, the 6th Earl of Leicester, and two other barons, in their rebellion against King Henry III. When all three barons were killed, Roger assumed leadership of the rebellion, causing him to be outlawed. He settled in Sherwood Forest, living there for four years, and defying the authorities. He was said to have been able to call upon 100 men but was eventually caught in 1272. This interpretation of Robin Hood's identity is at odds with the popular version that Robin served under King Richard the Lionheart, who died in 1199.

Benison then identified Reynold de Grey of Codnor Castle as a prime candidate for the legendary Sheriff of Nottingham.

It seems that Reynold de Grey and Roger Godberd might have started out as friends, going hunting together, and there is even a record of them being jointly charged with stealing the king's deer. Reynold was one of the youngest ever Sheriffs and had been a military leader, helping Edward I conquer Wales.

It was the Barons' Revolt between 1264 and 1267 which ended their friendship. During this bitter conflict, you were either on the side of the Barons or the Royals. Roger supported the barons, while The Sheriff sided with the Royals.

Fans of the Robin Hood's regular one-upmanship over the Sheriff might be disappointed to hear that it was the Sheriff of Nottingham who caused Roger Godberd's downfall. Reynold de Grey captured Roger in the grounds of Rufford Abbey, taking him to Nottingham Castle. Roger escaped the Castle, being recaptured and sent to trial at the Tower of London, where he was pardoned.

Codnor Castle

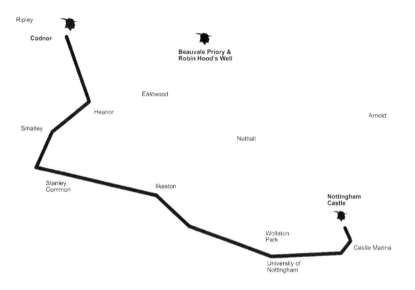

Ripley

Codnor

Beauvale Priory &
Robin Hood's Well

Eastwood

Heanor   Arnold

Smalley

Nuthall

Stanley
Common   Ilkeston

Nottingham
Castle

Wollaton
Park

Castle Marina

University of
Nottingham

Codnor Castle to Nottingham Castle

Codnor Castle to Nottingham: 16 miles - 1 hour

There is a faster, less scenic route of getting into Nottingham, straight down the A610. The trunk road route is more suited to larger vehicles. However, my recommended route takes in some more of Derbyshire's towns and villages, before entering Nottingham along Castle Boulevard. This route into the city, under the castle's shadow, seems a more appropriate way to end our journey.

- At the A610 traffic lights, take A6007, straight on through Loscoe, towards Heanor.

Loscoe has a history going back to at least the Viking era. The village name derives from Old Norse words lopt and skógr, meaning "wood with a loft house." However, it is the area's mineral wealth that helped the whole valley prosper, with the Norman Barons paying many Vikings to leave.

Driving downhill into the valley cut by Loscoe Brook and The Red River, look between the houses you pass. Amidst the more modern houses are a huge variety of historic cottages. These are both agricultural dwellings and Victorian mineworkers' cottages.

I based my historic novel *Blackrake* around Loscoe, as it fits nicely in the centre of the Ironstone Blackrake mining area. Many generations of my fictional Viking family mirrored the real population; arriving as Viking metal workers, becoming proficient archers, serving in campaigns like Agincourt, before going to work in the coal mines and the Butterley engineering company.

Loscoe Dam

All the surrounding villages have more than their share of history. Three miles away in Denby, a seam of clay was discovered in 1806 when a road was being constructed. Denby Pottery (Derby Road, Denby, DE5 8NX) was founded the following year, becoming famous for its distinctive salt-glazed pots. The pottery is still there, with a visitor centre, café, and garden centre.

Since we are on a road trip, it seems appropriate to tell you about Denby's claim to road building fame, as the birth-place of tarmac. In 1903, a wagon carrying barrels of tar collapsed, covering a stretch of road with wet tar. Local workers covered the spillage with slag from a nearby blast furnace. Nottinghamshire County Surveyor, Edgar Hooley, noticed the stretch of road was free of dust and wheel ruts. He asked locals what had happened and by 1902 he patented the process of heating tar, then adding slag and stones to form a road surface. Nottingham's Radcliffe Road became the world's first tarmac road. **www.denbypottery.com**

- Leaving Loscoe, we travel uphill, towards the more industrial town of Heanor.
- We see very little of Heanor, since the roundabout at the town's edge takes us right on the A608 into more rural scenery towards Smalley.

The road from Heanor to Smalley twists and undulates nicely through fields and farms, but beware the plethora of fixed speed cameras.

Smalley

Anyone who has been tempted by Scotland's NC500 might like to hear about Smalley's Bonnie Prince Charlie connection. In 1745, the Young Pretender and his Jacobite supporters reached as far south of Derby. Smalley was one of several villages that hosted the Bonnie Prince during his short time in Derbyshire.

Saint John the Baptist bell tower: Smalley

Smalley's other claim to fame is its rather large bell tower. In 1908, Reverend Charles Kerry left a set of five bells to his village church. These bells are the heaviest chime of five bells in England, and a new bell tower had to be added to the church of Saint John the Baptist to house them (Main Road, Smalley, DE7 6JX).

- At the hamlet of Smalley Cross, you see the Rose & Crown pub (Main Road, Morley, DE7 6DG) on your right.
- This former coaching inn dates back to around 1860.
- Turn left onto the A609 Ilkeston Rd. The scenic A609 takes us through the village of Stanley Common.

Stanley Common and West Hallam

A pleasant street called The Brickyard (Stanley Common, DE7 6FR) and, in the next village of West Hallam, a café built into an old pottery kiln, give an idea of the industrial heritage among these pretty villages.

The Bottle Kiln site at West Hallam (High Lane West, West Hallam, DE7 6HP) was originally a sawmill making pit-props. Then, in the mid-19th Century, a small brick works was built to use materials from a nearby clay pit. The bricks were fired in beehive kilns. Two bottle-neck kilns were built by the West Hallam Art & Earthenware Company in the 1920s. The pottery failed in 1933, with one kiln demolished in the 1950s. This prompted the remaining outer kiln shell to be registered as a listed building. In 1983, the café and craft centre complex were built around the bottle-shaped kiln shell. **www.bottlekiln.co.uk**

- The road continues winding its way through farm-land, to reach the Straw's Bridge Nature Reserve (High Lane East, West Hallam, DE7 5FG).

From here, the disused Nutbrook Canal and a network of nearby reclaimed mineral railway lines, provide plentiful walking and cycling opportunities. **www.waterways.org.uk/ waterways/discover-the-waterways/nutbrook-canal**

- Soon after Straw's Bridge, we re-enter an urban land-scape at Ilkeston.

Ilkeston
Anyone old enough to remember the TV show *Citizen Smith* might be interested to learn that despite his character leading The Tooting Popular Front, the show's lead actor, Robert Lindsay, was born in Ilkeston.

Like many towns in this mineral rich area, mining and iron working form a big part of its heritage. However, around the turn of the last century Ilkeston was also well known for framework knitting.

Anyone visiting Ilkeston during October might see the entire town centre taken over by The Charter Fair. Departing from Nottingham's Goose Fair, many of the showmen set up in Ilkeston's streets, following a tradition begun in 1252.

- Reaching Ilkeston's busy traffic island, we continue on A609 towards Nottingham.
- This section remains very urban, until you reach the Gallows Inn (Nottingham Road, Ilkeston, DE7 5BN) and cross the Erewash Canal.

The pub's somewhat gruesome name comes from a gibbet which stood on the spot during the 17th century.

The 12 mile (19km) long Erewash canal joins the Cromford Canal to the north and enters the River Trent as it flows into Nottingham. Along the way, it picks up the Derby Canal and the Nutbrook Canal, which we encountered at Straw's Bridge.

- Once you pass under the M1, we are now on Trowell Moor, another pleasant stretch of rural Nottinghamshire.
- At the end of Trowell Moor is a complicated, five-way traffic light junction. If you imagine it as a roundabout, take the third exit onto Wollaton Vale.

We are now in the suburbs of Nottingham, passing through a built-up area, but it does lead us to Nottingham's famous deer park. Watching the herd of red deer and fallow deer, I could imagine Robin Hood poaching meat from Wollaton Park. However, although the ancient Sherwood Forest undoubtably reached the outskirts of Nottingham, Wollaton Park has only existed since the early 19th century. The 6th Baron Middleton demolished the village of Sutton Passeys, and enclosed his new park with a seven mile (11 km) red brick wall. The park saw action during WWII when American troops were billeted there, waiting to be parachuted into Europe. Later in the war, German prisoners of war were also held here.

The Middletons' ancestral home of Wollaton Hall is rather older than the 6th Baron's deer park. The Elizabethan country house was built in the 1580s, atop a prominent hill. The hall, now owned by Nottingham City Council, houses their Natural History Museum and Industrial Museum. In 2011 Wollaton Hall starred in the Batman movie *The Dark Knight Rises*, where the Hall was used as Wayne Manor. **www.wollatonhall.org.uk**

Wollaton Hall

- At the bottom of Wollaton Vale, turn left at the roundabout, onto A52 Derby Road, keeping Wollaton Park on your left.
- The University of Nottingham's main campus is on your right (postcode NG7 2RD).

First opened as an adult education centre in 1798, the university is now part of the prestigious Russell Group.

- After Wollaton Park, we reach a busy traffic light controlled roundabout opposite the Queens Medical Centre (postcode NG7 2UH), which is itself part of The University of Nottingham.
- We turn right at the roundabout, briefly joining the Nottingham Ring Road.
- Immediately after the hospital, turn left onto A6005 Abbey Street. We are now entering the city's conurbation.
- At a small roundabout, turn right, taking A6005 Castle Boulevard into the centre of Nottingham.
- On your right is Castle Marina (postcode NG7 1TN), which as well as its boating marina, has many shops and eateries.
- Castle Boulevard runs parallel with the Nottingham Canal on your right, as we look up and get our first glimpse of Nottingham Castle (postcode NG1 6AA).

Nottingham

Before reaching the castle, The Park Estate on your left is worthy of mention. The upmarket, largely Victorian private residential estate began life as a deer park for Nottingham Castle, which our hero would have frequented. The 19th century industrialisation of Nottingham made The Park a valuable recreation space for city residents, but this did not stop the 4th Duke of Newcastle from building his grand houses. The Park remains an exclusive estate, with vehicle access controlled by bollards, requiring your registration number to be recognized by the cameras. Even pedestrian access is gated at most places overnight. The Park remains lit by gas street-lights, the largest such network in Europe.

- As we reach the centre of the city, Castle Road is on your left, leading, as its name suggests, to Nottingham Castle.
- There is parking for motorcycles and disabled permit holders on Castle Road, but other vehicles should use one of the city's many car parks.

Nottingham city centre is another place that already features in a great many guidebooks and websites. In selecting the highlights to give you, I have chosen the obvious Robin Hood location of Nottingham Castle. I have limited my coverage of attractions not directly connected with our hero, to a few of my personal favourites. These tend to be some of the city's older sites, along with the Galleries of Justice, which piqued my interest as a retired Policeman. **www.visitnottinghamshire.co.uk/explore/nottingham**

Nottingham Castle (Castle Road, Nottingham NG1 6AA)
Apart from Sherwood Forest, Nottingham Castle is probably the most famous of all the Robin Hood locations. It occupies a commanding position on a natural promontory called Castle Rock, with cliffs measuring 130 feet (40 m) high. **www.nottinghamcastle.org.uk**

Such a dominant position over the city will have been a defensive position since Nottingham was first settled. However, it is the Normans with whom we most associate the term "castle".

The first Norman castle on Castle Rock was a wooden motte-and-bailey, begun on the orders of William the Conqueror in 1068, two years after the Battle of Hastings. Sometime after coming to the throne in 1154, King Henry II began to replace the wooden structure with a far more defensible stone castle. When complete, the rebuilt castle had an Upper Bailey at the highest point on Castle Rock, a Middle Bailey containing the royal apartments, and a large Outer Bailey.

For centuries, Nottingham Castle was one of England's most important royal castles. It was strategically important for its location near a crossing of the River Trent. But it was also a place of leisure for nobles and royalty. It was close to Royal Hunting Forests at Tideswell, Barnsdale and Sherwood, as well as its own deer park in the area still known as The Park.

It is the period of the Third Crusade, between 1189 and 1192, where Nottingham Castle features most prominently in popular versions of the Robin Hood legends.

During this time, King Richard the Lionheart and his most trusted noblemen were overseas trying to recapture Jerusalem from the Muslim armies. With the King and his supporters away, his brother John rallied his supporters towards rebellion. The Sheriff of Nottingham was among Prince John's supporters, making Nottingham Castle a key location in the rebellion. The Walt Disney animated version of Robin Hood provides an amusing assessment of John's desire to become King John the First, describing him as "John the Worst."

One of the tunnels through Castle Rock bears the name Mortimer's Hole. This name relates to a piece of political intrigue in 1330, where the 17 year old King Edward III staged a coup against his Regents. Edward's mother, Isabella of France, and her lover Roger Mortimer, were acting as Regents during Edward's minority. They were living in Nottingham Castle and, aided by conspirators inside the castle, Edward and his followers entered the castle through a secret tunnel, arresting Isabella and Mortimer.

Lovers of legend might like the connection often made between Mortimer's Hole and the stories of King Arthur.

Scholars link a poem written in 1331 to Edward's coup, when the poem tells of caves beneath a castle being carved by Lancelot to hide Guinevere after their adulterous affair. This poem is thought to be the earliest reference to Lancelot and Guinevere's adultery.

Sadly, for visitors wanting to see the castle which hosted so much real and legendary action, the original Norman Castle was partially demolished in 1651, leaving just the original walls and gates.

In the 1670s William Cavendish, the 1st Duke of Newcastle, later built a ducal mansion on the site. It is this stately home which now dominates the skyline, but enough of the old castle walls remain to give an impression of the layout of the site.

Nottingham Castle maintained its place in history, well beyond the times attributed to Robin Hood. A visit to Nottingham will satisfy a broad range of historical interest.

The castle and surrounding streets played a key role at the very beginning of the English Civil War.

At the start of the Civil War, in August 1642, Charles I chose Nottingham to rally his armies. The castle had been badly damaged during earlier skirmishes, and Charles did not garrison his troops there – though soon after he departed, Castle Rock was made defensible again, and was held by the Parliamentarians. Cromwell's men repulsed several Royalist attacks, and they were the last group to hold the castle. In 1648 the Royalist commander, Marmaduke Langdale, was captured and held in Nottingham Castle, but he managed to escape and make his way to Europe. In 1651, two years after the execution of Charles I in 1649, the castle was destroyed to prevent it being used again.

After the restoration of Charles II in 1660, the Ducal Mansion was built by William Cavendish, 1st Duke of Newcastle. This Italianate palace was considered as one of the finest in England at the time.

The Industrial Revolution lessened Nottingham's appeal with the gentry, as the factories brought Nottingham the reputation of having the worst slums in the British Empire, outside India. When residents of Nottingham's slums rioted in 1831, they set fire to the mansion, doing a huge amount of damage.

Nottingham Castle

During post-fire renovations, Robin Hood returned to Nottingham Castle, in the form of the Robin Hood Rifles. The original exterior stairs on the eastern side of the mansion were demolished to create a parade ground for the soldiers. Modern amalgamations of British Army regiments saw the Nottingham regiment variously known as The Sherwood

Foresters, The Worcestershire & Sherwood Foresters and now The Mercian Regiment.

The Robin Hood Rifles were a Territorial Army unit, which once formed the 7th battalion of the local Sherwood Foresters Regiment. Although we think of *Dad's Army* as being a Home Front force, Nottingham's volunteers saw overseas action during the African Boer War from 1900 to 1902, and also during WWI. **www.nottsra.co.uk**

Their military service is remembered at a monument within Saint Mary's Church, in the Lace Market (High Pavement, Nottingham, NG1 1HN).

The Robin Hood Rifles story begins, appropriately, on Nottingham Castle Green in the 19th century. The battalion was formed in 1859, amid fears of war with France, when most counties created rifle regiments. The unit was formed on 30th May 1859 when six volunteers paraded at Nottingham Castle under Sergeant-Major Jonathan White, who remained with the Robin Hoods for 40 years, ending his career with the honorary rank of Colonel.

By October 1859, five separate company-sized Rifle Volunteer Corps (RVCs) had been raised in Nottingham. They were combined into a single battalion as the Robin Hood RVC, later becoming known as the 1st Nottinghamshire (Robin Hood) RVC.

The Rifles recruited exclusively from the City of Nottingham, with recruits often having worked together in civilian life. One company was raised by A.J. Mundella, from employees of his hosiery mill.

In 1900, men of the battalion volunteered for service in the Boer War and sailed for South Africa in February. During the campaign they took part in three battles and 25 smaller engagements. Sergeant Hickinbottom was awarded the Distinguished Conduct Medal, and the battalion was awarded its first Battle Honour.

When WWI began in 1914, one of the two Robin Hood Rifles battalions fought as part of the Nottinghamshire and Derbyshire Brigade, landing in France during February 1915. The Robin Hoods saw heavy fighting at the Battle of Hohenzollern Redoubt, where Temporary Captain Geoffrey Vickers was awarded the VC. The battalion was also involved in the first day of the Battle of the Somme, on 1 July 1916, and sustained severe casualties.

On 1st July 1916 they attacked in the first wave at 7.30am, as part of a diversionary attack. The Robin Hood Rifles went over the top with 536 men. Their casualties topped 391, with most falling within the first 10 minutes. Many streets in Nottingham, especially in the old Saint Ann's area, drew their curtains as a mark of respect.

The other battalion of Robin Hood Rifles (the 2nd / 7th Robin Hoods) was sent to Ireland in 1916, to help suppress the Easter Uprising in Dublin. They joined their comrades in France during 1917, taking part in the Battle of Passchendaele.

Coming from a coal mining area, the Robin Hoods played an important role in training soldiers to build the trenches.

At the end of WWI in 1918, the Robin Hood Rifles were disbanded, but the name of our legendary hero reappeared two years later. In 1920, Britain's Territorial Force was reorganised as the Territorial Army, and the 7th (Robin Hood) Battalion (TA) was formed.

The advent of air power reduced the need for infantry, and many rifle battalions were converted to an anti-aircraft role. Following their re-training, the battalion became the

42nd (The Robin Hoods, Sherwood Foresters) Anti-Aircraft Battalion, Royal Engineers.

Robin Hood Rifles badge

Ye Olde Trip to Jerusalem (Brewhouse Yard, Nottingham, NG1 6AD)
Many versions of the Robin Hood story depict Robin as one of Richard the Lion Heart's Crusaders. So, it should take little imagination to picture Robin enjoying a last drink before marching on the Holy Land.

The Grade II Listed, Ye Olde Trip to Jerusalem, is one of several pubs claiming to be the oldest in England. Nottingham has two of the other contenders: Ye Olde Salutation Inn and The Bell Inn. The most prominent claim from outside Nottingham is Ye Olde Fighting Cocks in Saint Albans, to the north of London.

The building rests against Castle Rock, and is attached to several caves, carved out of the soft sandstone. These were originally used as a brewhouse for the castle, during the medieval period, meaning that Robin's farewell drink was most likely brewed in the caves.

The pub claims to have been established in 1189, the year that Richard the Lionheart became king, and Pope Gregory VIII called for a Third Crusade to the Holy Land; however, no documentation exists to verify this claim.

The earliest reference to the name "Ye Olde Trip to Jerusalem" was in 1799. Before then, the pub was named "The Pilgrim", with references to this name dating back to 1751. Both names come from the belief that pilgrims or crusaders stopped at the inn on their journey to Jerusalem. Locals often use a shortened version, calling it simply "The Trip".

Several Nottingham guided tours visit Ye Olde Trip to Jerusalem, and The Original Nottingham Ghost Walk starts here on Saturday evenings.

Ye Olde Trip to Jerusalem

Inside Ye Olde Trip to Jerusalem

Old Market Square (Postcode NG1 2BS)

Visiting Nottingham's Old Market Square, we visit the location of Robin Hood's best known appearance.

Folklore says that it was in the Old Market Square where Robin Hood took advantage of an amnesty and won the silver arrow in a contest devised by the Sheriff of Nottingham. This contest forms the central plot to Disney's animated version of *Robin Hood*, where Robin wears stilts to disguise himself as a stork (all Disney's Robin Hood characters were portrayed as animals) to enter the competition.

There have been tales of Robin shooting for a gold and/or silver arrow since at least the 15th century. In most versions, Robin's identity is discovered at the contest, and he must fight his way to safety. The archery contest has become a fixture in most modern Robin Hood books and films. For example, an episode of the 1950s TV series *The Adventures of Robin Hood*, starring Richard Greene, features an archery tournament where the outlaws take refuge at Sir Richard's

356

castle. In later versions of the story, Robin splits his opponent's arrow down the centre, a development borrowed from Sir Walter Scott's 1819 novel *Ivanhoe*.

A Gest of Robyn Hode, composed around 1460, is probably the earliest mention of an archery contest. A tournament to win an arrow made of silver and gold makes for an exciting middle section of *The Gest*.

The concept reappeared in the ballads collected by Francis James Child, around 1888. Verse 23 of *Child Ballad* 152: *Robin Hood and the Golden Arrow*, features an arrow with a silver shaft and a golden head. "So, the arrow with the golden head, and shaft of silver white. Brave Robin Hood won, and bore with him, for his own proper right."

Today, The Old Market Square covers an area of approximately 12,000 square metres, or about three acres. It is one of the largest paved squares in Britain. Large as the square is today, it was once much bigger. From the 11th Century until 1928, the market square covered an area of about 5.5 acres, Because of its size, it was frequently referred to as the "Great Market Place."

In the days before the City of Nottingham was formed, this area was halfway between the Norman town of Nottingham, situated around Castle Rock, and the older Anglo-Saxon town (called Snottingham), which was based around what is now the Lace Market. The central point between the two towns became a key marketplace, putting the square at the centre of Nottingham's growth for hundreds of years. The two towns were once divided by a wall. The line of this historic wall was reinstated when the square was redesigned in the 2000s, with a stainless steel drainage channel down the centre of the Square.

The square was the original setting of Nottingham's Goose Fair, an annual fair held in October originating over 700 years ago. The Goose Fair was moved in 1928 for redevelopment of the square. The Goose Fair can still be visited each October on its new site, north of the city centre. Today's fair adopts a more contemporary amusement park style, somewhat different from the livestock market of 700 years ago.

Sports fans might remember trophies won by Nottingham Forest Football Club, including the European Cup and the FA Cup, being held aloft in front of crowds here.

In 2004, a memorial service for Nottingham Forest's manager Brian Clough was held in front of TV cameras and thousands of football supporters.

A statue of Clough was later built just off the square, at the junction of King Street and Queen Street, though my former Police colleagues remember "Cloughie" somewhat less favourably than the football fans seem to.

Nottingham ice skating legends Torvill and Dean also stood on the Council House balcony after their famous 1984 Olympic victory.

In December every year, the square hosts a Weihnachtsmarkt (German Christmas Market) and is the centre of local New Year's Eve celebrations. The Nottingham Christmas Lights switch-on event also takes place here.

The eastern end of the square is dominated by the Council House, which served as Nottingham's town hall until 2010, when the city's administration moved to more modern office accommodation. Formal Council meetings are still held within its grand Council Chamber.

Two large stone lions guard the Council House steps, becoming a popular symbol of the city. The Left Lion has since been adopted by locals as a meeting place. The lions were officially named "Agamemnon" and "Menelaus", after two brothers from Greek mythology. Locals tend to call them "Leo" and "Oscar".

Speaker's Corner: On 22nd February 2009, Nottingham's Speaker's Corner was officially opened by Jack Straw (at the time, UK Justice Secretary). This was the first official Speak-ers' Corner outside London.

Nottingham's Old Market Square

The Bell Inn (Angel Row, Nottingham, NG1 6HL)
Along with Ye Olde Trip to Jerusalem and Ye Olde Saluta-tion Inn, The Bell Inn claims to be the oldest pub in Notting-ham. The Grade II Listed building dates from around 1437 and sits on one side of The Old Market Square.

Sometime before 1271, the Whitefriars established a fri-ary on what is now Friar Lane. Around 1420 (according to dendrochronological dating of timbers), a guesthouse was added on the site of what is now the Bell Inn.

After the Dissolution of the Monasteries by Henry VIII in 1539, it became a secular alehouse, taking its name from the Angelus Bell that hung outside.

Entrance to the bars is down the central passageway, which used to lead to the stables, and retains its original flag-stones. To the right of the entrance are the leprosy windows, where customers had their fingers counted before being allowed to enter.

The original bars, known as The Long Room and The Elizabethan Bar, date back to 1437, and their original timber crown-posts and cross beams have been preserved. The Tudor Bar also features a piece of the original wallpaper among other historical artifacts on display. The Elizabethan Bar is dominated by a large stained-glass window, and restoration work in 2002 uncovered the original wooden floor.

The Snack Bar was once an outdoor courtyard with two wells used for brewing.

The first floor restaurant and function room were once the living quarters, with windows overlooking the Old Market Square.

The oak-panelled low-beamed room, which features an original fireplace, now houses The Belfry Restaurant.

The Crown Post Room is an extension to The Belfry used for private functions, and features the unusual crown post roof supports.

The cellars were hand-carved in the sandstone beneath the Snack Bar and adjacent buildings. Dating back to the Norman period, they were excavated by the Carmelite Friars and contain two wells (including the Monks Well). They are the site of the original kitchen, and a well-preserved bonded warehouse once used by a neighbouring wine merchant. The cellars are opened to the public on regular guided tours.

In 1998, the Channel 4 TV series *History Hunters* examined the claims of The Bell Inn, Ye Olde Salutation Inn and Ye Olde Trip to Jerusalem to be the oldest pub in Nottingham. The researchers concluded that of the three, Ye Olde Salutation was the oldest building, but the Bell was the first to be used as a pub.

Lace Market

The quarter-mile square of the Lace Market is one of Nottingham's most historic remaining areas. Nothing remains of the area's Saxon history, but it is thought to be the original Saxon settlement, from which Nottingham was built. At the height of the British Empire it was the centre of the world's lace industry and is now a protected heritage area. It was never a market in the sense of having stalls, but it was once packed with salesrooms and warehouses for storing, displaying and selling lace. Today the area earns its living through bars, restaurants and shops.

Most of the Lace Market is typically Victorian, with densely packed red-brick buildings of between four and seven stories high. There are iron railings, old gas lamps and red phone boxes, to give visitors a sense of going back in time to Victorian England. The Adams Building (Stoney Steet, Nottingham, NG1 1NG) (now a college campus) was built for Thomas Adams, a notable Quaker, who did much to improve the Victorian working conditions in his factories. Many other grand buildings of the Victorian age were designed by Watson Fothergill, a prolific local architect responsible for around 100 buildings in the area between 1870 and 1906. His Gothic style was very popular in Victorian times, resulting in many shops, banks, houses and even churches being decorated with turrets, gargoyles and other distinctive features.

Not everything in the Lace Market is Victorian. High Pavement is a handsome Georgian street, which is home to the Galleries of Justice and Saint Mary's Church.

Nottingham's Lace Market tells a tale of industrial decline, typical of many British cities. At its peak in the 1890s, Nottingham's hosiery industry employed around 25,000 (mostly female) workers. Advancements in technology reduced this number to below 5,000 during the 1970s, with many factories becoming derelict and the Lace Market falling into decline.

Nottingham City Council kickstarted gentrification of the Lace Market in 1978, offering grants to refurbish the historic buildings. Nearly all the old warehouses have now been renovated and repurposed as luxury apartments, offices and academic buildings. The industrial focus of the Lace Market has moved towards the creative sector, with several PR and design agencies making the Lace Market their home.

The Lace Market has also become one of the city centre's main tourist areas, with the National Justice Museum, and the Nottingham Contemporary Art Gallery being the two biggest draws.

The National Justice Museum (formerly known as the Galleries of Justice), on High Pavement (postcode NG1 1HN), are inside the old law courts and County Gaol. If you look above the entrance, you will see a mistake made by the stonemason, who misspelled the word Gaol as "County Goal". **www.nationaljusticemuseum.org.uk**

The Grade II Listed building is a former Victorian courtroom, prison and police station, where an individual could be arrested, tried, sentenced and executed.

The earliest confirmed use of the site for official purposes was by the Normans, so Robin Hood might easily have been put on trial here. The Normans appointed Sheriffs (a contraction of the words "Shire Reeve") to keep the peace and collect taxes; hence the site was sometimes known as the Sheriff's Hall, the County Hall or the King's Hall. The first written record of the site being used as a law court dates from 1375. The first written reference to its use as a prison is in 1449. The courts were still in use during the 1950s, as my mum told stories of being on duty there during her time as a Policewoman.

Until 1832, most Nottingham hangings took place at Gallows Hill, but in 1832 they moved to the Shire Hall. The last public execution was held in 1864, when Richard Thomas Parker was hanged for murder. Executions continued out of public view, in the rear yard, with Thomas Gray being the final execution in 1877. Anyone interested in further reading about capital punishment might investigate the case of Thomas Gray. He was hanged for the murder of Ann Mellors, allegedly for refusing his proposal of marriage. At an appeal hearing, several doctors successfully testified to his mental incapacity, but the appeal verdict came too late to stop his execution.

The Shire Hall continued in use as Nottingham's civil and criminal courts until 1991, when Nottingham Crown Court was opened on Canal Street.

The Galleries of Justice Museum first opened in 1995. It was refurbished and rebranded as the National Justice Museum in 2017.

The museum houses two courtrooms, an underground jail, and the site used for executions. The Crime Gallery includes a range of family activities, interactive exhibits and exhibitions relating to crime and punishment. It also houses the dock relocated from London's Bow Street Magistrates' Court.

The National Justice Museum

Nottingham Contemporary (Weekday Cross, Nottingham, NG1 2GB) is a modern art gallery in the Lace Market, which opened in 2009.

It is perhaps a little ironic that a modern art gallery should sit on one of Nottingham's oldest sites of habitation. Garners Hill once housed cave dwellings, a Saxon fort and a medieval town hall, until the Victorians destroyed all evidence in the construction of a railway line.

I confess to modern art not really being my thing. The gallery is very proud of its green exterior cladding, which is embossed with a traditional Nottingham lace pattern. Nottingham Contemporary had been open for some time before I realised the cladding was not a temporary construction site fence. **www.nottinghamcontemporary.org**

The Nottingham Contemporary modern art gallery in Nottingham's Lace Market

The Church of Saint Mary the Virgin (High Pavement, Nottingham, NG1 1HN) occupies a prominent spot in the Lace Market. It is Grade I Listed, one of only five Grade I Listed buildings in the city of Nottingham. It is the oldest religious building in the city, and its largest mediaeval building. The church is mentioned in the *Domesday Book* and is thought to go back well into Saxon times.

Of note on our **500RH** journey is the memorial within the churchyard to Nottingham's Robin Hood Rifles. The memorial is a permanent reminder of the contribution Nottingham people made to the British War effort. The local history society said that "Robin Hood Rifles were the city's own battalion made up entirely of Nottingham men, and they weren't professional soldiers, but lace workers, clerks, shop-keepers and teachers."

Nottingham Caves

Nottingham uses the term "caves" to describe the under-ground accommodations which are spread throughout the city centre. But "caves" is a little inaccurate, since most were carved by man, rather than being what we generally under-stand to be naturally occurring caves. However, this anomaly does not make the caves any less interesting. www.nationaljusticemuseum.org.uk/cityofcaves

Many of the caves were covered over and lost until 2016, when intensive surveys began by the City Archaeolo-gist. In the first two years of surveying, 200 caves were re-discovered. The total now exceeds 800 caves.

There are many opportunities to visit individual caves, mostly underneath Nottingham's older pubs. But City of Caves is a specific visitor attraction, located in a network of caves underneath the Broadmarsh Shopping Centre. (Note: The Broadmarsh area of Nottingham was under re-development at time of writing. The entrance to the City of Caves was at the bottom of the Garner's Hill Steps next to Nottingham Contemporary, but could be moved during the re-development. Postcode: NG1 1HF.)

Like the city's other caves, these too were carved out of sandstone, and were variously used as a tannery, public house cellars, and as an air raid shelter.

Construction of the Broadmarsh Centre in the late 1960s included plans to fill in the caves with concrete. This caused a public outcry, prompting the caves to be scheduled as an Ancient Monument, and forcing the developers to change their plans. The caves were cleared by volunteers from the Sherwood Air Cadets and Rushcliffe School, and were opened for public tours by the Friends of Nottingham Museum in 1978.

These caves are some of the oldest remaining in the city, with pottery finds dating from as long ago as 1270. They are known to have been inhabited from at least the 17th century, until 1845 when legislation banned the renting of cellars and caves as homes for the poor.

The recreated tannery in Nottingham's City of Caves

Two of the caves housed the only known underground tannery in Britain. The Pillar Cave was first cut around 1250, but was filled in by a rockfall around 1400. It was cleared and reopened as a tannery in 1500, with circular pits cut to hold barrels. A second cave was also cut with rectangular clay-lined vats. The small size of the vats in these caves indicates that they were probably used for sheep or goat skins, rather than cowhide. The caves opened to the River Leen, where the tanners washed their skins in the town's drinking water.

Basement walls visible inside City of Caves are all that remains of the buildings on Drury Hill, which was once a wealthy neighbourhood in the medieval city. By the 19th century, the whole area had degenerated into one of the worst slums in Britain. Poor families ate, slept and lived in single room basements. The overcrowded conditions and poor sanitation made it a breeding ground for cholera, tuberculosis and smallpox.

When WWII arrived, some of the caves here were joined together to form one of the 86 public air raid shelters cut into the sandstone beneath the city. A particularly severe bombing raid on 8th May 1941 has been recreated as part of the tour. Holes were also dug here, to supply the sand needed to fill the sandbags that helped to protect the city.

Caves are still being rediscovered under Nottingham's streets. As I wrote this, in December 2021, a new wine bar was opening in one of the latest discoveries.

Angelo Trivigno, made the discovery while investigating a damp patch in the Flying Horse Walk (South Parade - St Peter's Gate, Nottingham, NG1 2HN) fashion boutique run by his wife and daughter.

Angelo had no blueprint to give an indication about the scale of his 11th century medieval cellar, so he embarked on a massive risk in starting to excavate.

They removed 660 tonnes of rubble by hand, uncovering a 120 metre warren of cellars and caves, which have been transformed into a champagne bar.

The renovation came with restrictions, only allowing the removal of rubble and levelling of the floor. The walls and ceilings could not be touched.

The Salutation Inn (Hounds Gate, Nottingham, NG1 7AA)
A 13th century alehouse called The Archangel Gabriel Salutes the Virgin Mary, is thought to have been built on this site in 1240. So it could have been frequented by Roger Godberd, a candidate for being Robin Hood, as he was outlawed in 1265. In 1267, Godberd settled in Sherwood Forest, defying the authorities for four years until his capture in 1272. As with any interpretation of the legend, there are discrepancies. In this case, it is the fact that Richard the Lionheart, who is inextricably linked with Robin Hood, died in 1199, 41 years before the first Salutation alehouse was built.

The Inn's name refers to the salutation "Ave Maria, plene gratia," given by the Archangel Gabriel to the Virgin Mary. It was a name often given to inns belonging to religious houses, which might mean the Inn was built as a guest-house for the Carmelite or Franciscan friaries of Nottingham. I did wonder if I could link Friar Tuck to the Salutation, but the hermitage at Fountaindale, which we visited earlier on our journey, was founded by the Augustinian order, and Fountains Abbey (Yorkshire's claim to Friar Tuck) was Cistercian.

The current building, on the corner of Hounds Gate and Saint Nicholas Street (formerly Jew Lane), dates from the 15th century, so its customers may have toasted Henry V's victory at Agincourt. It is typical of the mediaeval houses and shops used by wealthier people living in England during the Wars of the Roses.

At several points on our journey, we have crossed paths with Tony Robinson's *Time Team* TV show. The Salutation featured in their spin-off series, *History Hunters*, who confirmed the building had stood since at least 1415, and was in use as a pub by at least 1725. The *History Hunters* concluded that the Bell Inn was the oldest pub in Nottingham, but the Salutation was its oldest building.

Many of Nottingham's historic buildings had cellars excavated from the city's soft sandstone bedrock. Being Nottingham's oldest building, it is no surprise that there are caves underneath which pre-date the building itself. I visited the Salutation's caves on one of the many Ghost Walks you can take through Nottingham. The History Hunters found that these caves were once used as a brewing house, suppling ale to the Inn above.

The Salutation Inn

The Royal Children Public House (Castle Gate, Nottingham, NG1 7AT)
The Royal Children pub, on Castle Gate, gets its curious name from James II's grandchildren. In 1688, when her father's grip on the throne was slipping, Princess Anne fled from James' court and sought refuge in Nottingham Castle.

Local tradition says that Anne's children were accommodated at the Inn, and played with the innkeeper's children. Local historians dispute this, since the Princess had no surviving children in 1688, but the Inn sign perpetuates the story by showing two well-dressed royal children, together with a more ordinarily dressed girl.

The pub sign does have an interesting, and probably more genuine, history – a history linking Nottingham with Whitby, which was an earlier stop on our **500RH**.

A few hundred years ago, whale oil was part of everyday life, and the whale fisheries of Whitby and other northeast ports were very prosperous. Whaling skippers distributed parts of the skeletons as advertisements. In the case of the Royal Children, a whale's shoulder-blade was presented, which subsequently became the Inn's sign.

The whalebone sign simply displayed the Inn's name. When the Inn was rebuilt, the whalebone was moved inside to a position above the bar, and the pictorial sign hung outside.

A plaque outside the pub tells us that this might be the only Inn sign of its kind in existence, and marks Nottingham's place in the technological advancements of the time. Shortly after the reign of James II, whale oil began to take the place of candles, and this Inn is said to have been one of the first to use oil lamps. The Innkeeper was also a retailer of whale oil to the people of Nottingham.

Royal Standard Place (Nottingham, NG1 6FS)
A short walk up Castle Road and Standard Hill brings you to Royal Standard Place. Other than an inscribed stone in the centre of the road and a modern flagpole, there is actually very little to commemorate where King Charles I raised his

Royal Standard on 22nd August 1642. This act was effectively the start of the English Civil War, where The Cavaliers, led by the King and the Parliamentarian Roundheads, led by Oliver Cromwell, fought a bitter conflict, lasting nine years.

Newark's Civil War Museum featured in one of the first stages of our journey, so a walk up Standard Hill on our final day seems a fitting way to round off an important part of our history.

Standard Hill and Royal Standard Place

The Robin Hood 500: 500RH
Just the Directions

This section has the same route description as the main body of the book, but without the visitors' notes and descriptions.

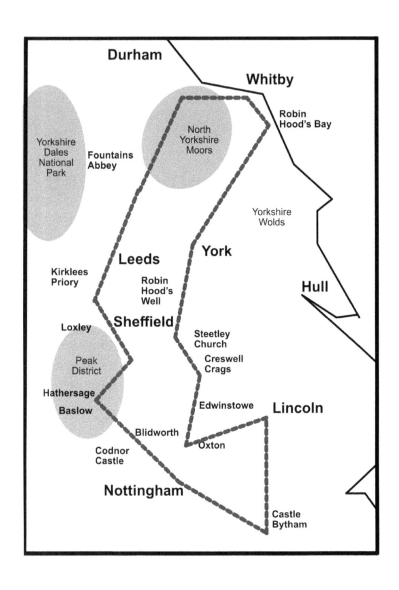

Part One
South Nottinghamshire – Leicestershire & Lincoln
106 Miles · 3 Hours travelling
Travelling time does not include time spent exploring the attractions en-route

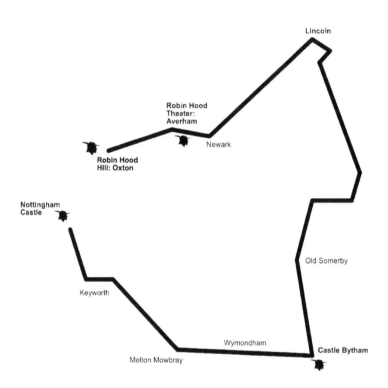

Nottingham Castle to Robin Hood Hill: Oxton

Nottingham to Castle Bytham: 36 miles – 1 hour

- Leaving Nottingham to the south is much like leaving any city. Once out of the historic centre, all there is to see is modern-day industrial and retail sprawl. Luckily, it is a fairly short ride along the A52 Trunk Road, before you turn south on the A606 into more rural Nottinghamshire.

- The first place of interest along the A606, is Keyworth.

- Back on the A606 we are into agricultural country, riding through some of the best scenery South Nottinghamshire and North Leicestershire has to offer.

- Continue on A606 to Melton Mowbray

- We leave Melton Mowbray, initially on the busy A607 towards Grantham, branching off very soon onto the much quieter B676 Saxby Road.

- Just before the village of Saxby, take a right turn onto the unclassified Melton Road, towards Wymondham.

- Drive through Wymondham.

- Another staggered crossroads takes you past the village of South Witham, before passing under the A1 and reaching our Robin Hood destination of Castle Bytham.

Castle Bytham to Lincoln: 40 miles - 1 hour

The next leg of our journey turns north towards Lincoln. Setting a satnav to Lincoln will plot a less interesting route, avoiding several pretty villages. If, like me, you are not technical enough to program a bespoke route, I recommend setting it first to Old Somerby (postcode NG33 4AB).

- There is a choice of equally scenic routes from the Castle Bytham.

- Turning right, the satnav will route you through Little Bytham.

- Turning left will take you back to the village centre, then north on A151 Water Lane.

- Then the B1176 takes us through Bitchfield, which is actually little more than two hamlets.

- The next village is Boothby Pagnal.

- We are now at Old Somerby, about three miles south of Grantham, where I stopped to reset my satnav for RAF Waddington (giving an indication of the area we are about to enter).

- From Old Somerby, we take the dead straight B6403 High Dyke, through Ancaster.

- Pass RAF Barkston Heath.

- The old Roman road joins the A17 at the hamlet of Byard's Leap.

- Facing you, on the other side of the A17, is the second of our RAF bases. This time it is the Air Force's Staff College at Cranwell.

- At this point, there is an option for anyone not wishing to visit Lincoln; by remaining on the A17, you join the A47 on its way to Newark.

- For those heading for Lincoln, we turn left for a brief spell along the A17, before turning right and driving north along the A607 towards RAF Waddington.

- Another four miles brings us into the centre of Lincoln and another stop on our Robin Hood journey.

Lincoln to Oxton: 30 miles - 1 hour

- I took the busy A46 Trunk Road away from Lincoln, towards Newark and back into Nottinghamshire.

- We leave Newark on the A617 Kelham Road, signposted for Mansfield, although we turn off before reaching there.

- Soon after passing through Kelham, you will see a brown tourist sign, pointing to the Robin Hood Theatre at Averham.

- Back on the A617, we very soon turn left onto A612, towards Southwell.

- Our first stop on the way to Southwell is at Upton.

- After leaving Upton, we pass through Eastthorpe and Westthorpe, before reaching the market town of Southwell.

- We leave Southwell on the B6386 Oxton Road.

- Along the way, we pass Brackenhurst Agricultural College (Brackenhurst Lane, Southwell, NG25 0QF).

- Finally, just before reaching the roundabout with the busy A6097, we turn right into Oxton Village (post-code NG25 0SS).

- Robin Hood Hill can be reached on foot, along a public footpath which starts near Oxton's Old Green Dragon Pub (Blind Lane, Oxton, NG25 0SS).

Part Two
Nottinghamshire
92 Miles - 3 Hours 10 Minutes travelling
Travelling time does not include time spent exploring the
attractions en-route

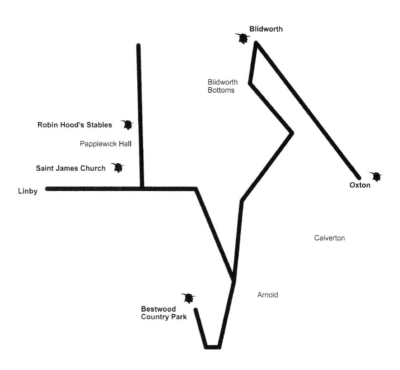

Oxton to Papplewick

Oxton to Blidworth: 4 miles - 10 minutes

- Follow Forest Road north out of Oxton. Looking up to our right, we get a view onto the tree-lined top of Robin Hood Hill.

- We meet and cross the busy Oxton By-Pass into Oaks Lane, passing Oakmere Golf Course (postcode NG25 0RH).

- Then we cross the busy A614 into Haywood Oaks, driving through the woods from which the lane takes its name.

- After about a mile of forest and farmland, we reach houses at the edge of Blidworth.

- Turn left onto Dale Lane, then left again at the petrol station, uphill on Main Street.

- Saint Mary of the Purification & Saint Lawrence Church (Main Street, Blidworth, NG21 0QX) is on your left, opposite the junction with Ricket Lane. This church reputedly has Will Scarlet's grave.

Blidworth to Bestwood Country Park: 9 miles - 20 minutes

- Backtrack slightly along Main Street until you reach the Black Bull pub (Main St, Blidworth, NG21 0QH), and turn right, downhill, onto Field Lane and back into open countryside.

- At the T junction at the bottom of the hill, turn left onto Blidworth Lane, entering the hamlet of Blidworth Bottoms, and passing the Fox & Hounds pub on your left (Calverton Rd, Blidworth Bottoms, NG21 0NW).

- Calverton Road becomes Blidworth Lane, running parallel to Haywood Oaks, along which we earlier entered Blidworth.

- Meeting the busy A614 Old Rufford Road, we turn right, crossing a roundabout after which the A614 becomes Ollerton Road.

- At the next roundabout, we turn left on A60 Mansfield Road, towards Nottingham. These are the suburbs of Nottingham, and our route becomes more urban.

- We now move on to Bestwood Lodge and Bestwood Country Park (Bestwood Lodge Drive, Arnold, Nottingham, NG5 8HT).

- At a very busy traffic light controlled junction, turn right onto B6004 Oxclose Lane.

- Then, take the first turn right onto Queens Bower Road. You may think you are going wrong as you drive into a Council Estate, but Bestwood Country Park is signposted from here.

- Take your first turning right onto Bestwood Lodge Drive. After a short distance, houses continue on your left, but farmland opens up on your right.

- After driving through an avenue of trees, the houses continue on Woodchurch Road to your left, and Bestwood Lodge Drive turns off to the right, becoming more rural. Bestwood Lodge Hotel is signposted at this junction.

- High vehicles should park on the unmade layby at this junction, as the official car park has a height restriction.

- Approximately 100 metres from the junction, a car park and toilets are on your right (car-park postcode NG5 8NQ).

- A forest footpath opposite the toilet block leads first into the gardens of Bestwood Lodge, then into the Country Park. Cyclists should continue up the tarmac drive.

Bestwood Country Park to Papplewick: 7 miles - 20 minutes

- Retrace your route back through the suburbs of Nottingham to the A60 / A614 roundabout.

- This time, take the A60 Mansfield Road northwards, towards Mansfield and returning into rural scenery.

- Soon after passing Police Headquarters, turn left on B6011 Forest Lane, signposted for Papplewick Village.

- We are back into farmland and on our way to another hot-spot of Robin Hood locations.

- Opposite the 300 year old Griffin's Head Pub (postcode NG15 8EN), turn onto Main Street.

- After 200 metres, Main Street takes a sharp right, then left turn, becoming B683 Blidworth Waye.

- Taking a left turn at this point, is a lane leading to Saint James' Church (postcode NG15 8FE). The lane is a private road but is designated as a Public Footpath and reaches the church in about 200 metres. Legend says that Robin Hood's minstrel Alan a Dale was married by Robin in this church.

- Robin Hood's Stables is a well-hidden cave, set into the sandstone near Papplewick Hall. The cave is within a small wooded hillside, called The Firs. The edge of the wood can be followed by walking along Hall Lane, from Top Farm (which forms part of the Robin Hood Way).

King's
Clipstone

Edwinstowe

King John's
Palace

Mansfield

Fountaindale

Papplewick
Hall

Papplewick Hall to Edwinstowe

Papplewick to Thieves Wood & Fountaindale: 4 miles - 7 minutes

- Continue uphill from Papplewick Hall on Blidworth Waye, until you reach the T junction with A60 (at a point where it changes from Mansfield Road to Nottingham Road).

- Turn left towards Mansfield, passing the main vehicle entrance to Newstead Abbey on your left.

- The A60 Nottingham Road drops downhill through farmland, before climbing again between Thieves Wood on your left and Harlow Wood (postcode NG18 4TJ) on your right.

- Bessie Sheppard's Stone is a good setting off point into Harlow Wood, sitting almost at the bottom of the hill, where the Robin Hood Way crosses the A60.

- Fountain Dale is an area associated with Friar Tuck. It is a 10 minute walk along the Robin Hood Way from Bessie Sheppard's Stone.

Thieves Wood & Fountaindale to Old Clipstone: 8 miles - 16 minutes

- After walking back to the road, and our vehicles, we continue on the A60 Nottingham Road, towards Mansfield.

We turn east before reaching Mansfield, but the area around Kings' Mill Reservoir is associated with Much the miller's son, through the *Ballad of the King and the Miller of Mansfield.*

- At the outskirts of Mansfield, turn right at busy traffic light junction, onto A617. This is a newly built by-pass road.

- At the first roundabout on the A617 by-pass road, turn left on A6117 Adamsway, towards Forest Town.

- The A6117 crosses the A617 at a busy traffic light junction, then continues downhill as Oak Tree Lane.

- At the traffic light controlled crossroads in Forest Town, turn right on B6030 Clipstone Road West, towards Clipstone.

A lane to your right in Clipstone takes you to Vicar Water.

- We return up the Vicar Water access lane, to re-join the B6030, now named Mansfield Road, turning right towards Kings Clipstone (postcode NG21 9BT).

- As we drive down a spiralling set of bends known as The Rat Hole, we reach a much smaller village sharing the name Clipstone.

- Soon after the Rat Hole bends, we see the Dog & Duck pub on our right.

King John's Palace (postcode NG21 9BT), is on private land, but can be seen from the Bridleway between Vicar Water and the Dog & Duck pub.

King's Clipstone to Edwinstowe: 3 miles ∕ 5 minutes

- Continue on B6030 through a rural area, then after a short distance turn left onto Mill Lane, signposted Edwinstowe.

- You will see Sherwood Pines Forest Parks (postcode NG21 9JL) on your right, which is worthy of a visit.

Sherwood Pines has many walking and cycling trails, a café and visitors centre, and accommodation in the form of forest lodges.

- Mill Lane ends at a T junction in Edwinstowe, which is another hot spot of Robin Hood locations.

- Turn left and negotiate the one way system, to reach the Sherwood Forest Visitors' Centre car park (postcode NG21 9JZ).

Saint Mary's Church (Church Street, Edwinstowe, NG21 9QA) stands against Barnsdale's claim to have hosted Robin and Marian's wedding. The High Street has a statue in their honour.

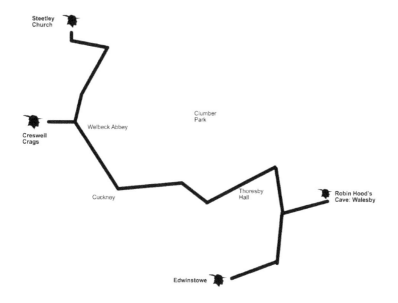

Steetley
Church

Creswell
Crags

Welbeck Abbey

Clumber
Park

Cuckney

Thoresby
Hall

Robin Hood's
Cave: Walesby

Edwinstowe

Edwinstowe to Steetley Church

Edwinstowe to Walesby: 5 miles - 10 minutes

- Leave Edwinstowe on B6075 Ollerton Road. At the busy five-way roundabout, take A614 Blyth Rd (second exit).

- After about two miles, opposite one of the gates to Clumber Park, turn right onto Whitewater Lane, towards Walesby.

- Just after the hump-back bridge, there are several rough parking areas outside Walesby Forest Scout Camp (postcode NG22 9NG).

- At a point where Whitewater Lane turns a sharp right, park on the rough layby.

Robin Hood's Cave (off Whitewater Lane, Walesby, NG22 9NG), is on a Public Bridleway, which is part of the Robin Hood Way. The Bridleway heads north from the layby. About 500 metres along this Bridleway, the rock forms a low cliff over the bank of the river Maun. This is Robin Hood's Cave, which is said to have sheltered Robin Hood.

Walesby to Creswell: 12 miles - 20 minutes

- Retrace your route along Whitewater Lane and turn right onto A614.

- After passing Clumber Park, we turn left onto Netherfield Lane, passing Thoresby Hall (postcode NG22 9WH) on our left.

- At the end of Netherfield Lane, we reach a pair of roundabouts, turning left at the first, then right at the second.

- Follow A616 Budby Road into the pretty village of Cuckney (postcode NG20 9NQ) which has lots of history.

The village of Church Warsop (postcode NG20 0SF) is a short detour to your left. Legend says that the people of Church Warsop never locked the doors of their homes, because Robin Hood was always welcome.

- For those of us not visiting Church Warsop, turn right onto A60, towards Worksop.

- Before long, we reach the Dukeries Garden Centre (postcode S80 3LT), set around the former Welbeck Abbey.

- Soon after passing Welbeck Garden Centre, turn left on B6042 Hennymoor Lane.

- At a T junction turn right on Craggs Rd, to see the Creswell Crags Visitors Centre car park on your left (postcode S80 3LH).

Creswell Crags was reputedly frequented by Robin Hood, and one of the caves bears his name.

Creswell to Steetley Church: 3 miles - 9 minutes

- Leave Creswell Crags, turning right from the car park, and retrace your route back to the A60.

- Turn left onto A60 towards Worksop.

- At an oddly shaped roundabout, turn left onto A619.

- After approximately one mile, Steetley Lane is on your right, signposted Shireoaks and Thorpe.

Beware, parking and turning for larger vehicles will be difficult after taking this turn. We are now less than 500 metres from the church, so parking a motor-home and walking in, is not an onerous task.

- After about 500m, turn left into Scratta Lane, then almost immediately left into the church's unmade car park (postcode S80 3DZ).

All Saints' Chapel Steetley (3 Field View, Steetley, Worksop, S80 3DZ) was referred to in Sir Waiter Scott's *Ivanhoe* as Copmanhurst. Legend says the Church Clerk was Friar Tuck, who entertained the Black Prince (King Richard I) there, when the church was just 50 years old.

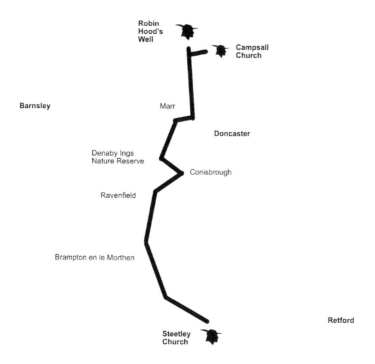

Robin
Hood's
Well

Campsall
Church

Barnsley

Marr

Doncaster

Denaby Ings
Nature Reserve

Conisbrough

Ravenfield

Brampton en le Morthen

Retford

Steetley
Church

Steetley Church to Robin Hood's Well: Skellbrook

Steetley Church to Skellbrook / Barnsdale: 37 miles - 1 hour

This is a long section, which could be driven along major roads to reach Robin Hood's Well quite quickly. The most straightforward route covers the distance in 35 minutes. However, you would miss out on many nice roads and villages along my recommended route. By necessity, we skirt the edges of some industrial towns along the way, but we are through them quickly and back into rural scenery and along lightly used roads. So, for those coming with me on the scenic route, get out your map, or program your sat-nav.

- Retrace your route from Steetley to the A619, turning left towards Worksop. Then, join the A60 Mansfield Road towards Worksop.

- At a large roundabout, take the second exit, onto A57.

- Stay on the A57, going straight through the next three roundabouts.

- The A57 begins as a dual carriageway, but quickly becomes a more rural single carriageway.

- At the fourth roundabout, with the Red Lion pub (postcode S26 1DJ) on your left, turn right, taking the fourth exit for B6463 Todwick Road.

- After 500 metres on Todwick Road, turn left onto the delightfully named Pocket Handkerchief Lane (postcode S26 1HD).

- Reaching a T junction with Common Road, turn left.

- The road name soon changes to Long Road then once again becomes Common Lane as we enter the village of Brampton-en-le-Morthen (postcode S66 9AT).

- Our short journey through Brampton-en-le-Morthen takes an inverted S shape, and we leave the village on Brampton Road.

- Reaching a roundabout, with a hotel (postcode S66 9JA) on your left, take the first exit onto B6060 Morthen Road and cross over M18.

- Continue on B6060 Morthen Road as it bends to the right and passes through a modern, but pleasant, residential area into Wickersley (postcode S66 1JL).

- At the roundabout in Wickersley, take the fourth exit, onto A631 Bawtry Road.

- This is an area where historic villages have grown to join with each other as suburbs of nearby conurbations, and Wickersley blends seamlessly into Bramley.

- We turn left onto Church Lane, immediately before Bramley Park (postcode S66 2RU) and head towards open countryside.

- At the first roundabout, we take the first exit, onto B6093 Main Street, entering Ravenfield (postcode S65 4LZ), another of Rotherham's villages turned suburb.

- At the next roundabout, take the second exit, turning right, remaining on the B6093 Moor Lane.

- As the name suggests, we are about to get a view of moorland.

- Houses remain to our left, but the view to our right opens up nicely.

- This is quite a long section, but is easy to navigate since Moor Lane ends at a T junction with A630.

- At the T junction, turn right onto A630 Doncaster Road.

- Immediately before the Hilltop pub (postcode DN12 2AY), turn left onto Old Road.

- Then after about 500m, at a school's green railings (postcode DN12 3LR), turn left onto Hill Top Road.

- We are still navigating Rotherham's suburbs as we reach a roundabout in the former village of Conisbrough. On the roundabout is an Asda supermarket (postcode DN12 4TJ).

- At the roundabout, take the first exit, turning left onto A6023 Doncaster Road.

- The River Don has split into two channels here and we cross over both of them.

- At traffic lights, soon after the second river crossing, turn right onto Pastures Road and back into the countryside.

- Just like the Don, the River Dearne has also split into two channels, which we cross, passing through the Denaby Ings Nature Reserve (postcode S64 0JJ).

- After the second crossing of the River Dearne, turn left onto Melton Mill Lane (postcode DN5 7TF).

- At the end of Melton Mill Lane, we navigate two junctions close together, both of which are formed around triangles of grass.

- At the first of these junctions, turn left onto Doncaster Road.

- Then, after 100m, turn right at a similar junction, onto Hangman Stone Road (postcode DN5 7EE).

- This is a long rural section, and the road name changes to Blacksmith's Lane as we drive through a wind farm.

- Navigating off Blacksmith's Lane is easy, as it ends in a T junction with A635 Barnsley Road (postcode DN5 7AX).

- Turn right onto A635 Barnsley Road, then after 100m turn left onto Church Lane.

- At a rather complicated five-way junction, take the one-o-clock option, onto Red House Lane, which runs parallel with A1M.

- We are now almost opposite Robin Hood's Well, but on the wrong side of the A1, so our next section loops us onto the southbound A1.

- Turn left onto A638 Doncaster Road, then at roundabout, turn right onto A6201 Wrangbrook Lane. This brings us to Barnsdale Bar roundabout (postcode WF8 3JF).

We are now in an area of South Yorkshire known as Barnsdale. The region has for a long time contested Sherwood Forest with an alternative claim to Robin Hood. The most modern manifestation of this claim was in naming Doncaster's airport as Robin Hood Airport. (First Ave, Doncaster DN9 3RH)

- From Barnsdale Bar roundabout, we can take a 10 minute detour to a church with an alternative claim to Robin & Marion's wedding venue.

- Cross straight on from the roundabout, into Wood-field Road.

- At the T junction in Campsall village, turn left, then right onto High Street, which takes us straight to Saint Mary Magdalene Church (postcode DN6 9LH).

Saint Mary Magdalene Church, at Campsall (High St, Campsall, Doncaster, DN6 9LH)
Locals claim that Robin Hood married Maid Marian at this church.

- After visiting the church at Campsall, we retrace our route back to Barnsdale Bar roundabout (postcode WF8 3JF), where we take the A1 south.

- Our destination is a minor road on our left, called Robin Hood's Well. (Skelbrooke, DN6 8LS). NB: the road has a street-sign calling it Robin Hood's Well, but Google Maps shows it as Great North Road.

- This village of Skelbrook was bisected by the A1, leaving Robin Hood's Well as little more than a lay-by. There is a light industrial works and a couple of houses. The remainder of the road stub is hidden be-hind a screen of trees, making a useful camper-van stop.

Part Three
North Yorkshire Coast & Moors
75 Miles ⸰ 2 Hours 30 Minutes travelling
Travelling time does not include time spent exploring the
attractions en-route

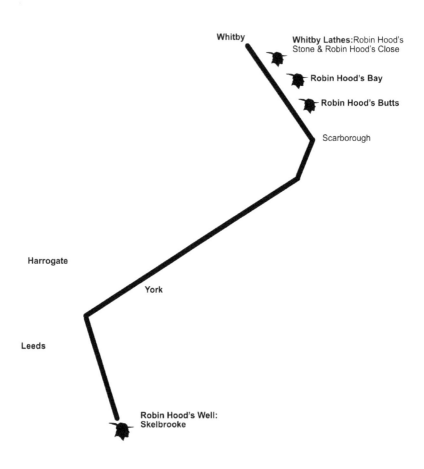

Whitby

Whitby Lathes:Robin Hood's
Stone & Robin Hood's Close

Robin Hood's Bay

Robin Hood's Butts

Scarborough

Harrogate

York

Leeds

Robin Hood's Well:
Skelbrooke

Skelbrooke to Whitby

Barnsdale to Ravenscar: 84 miles - 1 hour 48 minutes

- The most straightforward route allows a stop in York.

- Take the A1 north, then the A64 to York.

- From York take the A64 and A170 towards Scarborough.

I have not described the junctions along this section of the route, as it is straightforward to navigate

- From Scarborough take the A171 north. This appears to be a coastal road on a map, but high ground prevents a view of the sea.

- Pass through the villages of Scalby (postcode YO13 0NW),Burniston (postcode YO13 0HJ) and Cloughton (postcode YO13 0AE).

- Continue on A171 until just after Wayside Farm holiday cottages (postcode YO13 0DX).

- Turn right onto minor road (signposted: Staintondale and Ravenscar) There is also a brown tourist sign: Coastal Centre and Hotel.

- After a short distance, turn right onto Stubbs Lane (signposted Staintondale and Ravenscar). There are brown tourist signs to: Shire Horse Farm, Hotel and Coastal Centre. There is also a blue cycle route sign.

- Stubbs Lane soon changes name to Gainforth Wath Road, then Rudda Road.

- At T-junction turn left onto Bloody Beck Hill (signposted Ravenscar). There are brown tourist signs to: hotel and Coastal Centre. This road appears narrower on Google Maps, but is very similar to the one we have just turned from.

- Bloody Beck Hill crosses Bloody Beck (a stream), then changes name to Scarborough Road.

- We reach a disused windmill, which has been converted to a house (postcode YO13 0ER). This is labelled Beacon Windmill on the OS map.

- The road takes a 90 degree right turn here, changing name to Raven Hall Road.

- Take the narrower straight on option, onto Scarborough Road signposted as a dead end. Ahead of you is a TV mast, where there is car parking.

Note that it is possible to continue downhill on Scarborough Road. But it is steep and single track, with few passing places. I did drive down with my small camper van. There is some parking where a Bridleway splits left, slightly uphill, and the road (Cleveland Way) drops steeply ahead.

The road ends at Stoupe Bank Farm (postcode YO13 0NQ), where there is a turning circle, but no parking available.

Robin Hood's Butts are historic burial mounds, on Brow Moor. There are several walking options to visit them.

Ravenscar to Robin Hood's Bay: 11 miles - 25 minutes

- After leaving Robin Hood's Butts, we re-trace our route back to the A171.

- Turn right onto A171 (signposted Whitby)

- Turn right from A171, on a local road (signposted Fylingthorpe and Robin Hood's Bay) to Robin Hood's Bay.

Robin Hood's Bay to Whitby Laithes: 4 miles - 10 minutes

- After visiting Robin Hood's Bay, return along the same route, to the A171.

- Turn right onto A171 (signposted Whitby).

- Pass through the hamlet of Normanby and the village of Hawsker.

- Opposite a cycle hire centre (postcode YO22 4LB), with railway dining cars, turn right onto Hawsker Lane (signposted P, Abbey Headland, and Whitby Abbey on Brown tourist sign). This road is also a back way into Whitby.

- Pass through a delightful village, with a historic church and an old red brick barn on your right.

- Reach Manor House Farm caravan site (postcode YO22 4JZ).

Footpaths lead from opposite the caravan site, towards Whitby Lathes Farm.

Robin Hood's Stone and Little John's Stone are in fields behind Whitby Lathes Farm.

But there is no parking here, unless you are staying on one of several sites along Hawsker Lane.

Better parking is available a little further along the A171 on Enterprise Way industrial estate.

- To reach Enterprise Way, continue along the A171 until you reach the 30 MPH sign and the boundary sign for Whitby.

- Turn right into Enterprise Way (postcode YO22 4NH). Robin Hood's Stone and Little John's Stone can be reached on foot from here.

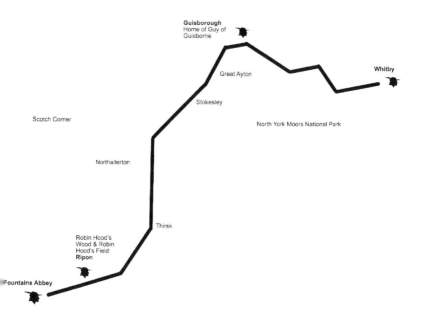

Guisborough
Home of Guy of
Guisborne

Whitby

Great Ayton

Stokesley

Scotch Corner

North York Moors National Park

Northallerton

Thirsk

Robin Hood's
Wood & Robin
Hood's Field:
Ripon

Fountains Abbey

Whitby to Fountains Abbey

Whitby Laithes to Fountains Abbey: 70 miles ⁄ 1 hour 30 minutes

- From Whitby Laithes, continue north on the A171 towards Whitby.

- Leave Whitby on the A171 (signposted Teeside, Guisborough, Pickering and Ruswarp), skirting the northern edge of the North Yorkshire Moors National Park.

- This stretch of the A171 is a stunning road which is easy to navigate. It becomes slightly more built up around Guisborough, but is still very much North Yorkshire

- Continue on A171, passing north of Guisborough, to a roundabout with A173 (postcode TS14 6QS). Guisborough enters the Robin Hood legend as a possible home for Guy of Gisborne.

- After passing around Guisborough, at roundabout (postcode TS14 6QS), take first exit, turning left (south) on A173 (signposted Great Ayton).

- Continue along the A173 to drive through Great Ayton. The Cleveland Hills dominate the view to our left along the whole length of this road.

- At roundabout outside Stokesley (postcode TS9 5NY), take second exit (left), to join A172 southbound (signposted Thirsk).

- Meet A19 turn left / southbound. Be careful not to miss this Y junction, which does not look like a major A road junction.

- Take the left fork onto A19 (signposted Northallerton and Osmotherley on a white local sign before the junction) (Signposted The South A19 Thirsk on a green A road sign at the junction.)

- On the outskirts of Thirsk, the A19 becomes the A168 without a junction.

- The A19 continues off a slip road (signposted A19). Do not take A19.

- We continue on the main carriageway along A168.

- Near the village of Dishforth, the A168 meets the A1M.

- Leave the main carriageway of the A168 at Junction 49 (signposted Ripon), to continue on A168.

- Do not go onto the A1M.

- The A168 now runs parallel with the motorway.

- At roundabout turn right onto B6265 towards Ripon.

- Brown tourist signs for Fountains Abbey begin here.

- Follow brown tourist signs for Fountains Abbey through Ripon, alongside the Ripon Canal.

- Continue along B6265, following Fountains Abbey signs, until just after Ripon Cathedral.

- To visit Robin Hood Wood and Robinhood Field, leave the B6265 turning left onto a weight restricted road, Low Skellgate.

- Cross the River Skell on a stone bridge.

- Low Skellgate becomes A61 Harrogate Road.

On your right, at the corner of Borrage Green Lane, is a children's' park (Harrogate Road Playground, HG4 1SW). This is all that remains of the once large Borrage Green area, of which Robin Hood Wood and Robinhood Field once formed a part.

It is possible to start a walk here, but there is very limited parking. A better place to start is the car park for Hell Wath Nature reserve.

- Continue past the park, along Harrogate Road, taking your third right, into Whitcliffe Lane, which is a residential estate.

- Whitcliffe Lane is a long road. On a map, it appears to go straight on, with Hell Wath Lane turning to the right. On the ground, the opposite is true. Whitcliffe Lane narrows and is marked "Unsuitable for motors" Hell Wath Lane is the natural continuation.

- After a short distance you will see car parking areas at the junction with Hell Wath Grove (postcode HG4 2JT).

From Hell Wath, we continue our journey to Fountains Abbey.

- Retrace your route along Whitcliffe Lane, and back through Ripon to re-join the B6265.

- Turn left onto the B6265 Somerset Row.

- We are once again following brown tourist signs for Fountains Abbey. All subsequent junctions are well signposted.

- Turn left onto minor road to Fountains Abbey.

- Follow National Trust signs for the main car park and Visitors' Centre (postcode HG4 3DY).

Part Four
South Yorkshire
47 Miles ⁄ 2 Hours travelling
Travelling time does not include time spent exploring the
attractions en-route

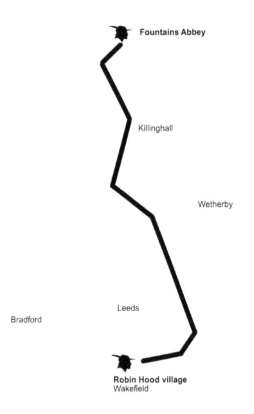

Fountains Abbey

Killinghall

York

Wetherby

Leeds

Bradford

Robin Hood village
Wakefield

Fountains Abbey to Robin Hood (Wakefield)

Fountains Abbey to Robin Hood Village (Wakefield):
35 miles - 1 hour 20 minutes

- Exit Fountains Abbey via the West Gate (postcode HG4 3EA), not the main entrance by which you arrived. National Trust signposts direct you around the estate's network of roundabouts.

- This first section of our journey is winding and rural. The roads are a little narrow, but do not present any difficulties.

- At the estate's West Gate entrance, turn right (south) onto Fountains Lane.

- After crossing a small river, reach a Y junction, with the road signs set on a triangle of grass.

- Take the left fork (signposted Markington and Harrogate)

- Continue along same road as it changes name many times to: How Hill Road, and Watergate Road.

- At T junction with Fountains Abbey Road, turn left (signposted Ripley, Knaresborough and Harrogate).

- Continue along same road as it changes name many times to: Oakwood Park, High Kettlespring Farm, Fountains Road, Scarah Bank, and finally Fountains Road again.

- At T junction with B6165, turn left (signposted Ripley, Knaresborough and Harrogate). Ripley Castle is also signposted from here on a brown tourist sign.

- Follow B6165 to roundabout junction with A61 Ripon Road.

- Take second exit from the roundabout onto A61 (signposted Knaresborough and Harrogate).

- At next roundabout, continue on A61 Ripon Road (signposted Harrogate).

- Cross the River Nidd, continuing on A61 Ripon Road.

- In the village of Killinghall, just after a pelican crossing and the Greyhound Inn (postcode HG3 2DG), turn right onto B6161 Otley Road (signposted Otley).

- At roundabout with A59 (Old Spring Well Pub - postcode HG3 2AP), continue straight on, following B6161 as name changes to Oaker Bank (signposted Otley).

- At Jubilee Roundabout, continue straight on, following B6161 Oaker Bank (signposted Beckwithshaw, Leathley and Otley).

We are now starting to see slightly more urban development, with military housing to the right, and the outskirts of Harrogate to the left.

A short detour into Harrogate is possible from here.

- Continue to follow B6161 as name changes to Pot Bank.

- At the beginning of Beckwithshaw village (postcode HG3 1QP), go straight on (second exit) at a roundabout, onto Otley Road (signposted Harrogate and Knaresborough).

- In Beckwithshaw turn left onto Shaw Lane (signposted North Rigton).

- We return to very rural scenery.

- Continue along same road (through crossroads with your priority) as name changes to High Moor Road.

- The road briefly changes name to Rigton Hill, as you enter the village of North Rigton, just before the next turning.

- At Square and Compass pub in North Rigton (postcode Leeds LS17 0DJ), turn left at mini-roundabout, onto Hall Green Lane (signposted Harrogate and Harewood).

- Cross the busy cross-roads junction with A658, onto Dunkeswick Lane. (Heading towards a railway level crossing).

- At T junction turn right onto A61 Harrogate Road (signposted Leeds).

- Cross the River Wharf on a historic stone bridge.

- Continue on A61 Harrogate Road (signposted Leeds).

- Opposite Lofthouse Lodge B&B (postcode LS17 9LU), turn left onto Wike Lane, which changes name to Forge Lane (signposted Wike).

- NB: this is a narrow road, along which inconsiderate parking can cause difficulties in passing.

- In Wike village, turn left onto Backstone Gill (signposted East Keswick).

- This is an unusual, triangular shaped junction, which in effect, operates as a T junction.

- After 100m, at Moor Allerton Golf Club (postcode LS17 9NH), turn left onto Coal Road (signposted Scarcroft).

- Continue through crossroads (with your priority) onto Brandon Lane.

- Bay Horse Lane merges from your left. Bear right as road name changes to Bay Horse Lane.

- Pass through crossroads (with your priority) as road name changes back to Coal Road.

- At T junction with A58, turn right onto A58 Wellington Hill, which becomes Weatherby Road.

- At roundabout, turn left onto A6120 (signposted Ring Road, M1, M62 and A1M).

- We are now entering the suburbs of Leeds, and the scenery changes accordingly.

- Continue on A6120 Ring Road Seacroft, straight across four roundabouts.

- This is an outer city ring road, but it is not as busy as some I have driven on.

- At the fifth roundabout, turn right onto Stile Hill Way (signposted Oulton, Newson Green and Colton). (If you reach the M1 roundabout, you have gone too far).

- This is a busy and complicated, traffic light controlled roundabout, with a retail park on your right (Colton Retail Park, Leeds, LS15 9JA).

- At roundabout, go straight on, onto Bullerthorpe Lane.

- This is a long stretch of road, which crosses over the M1.

- We are still in the suburbs of Leeds, but this road is more rural than the ones we have just travelled along.

- At T junction with A642 (Bridge Farm Hotel, postcode LS26 8PZ), turn right onto A642 Aberford Road.

- Cross the River Aire and the Aire & Calder Navigation, continuing on A642.

- A642 Aberford Road briefly changes name to Calverley Road, before reaching a roundabout.

- At roundabout, go straight over, onto A654 Rothwell Lane, passing Oulton Hall Golf Club (postcode LS26 8HN) (signposted Rothwell and Oulton Hall).

- Continue on A654 Aberford Road as it changes name to Oulton Lane, then Carlton Lane, then Leadwell Lane.

- The Village of Robin Hood is located off the A654, just before you cross the junction with Leeds Road, where the A654 becomes Thorpe Lower Lane. The Halfway House Public House is a good Sat Nav setting (postcode WF3 3AB).

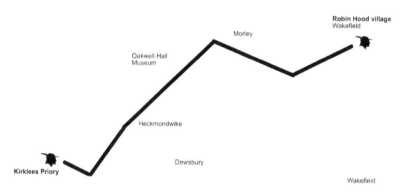

Bradford

Robin Hood village
Wakefield

Morley

Oakwell Hall
Museum

Heckmondwike

Dewsbury

Kirklees Priory

Wakefield

Robin Hood Village (Wakefield) To Kirklees Priory

Robin Hood Village (Wakefield) To Kirklees Priory: 16 miles – 40 minutes

After visiting the village of Robin Hood, we resume our journey to Kirklees Priory.

- Turn left out of the Halfway House car park and go straight through traffic light crossroads, onto A654 Thorpe Lane.

Note: for the Coach House pub and Robin Hood FC, you should turn right at this set of traffic lights, onto A61 Leeds Road / Wakefield Road. (Postcode LS26 0SF)

- Pass under the M1 motorway.

- At T junction turn right onto A654 Middleton Lane (There is no directional signpost, but there is a street sign for Middleton Lane). This is the village of Thorpe on the Hill (postcode WF3 3BX).

- Cross over M62 motorway.

- Soon after crossing motorway reach a traffic light controlled T-junction.

- Turn right onto A650 (signposted M62 Bradford and Dewsbury).

This T-junction marks the start of more urbanisation with council housing ahead of us.

- Reach the large and complicated Tingley Interchange roundabout (postcode WF3 1JX).

- We are taking the A650 Bradford Road, which is the second exit (signposted Bradford and Morley).

- Soon after Tingley interchange Bradford Road changes name to Tingley Common.

- Reach a complicated traffic light junction, which operates almost like a roundabout.

- We are continuing straight on, along the A650 Britannia Road. This would be the second exit if it was a roundabout (signposted Bradford).

The area around Britannia Road is quite built-up, but there is still evidence of industrial revolution stone buildings.

- A650 Britannia Road changes name to Bruntcliffe Road, near another Halfway House pub (postcode LS27 0BJ). This is the Leeds suburb of Morley.

- Continue along Bruntcliffe Road, to a traffic light controlled cross-roads, just before a large public house (postcode LS27 0LY).

- Turn left at this junction onto A643 Howden Clough Road (signposted Birstall).

We leave the urban area and the view opens ahead of us.

- Cross over the M62.

- A643 Howden Clough Road changes name to Leeds Road.

After passing over the motorway we descend on a hilly road through woods, and back into countryside.

At the bottom of the hill, we enter the District of Kirklees, and are nearing our destination of Kirklees Priory.

Be careful of speed cameras in Howden Clough village.

- Reach a traffic light controlled crossroads.

- Turn left onto A62 Huddersfield Road (signposted Huddersfield). There is also a brown tourist sign for Oakwell Hall Museum.

The A62 looks a major route on the map but in fact goes through some lovely rural scenery. We follow this road all the way to our destination at The Three Nuns.

- Take care as you approach The Three Nuns, as it is a complicated junction.

- There is a petrol station on the left.

- The Three Nuns car park entrance is in the middle of the junction, to your right.

- END POINT: Three Nuns Inn, Leeds Road, Dews-bury, WF14 0BY

Kirklees Priory & Robin Hood's Grave

The remains of Kirklees Priory & Robin Hood's Grave are on private land, within the Kirklees Estate.

There is a vast network of footpaths surrounding the Kirklees Estate, which can be turned into circular walks.

The best option for getting close is to use the public footpath on the east of the estate. This footpath starts just east of the Three Nuns and runs north towards the village of Hartshead, where it links to a network of paths, including The Bronte Way, The Kirklees Way, The Spen Way Heritage Trail, The Luddite Trail and The Brighouse Boundary Walk.

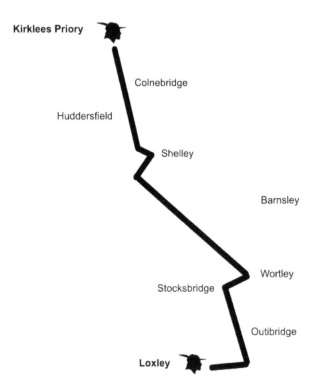

Bradford

Kirklees Priory

Colnebridge

Huddersfield

Shelley

Barnsley

Wortley

Stocksbridge

Outibridge

Loxley

Kirklees Priory to Loxley

Kirklees Priory to Loxley: 30 miles - 1 hour

- Leaving the Three Nuns car park and getting onto the A62 is not straightforward, since the exit falls inside a busy traffic light controlled junction.

- Ideally, we would turn right from the car park, but this is not possible.

- Turn left out of the car park onto A62 Leeds Road (travelling in the opposite direction to our route), then find a safe way of returning to the junction.

- A good satnav setting from here is the superstore, on Penistone Road, Waterloo (postcode HD5 8QW). There is a petrol station here and the onward navigation is straightforward.

- Pass the Three Nuns on your right, continuing straight on to the traffic island.

- Take first exit onto A62 Cooper Bridge Road, which soon becomes Leeds Road.

- At traffic lights (postcode HD5 0RP), turn left on B6118 Colne Bridge Road.

- Go straight across a traffic island at an industrial estate, continuing on B6118 Colne Bridge Road.

- Just after crossing a stone built road bridge, turn right onto Dalton Bank Road (signposted Dalton).

- Continue on Dalton Bank Road, passing Dalton Bank Nature Reserve on your left.

- Dalton Bank Road becomes Nettleton Road.

- At a roundabout on a housing estate, take first exit, onto Sutton Avenue. This might look like a wrong turn into the housing estate, but it makes for an easier left turn at the next junction.

- At T junction, turn left onto Crossley Lane.

- At roundabout, take second exit, turning right onto School Lane. Entering village of Kirkheaton.

- At mini roundabout, take second exit onto Waterloo Road.

- At the end of Waterloo Road, we reach a complicated series of junctions. We are going onto A629 Penistone Road.

- Care needs to be taken at this junction. The A629 turning is give way, but all other parts of the junction are traffic light controlled.

- The superstore (postcode HD5 8QW) is on your left soon after this junction.

- The next waypoint for your satnav is: The Bridge Inn, Cote Lane, Thurgoland, Sheffield, (postcode S35 7AE).

- If you have stopped at the superstore leave the car park turning left onto A629.

This long stretch of A629 provides easy navigation. It is a good class road, allowing reasonable progress, yet still affording pleasant views.

The Trans-Pennine Trail criss-crosses our route all along the A629.

- The A629 passes through several villages on the way to our next turning, including: Shelley village, Shepley village, Birds Edge and High Flatts.

- At Hoylandswaine roundabout, take second exit, continuing straight on, along A629 (signposted Rotherham.)

- At the village of Thurgoland turn right just after the Green Dragon pub (postcode S35 7AE), onto Cote Lane (there is no signpost).

- The road heads downhill into a valley and becomes more rural.

- We soon reach the Bridge Inn, which we used as a satnav way-point (postcode S35 7AE).

- Our next satnav way-point is the Co-op on Langsett Road South, at Oughtibridge, S35 0GY.

- Leaving the Bridge Inn, continue on Cote Lane, which becomes Forge Lane just after a very narrow stone bridge.

- Cross the River Don on another old stone bridge. Forge Lane bends to the right and loosely follows the line of the river.

- Just before you would pass under an arched railway bridge, turn right onto Soughley Lane.

- Soughley Lane winds through woodland area, interspersed with the remains of its former industrial past.

- At T junction, turn right on A6102 Wortley Road (signposted Oughtibridge, Stocksbridge and Deepcar)

- A6102 Wortley Road becomes Manchester Road. The road winds through a mix of rural and industrial areas, on its way to the outskirts of Sheffield.

- The A6102 passes through the villages of Deepcar and Wharncliff Side.

- We soon reach the village of Oughtibridge.

- The White Hart Inn on Langsett Road (postcode S35 0GX) sits in the fork of a one-way system of roads. Take the left side of the pub, onto Orchard Street.

- If you are looking on a map, we need to turn right onto Bridge Hill, but we are prevented from doing so, by the one-way system.

- Where the two roads re-join, double back onto the opposite carriageway. The turn is not signposted, but you drive around a pretty, stone-walled park area.

- At a zebra crossing, with a parade of stone-built shops on your right, turn left onto Church Street (signposted Worrell & Bradfield)

- Pass the Hare & Hounds pub (postcode S35 0FW) on your right.

- Drive uphill through Oughtibridge village. Take care in larger vehicles, as cars park on both sides of the hill, narrowing the road.

- Opposite number 128 Church Street, turn left onto Haggstones Road (signposted Worrall and Sheffield).

- Enter the village of Worrall, which is still quite built up.

- At the end of Worrell village, and just after a zebra crossing, turn right onto Kirk Edge Road (signposted Loxley & Bradfield).

- After a short distance on Kirk Edge Road, turn left onto Long Lane (signposted Loxley & Stannington).

- Hillsborough Golf Course (postcode S6 4BE) is on both sides of the road as you drive down Long Lane.

- At the end of Long Lane, reach the T-junction with B6077 Loxley Road.

- Turn left (signposted Sheffield & Wadsley). A view into the Loxley River valley opens up ahead of you.

- Turn left onto B6077 Loxley Road.

- Soon after turning onto Loxley Road, the Admiral Rodney public house (postcode S6 6RU) is on your left. Just after the pub is a row of stone troughs, presumably placed there to refresh horses coming up the steep hill from Sheffield.

- Just after these stone troughs turn left uphill onto Rodney Hill.

- Look for Loxley Primary School on your left (postcode S6 6SG).

There is a long parking layby opposite the school and in front of a row of houses (probably best to avoid the school's drop-off and pick-up times).

Robin Wood is an area of ancient woodland, which is owned by Loxley Primary School. This is where teacher Dan Eaton found the lost marker stone, which he believes marks to location of Robin Hood's birth. The woods are open to the public, with a nature trail and information about the flora and fauna you will find there.

Robin Wood is only a short walk from the school, and you are best to remain parked on Rodney Hill.

- With your back to Loxley Primary School start walking downhill, to your right. Take the first right turn into Chase Road uphill. Then the next right into Philips Road.

- Turn right at number 28 Philips Road at a hilly lawned area. Follow the footpath in front of houses to the entrance of Robin Wood.

- Go through the entrance and follow the rough paths anti-clockwise around the wood.

Part Five
Derbyshire & Nottingham
80 Miles - 3 Hours travelling
Travelling time does not include time spent exploring the
attractions en-route

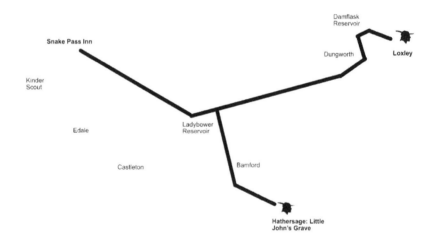

Loxley to Hathersage

Loxley to Hathersage: 16 miles - 30 minutes

- Re-trace your route down Rodney Hill, to the junction with B6077 Loxley Rd.

- Turn right, to leave Loxley heading west on B6077 Loxley Rd.

- At the start of Damflask Reservoir, turn left on B6076 New Road, driving along the top of the dam. (signposted: Dungworth, Low Bradfield & Stannington).

- Begin driving along the opposite side of Damflask Reservoir.

- Turn left from B6076 New Road onto B6076 Briers House Lane (signposted Dungworth & Stannington).

- Take care with navigation, as the map gives the impression that this is a natural continuation of New Road. It is actually a very tight left turn, onto a distinctly different road.

- Briers House Lane is very steeply uphill, with several tight corners. It is not suitable for caravans.

- Continue to follow B6076 through Dungworth Village (postcode S6 6HF), as the road name changes to Yewes Lane and Cliffe Hill.

- At a point where Cliffe Hill bends to the left, take a right turn onto Skye House Lane, just before a detached stone house.

- At a T junction, turn right onto Game Lane (signposted Glossop).

- Game Lane changes name to Beaton Green.

- At T junction, turn right onto Rod Side. You are on quite a remote road, with a stone built farm on your right.

- After a long stretch of straight road through open country, Rod Side takes a series of sweeping S bends, before reaching a T junction with A57 Manchester Road.

- Turn right onto A57 (signposted Glossop).

- This road twists and undulates through moorland, eventually reaching Ladybower Reservoir.

- Soon after this turning we enter the Derbyshire Peak District. The A57 may sound like a major road classification, but it is a delightful stretch of road.

- At the bottom of the hill, we reach a set of traffic lights at Ladybower Reservoir and Ladybower Inn (postcode S33 0AX).

- We will be turning left at these lights, onto the A6013 towards Bamford, but there is lots to explore in this area first.

Continuing on the A57 towards Glossop will take us up Snake Pass.

- Returning to our official route, we leave the A57 at the traffic light controlled junction, turning left on A6013 towards Bamford, entering Derbyshire's Peak District.

- After passing through Bamford, we reach the traffic light controlled T junction with the A6187.

We will be turning left towards Hathersage and Little John's grave, but a five mile detour to your right, towards Castleton, is worth taking.

- Having exhausted all that Castleton has to offer, we re-join the A6187 towards Hathersage, resuming our search for Robin Hood locations.

- We continue through the town, in search of Little John's Grave.

- Soon after passing the last of the shops, we turn left onto School Lane, which becomes Church Lane.

- These roads are narrow, with limited parking.

- The pretty Church of Saint Michael the Archangel is 200 metres along Church Lane in Hathersage. Stones in the churchyard mark the grave of Little John.

Robin Hood's Cave is set into Stanage Edge (Hooks Carr car park, Hope Valley, S32 1BR), the cliff face that towers over Hathersage to the north.

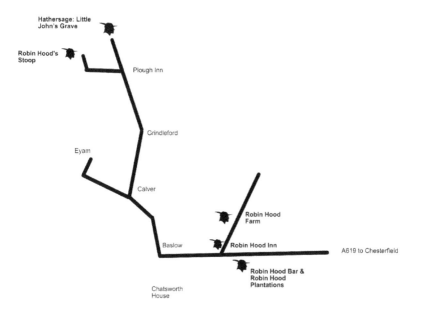

Hathersage: Little
John's Grave

Robin Hood's
Stoop

Plough Inn

Grindleford

Eyam

Calver

Robin Hood
Farm

Baslow

Robin Hood Inn

A619 to Chesterfield

Robin Hood Bar &
Robin Hood
Plantations

Chatsworth
House

Hathersage to The Hamlet of Robin Hood (Baslow)

Hathersage to Baslow: 7 miles - 15 minutes

- Retrace your route into the centre of Hathersage.

- Then, turn left onto B6001 Station Rd, passing the Little John Pub (postcode S32 1DD).

We detour from the B6001 on narrow and steep roads, to visit Robin Hood's Stoop, on Offerton Moor.

This Robin Hood location is not easy to reach, in fact it is really only practical on foot or by cycle. The area is very well serviced by foot and cycle rights of way.

- After visiting Robin Hood's Stoop, we re-trace our route to the Plough Inn (Leadmill Bridge, Hather-sage, S32 1BA) and turn right onto the B6001.

- Cross over the River Derwent, from where the B6001 runs parallel with the river and is sheltered by a canopy of trees.

- At T junction turn right on B6521 Main Road.

- The B6521 merges with the A625 and continues to traffic lights near Calver Sough (postcode S32 3WY).

A short detour up the A623 to our right, brings us to the villages of Stoney Middleton and Eyam.

- We return to the traffic lights at Calver Sough going straight across, and continuing on the A623 Kingsgate, towards Baslow.

- We leave Baslow on the A619, turning left at a roundabout, passing through Nether End and past Chatsworth's Golden Gates.

- At a much larger roundabout, we continue on the A619, towards Chesterfield.

- After a very short distance, we see a minor road on our left and the Robin Hood public house (Chesterfield Rd, Baslow, DE45 1PQ).

- Around the Robin Hood public house are the Robin Hood locations of: The Hamlet of Robin Hood, Robin Hood Bar, Robin Hood Farm and Robin Hood Plantations.

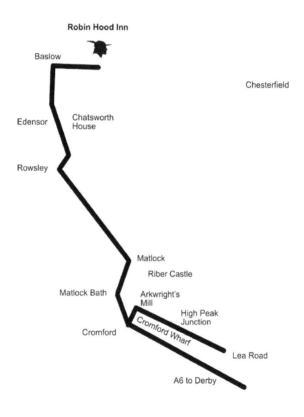

Robin Hood Inn

Baslow

Chesterfield

Edensor

Chatsworth House

Rowsley

Matlock

Riber Castle

Matlock Bath

Arkwright's Mill

High Peak Junction

Cromford Wharf

Cromford

Lea Road

A6 to Derby

The Hamlet of Robin Hood (Baslow) to Cromford

Baslow to Annesley: (including the Whatstandwell hamlet of Robin Hood)
26 miles ⁄ 40 minutes

- After visiting Baslow's hamlet of Robin Hood, we re-trace our route back along the A619 to the roundabout adjacent to Baslow sports field (postcode DE45 1SP).

- At the roundabout, we turn left, continuing on the A619 (signposted for Chatsworth House) for a short distance.

- On a map, you appear to reach a road junction, with the B6012 turning off to your left. On the ground, it is the continuation of the A619 which is marked as a right turn, with the B6012 continuing straight on.

- We continue onto the B6012 Bakewell Road, heading for Chatsworth.

- At the next minor road junction, continue left on the B6012 to Edensor.

- After driving through Chatsworth Park and enjoying views of Chatsworth House, the B6012 winds its way over a hump-back bridge, before meeting the A6 at Rowsley (postcode DE4 2EH).

- Turn left onto the A6, towards Matlock. Beware, this stretch of road between Rowsley and Matlock has several static speed cameras.

There is also a lot to capture our interest on the route into the Victorian town of Matlock.

- From Matlock, we follow the A6, alongside the River Derwent, to Matlock Bath.

- Following the A6 towards Cromford, we encounter the imposing Masson Mill, on the left of the road. This is the start of the 15 mile long, Derwent Valley Mills: UNESCO World Heritage site.

- Continuing along the A6, we soon reach the mill town of Cromford.

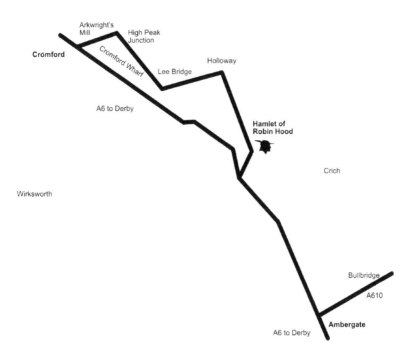

Matlock Bath

Arkwright's Mill

High Peak Junction

Cromford Wharf

Cromford

Lee Bridge

Holloway

A6 to Derby

Hamlet of Robin Hood

Crich

Wirksworth

Bullbridge

A610

A6 to Derby

Ambergate

Cromford to Ambergate

Our next stop after leaving Cromford puts us back on the Robin Hood trail. Close to the village of Whatstandwell, there is a hamlet known as Robin Hood.

We have a choice of routes to get there, dependent on the size of your vehicle.

Option 1:

- The simplest route is to follow the A6 south, through the Derwent Valley, until the A6 takes two right angle turns across the River Derwent.

- Immediately after the road bridge and Family Tree public house (postcode DE4 5HG), turn left, onto B5035.

- After a short distance uphill, cross the Cromford Canal and reach one of the Cromford Canal car parks (2 Stoney Wood Drive, DE4 5EE), which is ideal for a walk or cycle along the canal.

- Turn left onto Robin Hood Road, signposted Holloway. (Narrow and unsuited to larger vehicles).

- After approximately 600m, Robin Hood Road becomes Leashaw Road, and you have reached the hamlet of Robin Hood (postcode DE4 5HF).

- The old sawmill, which is now a B&B called Robin Hood Tower is on your left, looking downhill, towards the canal and river.

Option 2: (Unsuited to larger vehicles).

- Leave Cromford Mill on Mill Lane, crossing the River Derwent and passing the junction with Willersley Lane, which leads uphill to Willersley Castle.

- After the bridge, Mill Lane becomes Lea Road, which we follow to the hamlet of Lea Bridge.

- Here, we take the right fork, onto Mill Lane.

- Where Mill Lane becomes a steeper uphill road, it changes name to Yew Tree Hill. Follow this into Holloway.

- In Holloway, turn right, downhill, onto Bracken Lane.

- Bracken Lane becomes Leashaw Road, which soon reaches the hamlet of Robin Hood (postcode DE4 5HF).

The old sawmill, which is now a B&B called Robin Hood Tower is on your right, looking downhill, towards the canal and river.

- After visiting the hamlet of Robin Hood and Robin Hood Tower we retrace our route to the A6 and the Family Tree public house (postcode DE4 5HG), turning left towards Ambergate.

- At the Hurt Arms, we leave the A6 and the Derwent Valley, turning left onto the A610 and entering the Amber Valley.

A short (1.6 mile) detour from the A610 allows us to visit Heage Windmill (Unsuitable for large vehicles)

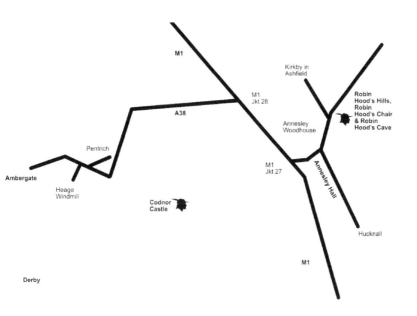

Ambergate to Robin Hood Hills (Annesley)

Ambergate to Robin Hood Hills (Annesley)

- If you have visited Heage Windmill, retrace your route back to the A610, turning right.

Another short detour away from the A610 allows a visit to Pentrich, the site of England's last revolution, which happened on 9th June 1817. It is a story that might well have involved Robin Hood, had he still been around during the 19th century.

- Continuing along the A610, we reach a large roundabout and join the A38 Trunk Road turning left, towards the M1.

- Take M1 South for one junction, leaving at J27.

- Take A608 towards Mansfield (best avoided at peak times, as the business estates on your left cause congestion).

- On your right is Annesley Hall, where Robin Hood's boots were once kept.

- At traffic lights, turn left on A611 Derby Rd, signposted Mansfield.

Within a short distance, you are back among rural scenery.

- Robin Hood's Hills, Chair & Cave are all in the vicinity of the junction with B6021 Nottingham Rd

- There is a limited amount of parking on a wide grass verge, along the south side of Derby Road. There is also plenty of roadside parking down Shoulder of Mutton Hill, after its name changes to Nottingham Road.

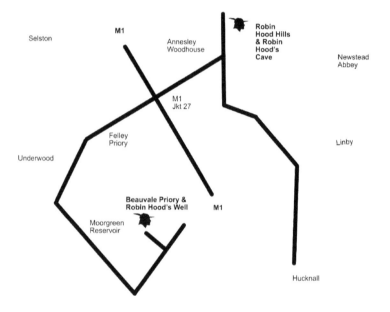

Selston

M1

Annesley
Woodhouse

Robin
Hood Hills
& Robin
Hood's
Cave

Newstead
Abbey

M1
Jkt 27

Felley
Priory

Linby

Underwood

Beauvale Priory &
Robin Hood's Well

M1

Moorgreen
Reservoir

Hucknall

Eastwood

Robin Hood Hills (Annesley) to Beauvale Priory

Annesley to Beauvale Priory: 7 miles - 15 minutes

- Retrace your route along the A611 and A608 back to M1 J27.

- Cross the motorway, continuing on A608, passing Felley Priory on your left.

- At a T junction, turn left onto B600 Willey Lane, passing Moorgreen Reservoir (Willey Lane, Nottingham, NG16 3QS), built originally to feed the Nottingham Canal, but now a carp fishery. There are several walks and cycle rides in the hills around the reservoir.

- Just after Horse & Groom pub (Moorgreen, Newthorpe, Nottingham NG16 2FE), turn left onto minor road, New Road, signposted with a brown tourist sign for Beauvale Priory.

- New Road is quite narrow, and perhaps not suitable for larger motorhomes or caravans.

- Beauvale Priory is off New Road to your left, down an even narrower lane (Beauvale Abbey Farm, New Road, Moorgreen, Nottingham, NG16 2AA). Robin Hood's Well sits in the private High Park Wood, overlooking Beauvale Priory from the north.

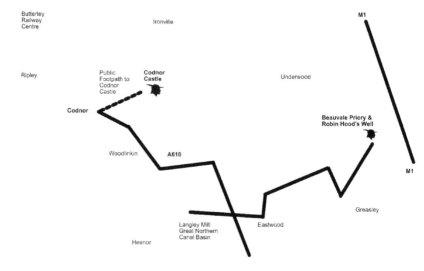

Butterley
Railway
Centre

Ironville

M1

Ripley

Public
Footpath to
Codnor
Castle

**Codnor
Castle**

Underwood

Codnor

**Beauvale Priory &
Robin Hood's Well**

Woodlinkin

A610

Greasley

Langley Mill:
Great Northern
Canal Basin

Eastwood

M1

Heanor

Beauvale Priory to Codnor Castle

Beauvale Priory to Codnor Castle: 7 miles · 25 minutes

- Retrace your route along New Road to the Horse & Groom pub.

- Opposite the pub, take B6010 Moorgreen.

- At T junction in Eastwood turn right on Nottingham Rd.

- After passing through Eastwood town centre, at traffic lights take A608 Derby Road.

- At the roundabout turn right on A610 (A short detour ahead takes us to Langley Mill and The Great Northern Canal Basin).

- Just before reaching the village of Codnor, you will see the Codnor Castle Inn and golf course on your right (Nottingham Road, Codnor, DE5 9RL).

- At the traffic light controlled T junction in Codnor, turn right, remaining on A610.

- Parking is available on the former marketplace, for a walk to Codnor Castle. (Note, there is a height restriction barrier on the car park.)

The only vehicle access to Codnor Castle is along private farm roads, but there are a choice of several walking and cycling routes to the castle.

The most direct walking route starts on the left of the Poet and Castle pub (2 Alfreton Road, Codnor, DE5 9QY), taking just over a kilometre along Public Footpaths to reach the castle remains.

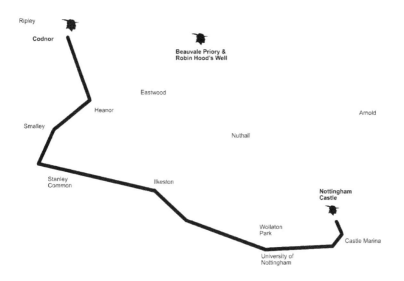

Ripley

Codnor

Beauvale Priory &
Robin Hood's Well

Eastwood

Heanor

Smalley

Arnold

Nuthall

Stanley
Common

Ilkeston

Nottingham
Castle

Wollaton
Park

Castle Marina

University of
Nottingham

Codnor Castle to Nottingham Castle

Codnor Castle to Nottingham: 16 miles · 1 hour

There is a faster, less scenic route of getting into Nottingham, straight down the A610. The trunk road route is more suited to larger vehicles. However, my recommended route takes in some more of Derbyshire's towns and villages, before entering Nottingham along Castle Boulevard. This route into the city, under the castle's shadow, seems a more appropriate way to end our journey.

- At the A610 traffic lights, take A6007, straight on through Loscoe, towards Heanor.

- Leaving Loscoe, we travel uphill, towards the more industrial town of Heanor.

- We see very little of Heanor, since the roundabout at the town's edge, takes us right on the A608 into more rural scenery towards Smalley.

The road from Heanor to Smalley twists and undulates nicely though fields and farms, but beware the plethora of fixed speed cameras.

- At the hamlet of Smalley Cross, you see the Rose & Crown pub (Main Road, Morley, DE7 6DG) on your right.

- This former coaching inn dates back to around 1860.

454

- Turn left onto the A609 Ilkeston Rd. The scenic A609 takes us through the village of Stanley Common.

- The road continues winding its way through farmland, to reach the Straw's Bridge Nature Reserve (High Lane East, West Hallam, DE7 5FG).

From here, the disused Nutbrook Canal and a network of reclaimed mineral railway lines provide plentiful walking and cycling opportunities.

- Soon after Straw's Bridge, we re-enter an urban landscape at Ilkeston.

- Reaching Ilkeston's busy traffic island, we continue on A609 towards Nottingham.

- This section remains very urban, until you reach the Gallows Inn (Nottingham Road, Ilkeston, DE7 5BN) and cross the Erewash Canal.

- Once you pass under the M1, we are now on Trowell Moor, another pleasant stretch of rural Nottinghamshire.

- At the end of Trowell Moor is a complicated, five-way traffic light junction. If you imagine it as a roundabout, take the third exit onto Wollaton Vale.

- At the bottom of Wollaton Vale, turn left at the roundabout, onto A52 Derby Road, keeping Wollaton Park on your left.

- The University of Nottingham's main campus is on your right (postcode NG7 2RD).

- After Wollaton Park, we reach a busy traffic light controlled roundabout opposite the Queens Medical Centre (postcode NG7 2UH), which is itself part of The University of Nottingham.

- We turn right at the roundabout, briefly joining the Nottingham Ring Road.

- Immediately after the hospital, turn left onto A6005 Abbey Street. We are now entering the city's conurbation.

- At a small roundabout, turn right, taking A6005 Castle Boulevard into the centre of Nottingham.

- On your right is Castle Marina (postcode NG7 1TN), which as well as its boating marina, has many shops and eateries.

- Castle Boulevard runs parallel with the Nottingham Canal on your right, as we look up and get our first glimpse of Nottingham Castle (postcode NG1 6AA).

- As we reach the centre of the city, Castle Road is on your left, leading, as its name suggests, to Nottingham Castle.

- There is parking for motorcycles and disabled permit holders on Castle Road, but other vehicles should use one of the city's many car parks.

Author's Afterword

500RH

WHEN my publisher asked me to write a conclusion to the Robin Hood 500, I was not entirely sure what I could add to everything I had already written on my journey. Then, by chance, that same evening, I went to An Evening with Sir Tony Robinson. During the evening, Sir Tony described his career in show business, a career that has its roots as much in history, as it does in comedy.

Sir Tony reminded me that history can be fun. In fact, he described the pitch from the producers of the Time Team TV show as, "wanting to get Britain's most stupid man to explain the archaeology". As it turned out, an extra-curricular course while at university, meant that he actually understood most of what the archaeologists were doing, before describing it in a way that Baldrick might understand.

For anyone unfamiliar with Sir Tony Robinson's TV career, it has dipped into history several times, none of which could be described as stuffy or academic.

First up was the Blackadder situation comedy series in which he co-starred with Rowan Atkinson. Its four series took Sir Tony's hapless Baldrick character from The Middle Ages (1485), through to The First World War (1914-1918). Given its genre, the show was played for comedy, but it also told Britain's history to people who might not otherwise have studied it.

Next came Time Team, which shortened an entire archaeological dig into just three days. We encountered Time Team during our visit to Codnor Castle, and a possible candi-date for the evil Sheriff of Nottingham.

Finally, Sir Tony re-visited the Robin Hood legends with Maid Marion and Her Merrie Men. This comedy show was inspired by Sir Tony's own daughter Laura taking control of a playground game, and bossing about the boys in her class.

Listening to Sir Tony speak, I realised my own take on history is very similar. We are lucky to live in a country with such a rich history. Learning about that history is fascinating, but we do not have to always take it too seriously. Many of the Robin Hood tales we encountered have been greatly embellished over time, but they still make a good story. Traveling around the **500RH** and reading the stories I uncovered provided a very enjoyable journey, along with learning about the history I trav-elled through.

I hope you enjoy your journey as much as I did. I will be developing a Robin Hood 500 website to help you delve even deeper into the **500RH**.

Useful Websites

500RH

I HAVE included website references to individual attrac-tions along the **500RH**, as we encounter them. The fol-lowing list is intended to provide wider research opportu-nities in planning your journey.

Tourism

- Leicestershire Tourist Information
  www.visitleicester.info

- Lincolnshire Tourist Information
  www.visitlincoln.com

- Nottinghamshire / Nottingham Tourist Information
  www.visit-nottinghamshire.co.uk

- Historical information about Lincolnshire's RAF ba-ses **www.raf-lincolnshire.info**

- Bomber County: historical information about Lin-colnshire's bomber squadrons **www.bcar.org.uk**

- The National Trust **www.nationaltrust.org.uk**

- The Robin Hood Way: long-distance footpath
  www.robinhoodway.com

- Sherwood Forest Visitor Attractions
  www.visitsherwood.co.uk

- Enlgish Heritage **www.english-heritage.org.uk**

Robin Hood Information

- International Robin Hood Bibliography
  www.irhb.org

- Encyclopaedia Britannica
  www.britannica.com/topic/Robin-Hood

- BBC Countryfile
  www.countryfile.com/people/historical-figures/guide-to-robin-hood-history-of-the-legend-and-best-places-to-visit

- Robin Hood Legend .com
  www.robinhoodlegend.com

Join the whole Robin Hood 500 Experience
www.500RH.co.uk

The **500RH** website takes you beyond our guidebook, exploring the locations in greater detail. We suggest different itineraries to suit your own way of experiencing the **500RH**.

Joining as a **500RH** Member gives you access to even more detailed itineraries, as well as regular newsletters about events and opportunities around the **500RH**. We are constantly negotiating new discounts, which are only available to **500RH** Members.

Be Proud of Your **500RH** Journey
A range of **500RH** merchandise is available through our website to help you remember your Robin Hood experience. Discounts are also available to **500RH** Members.

For details of new and forthcoming books
from Extremis Publishing, including our
podcasts, please visit our official website at:

www.extremispublishing.com

or follow us on social media at:

www.facebook.com/extremispublishing

www.linkedin.com/company/extremis-publishing-ltd-/